70: JESUS' EXPANSION STRATEGY

I am suggesting a way that the Church, up and down the spectrum, from a mini church, megachurch, cell church or church plant, can, by using Jesus' relationship groups of 3/12/70, experience expansion rather than just growth.

WILLIAM A. BECKHAM

Copyright © 2015 by William A. Beckham

Published by CCS Publishing
23890 Brittlebush Circle
Moreno Valley, CA 92557 USA
1-888-511-9995

All rights reserved. No part of this publication may be reproduced, stored in a retrieval system, or transmitted, in any form or by any means, electronic, mechanical, photocopying, recording, or otherwise, without the prior written permission of the publisher.

Printed in the United States of America.

ISBN: 978-1-935789-73-4

All Scripture quotations, unless otherwise indicated, are from the Holy Bible, New International Version, Copyright ©1973, 1978, 1984 by International Bible Society. Used by permission.

CCS Publishing is the book-publishing division of Joel Comiskey Group, a resource and coaching ministry dedicated to equipping leaders for cell-based ministry.

Find us on the World Wide Web at www.joelcomiskeygroup.com

I dedicate this book to pastors Jorge Leal and Victor Marte who were part of my first Prototype Mentoring Triad in Houston. They represent pastors around the world who are learning the mechanics and dynamics of Jesus' simple group strategy of a friendship triad that is contagious in discipling believers and reaching unbelievers, a cell community that nurtures believers and edifies the church, and groups of seventy that supervise and organize expansion. Such pastors are God's promise of a New Testament-like people epidemic in the 21st Century.

Charts

Quality & Quantity	56
Commitment Bus	87
Prototype Decision Process	94
Five Levels of Being Phenomenal	95
Adopting Change: Who will do it?	97
Innovation-Decision Period	98
Value Levels of Life	101
Anatomy of Innovation	115
Simple Prayers	145
Johari Window	175
Test the Spirit of Practical Prophecy	176
Friendship Triad Triangle	185
Friendship Triad Mainframe	188
Friendship Triad Process	195
Triad Checklist	201
Friendship Triad & Community Cell Contrast	203
Holistic Cell Hand Illustration	205
Evaluate a Group with Seven Elements	222
Jesus' Eight Guiding Principles of Leadership	228
Traditional Attraction Model	229
Expansion Cluster of Seventy	230
Two Church Wings	231
Basic Five-Point Process	236
Triad, Cell & Cluster Prototype	237
Two Church Paradigms	245
Visualizing Jesus' Strategy	297
Three-legged Stool	314
Triad: Contagious Internally & Externally	316
Jesus' Integrated Expansion System of 3/12/70	318
The Flow of Disciplines in a Triad	321
Friendship Triad Process	334
Parallel Strategy	337
Large Group Danger-Safe Zones	347
Three Large Group Options	348
Where We Are-Where We Want to Be	357
Traditional Large Group Public Model	360

Charts

New Large Group Public Model	364
Strategy Continuum	365
Expansion Building Blocks	371
Triad, Cell & Cluster Prototype	372
Friendship Triad Process	373
Men's & Women's Triad Chains	374
Leadership Hats	381
Cathedral Church Plant	391
Expansion Church Plant	392
The Triad is the Church Planting Seed	403
Umbrella: Cathedral, Creative, and Cell Church Models	407
Five Options for Participating in Expansion	409
Cathedral Church and Creative Church Umbrella Contrast	413
Cell Church Internal Growth & External Expansion Umbrellas	415

Contents

Foreword: Ralph Neighbour	11
Preface: Becoming the Strategy	15
Introduction: Decentralizing the Tower of Babel	23

SECTION I: FACTORS IN EXPANSION

Chapter 1: Characteristics of Jesus' Strategy	41
Chapter 2: Where Are the Working Models?	61
Chapter 3: Jesus' Great Vision	83
Chapter 4: Decision Process and Values	93
Chapter 5: The Dark Night of the Soul	111

SECTION II: PROTOTYPE DYNAMICS & MECHANICS

Chapter 6: Prototype Presence	127
Chapter 7: Prototype Prayer	143
Chapter 8: Prototype Edification	159
Chapter 9: Prototype Friendship	181
Chapter 10: Prototype Community	205
Chapter 11: Prototype Supervision	223

SECTION III: PARADIGM PERSPECTIVES

Chapter 12: A Trip to the First Century	243
Chapter 13: The Danger of Paradigm Paralysis	255
Chapter 14: Jesus' Great Commission Strategy	269
Chapter 15: Movements Are Built on Governing Principles	281
Chapter 16: Jesus' Strategy Overview	297

SECTION IV: STRATEGIC CONVERSATIONS

Chapter 17: A Conversation about Jesus' Integrated Strategy	313
Chapter 18: A Conversation about Your Strategy	323
Chapter 19: A Conversation about the Large Group	345
Chapter 20: A Conversation about Two Strategic Points	357
Chapter 21: A Conversation about Three Strategy Building Blocks	367
Chapter 22: A Conversation with Church Planters	389
Chapter 23: A Conversation with Pastors	405
Conclusion: The Spirit of Naaman	423

FOREWORD

I have marveled at the brilliance of the concepts presented in this book. One word kept flashing through my mind as I read the final version: *"This is anointed!"* The concepts have been so thoroughly developed that little is left to ponder. This book has taken years to create and has been through dozens of revisions. I prayed guidance for Bill through that period, knowing it would impact the future of church life. I am delighted it is being released simultaneously in Brazil as well as the USA. More translations will surely follow!

Bill Beckham and I first met in 1966 when I was with the Evangelism Division of the Baptist Convention of Texas. I conducted a Personal Evangelism Institute in his East Texas church. Little did we realize the way God would entwine our lives!

We were surprised a few years later when our two families arrived in the Missionary Orientation Center in Pine Mountain, Georgia. As the Beckhams left for Thailand we were to go to Singapore but our visas did not come through, so we were in Saigon during the closing days of the Viet Nam War. We then connected with them again in Bangkok while continuing to wait for our Singapore visa. There followed months of strategizing as I frequently returned to Bangkok to consult the urban strategy team Bill was part of.

By the time God led Bill and Mary back to Texas fifteen years later, we were in the final phase of our cell church journey and were beginning a new cell church in Houston. They drove down to Houston to visit us. He recalls September, Labor Day, 1990:

> *We drove down to Houston from Dallas after settling there with the intent of beginning a "different kind of church" in North Dallas. On the way back to Dallas with Mary, Joey, and Connie asleep, God spoke four words: "Attach yourself to Ralph." He never explained beyond that sentence and never withdrew it. And, God has blessed me beyond anything I could have expected because of our relationship.*

From that time, we have been closer than blood brothers, serving in conferences, co-pastoring the TOUCH FAMILY cell church, and endlessly mingling insights until we no longer know who shared them first. I had the honor of being the professor guiding his D. Min. in Cell Church Administration. His thesis was superb!

God created Bill with a powerful right/left brain interaction that has caused him to "see" concepts expressed through diagrams, as well as a great skill using words. His passion to focus in doing research has often driven him to work into the middle of the night.

As this book is released, we are at the beginning of the demise of the unbiblical Constantine church. God has given us in these pages a glimpse into the Last Days church, predicted by Joel and referenced by Peter at Pentecost. The home cell movement is a preliminary stage, and as Beckham carefully points out, the understanding of the Triad of two or three persons is now a further development of the Holy Spirit.

In the Regeneration movement in the Ukraine they are fulfilling the Last Days Church prophecy: *"Your sons will prophesy, also your daughters; your young men will see visions, your old men dream dreams. When the time comes, I'll pour out my Spirit on those who serve me, men and women both, and they'll prophesy."* There I have witnessed a 19-year old young man healing and delivering scores of people in Kiev and a 24-year old young woman pastoring the original cell church in Dnepropretskov! The movement now includes hundreds of new church plants and Internet cells scattered across the Russian-speaking world.

Bill's clear insights defined as "Practical Prophecy" defines the future lifestyle of Christ's Body, described in 1 Corinthians 14:3 along with 14:24-25. The norm for body life is for all believers to reveal evidence that "God is in their midst." The task of Christ in His present body is clearly to reveal His Presence and Power and Purpose – making Him the cause of conversions.

Thus, this book will grow in value in the coming years. It is a pilot, a guide, for the coming generations and a stimulus for those who are now ready to abandon leaky wineskins.

Ralph W. Neighbour, Jr.
March 2015

PREFACE

BECOMING THE STRATEGY

"We must become evidence of what we want practiced."
• Ralph Neighbour

Can I be frank with you reader? I believe we are living in a day and age where God is restoring something that has been lost from the original design of the church. I believe God is preparing us for an evangelism epidemic, an expansion people movement that will once again fulfill Jesus' mandate to make disciples of all nations. I don't believe our problem has been a lack of effort. It's a matter of focusing on Jesus' organic and relationship strategy. Does your own heart yearn to be part of that movement? I believe God intended for you to pick up this book.

Ralph Neighbour and I were recently discussing church strategy for the 21st century with several Spanish-speaking pastors. I was making the point that leaders must experience and prototype the dynamic life of a strategy as well as the mechanical nuts and bolts.

Ralph summed up the discussion with an important foundation truth of this book on strategy. "We must become evidence of what we want practiced." Leaders cannot just teach about a strategy. Leaders must become the strategy. The strategy must be who the leader is, not just what he/she does. A leader cannot help others implement a strategy until personally experiencing and internalizing the strategy. Psychologist Carl Jung understood the importance of our inward experience: "Your vision will become clear only when you look into your heart ... Who looks outside, dreams. Who looks inside, awakens."

This is a double-edged sword. Over a period of time a leader will *become* the strategy (good or bad) that is implemented. The strategy then becomes the leader's perspective, experience, frame of reference, and filter of theology. This is why it is so important that ultimately pastors and church leaders become "evidence of what GOD wants practiced."

Jesus Is the Strategy

The Gospels present a biographical rather than strategic account of how Jesus began the prototype of His church. He told the Disciples "follow me" (Matt. 4:18; 16:24) and demonstrated who a Christian is, what a Christian is to do, and how His followers were to be His spiritual body on earth. "I have set you an example (John 13:15).

The Gospel writers record Jesus' relationships, teachings, thoughts, and actions, not his strategy. But from His life we can reconstruct the strategic principles that guided Him. These principles reveal the nature of the church and His prototype.

"Jesus had built into his disciples the structure of a church that would challenge and triumph over all the powers of death and hell."[1] Jesus lived out the characteristics of His strategy that would guide every generation of the church. Within the characteristics of Jesus' church are the methodologies, systems, and

---

1. Robert E. Coleman, *The Master Plan of Evangelism* (Grand Rapids, ILL: Revell, 1993), 100.

design of the church of every age. Leaders who plan around His characteristics and principles naturally implement His methods and design ... if another design (such as Constantine's) doesn't distort Jesus' design. I suggest ten characteristics of Jesus' strategy in Chapter 1.

Your vision will determine the type of strategy you need. If your vision is maintenance then you will have a traditional strategy of maintaining the preaching, teaching, and building model. You will keep doing what you are doing. A maintenance strategy maintains the status quo.

If your vision is growth then you will have a growth strategy. Creative pastors with a growth vision will develop a strategy to make the traditional church work better. You will work harder to produce more fruit. A growth strategy will grow but will not produce the kind of pandemic people movement we see in the New Testament.

If your vision is expansion then you will have an expansion strategy. You will use Jesus' decentralized relationship system. Pastors who receive a revelation from God can be part of an expansion strategy that will penetrate people groups in Jerusalem, Judea, Samaria, and the world.

In this book I am suggesting a way that the church, up and down the spectrum, from a mini church, mega church, cell church, or church plant, can, by using Jesus' relationship groups of 3/12/70, experience New Testament expansion rather than just growing or maintaining in a building.

This Book is for Learners

Michael Gerber believes leaders have a problem when "they think they know enough. And so they spend their time defending what they know, rather than discovering what they don't."[2]

It is important for a leader to be a learner because in "a time of drastic change it is the learners who inherit the future. The learned usually find themselves equipped to live in a world that no longer exists."[3] Learners have the capacity to be reborn to new ideas, even new paradigms that challenge how things operate. The learned are stuck in past paradigms that are part of a previous world.[4]

"Learned" leaders "cannot solve a problem with the same level of consciousness that created it."[5] To solve a problem one has to have a new perspective, revelation, or insight. Constantine's paradigm produces "learned" people not "learners." Learned leaders have closed minds and are one of the greatest obstacles in changing the traditional model.

Nicodemus was an educated man with much knowledge about tradition and religion. However, he could not understand God's

---
2. Michael E. Gerber, *The E-Myth* (New York: Harper Collins, 1986), xiii.
3. Eric Hoffer, *Reflections on the Human Condition* (New York, NY: Harper & Row, 1973), 32.
4. *The Second Reformation*, published in 1995, was about reshaping the Church, both theologically and structurally, for the 21st Century. In it I introduced the first part of the structural church reformation of small groups. In a recently published book (2015), *The Second Reformation: Stage 2*, I lay a theological and conceptual base for a mid-level group (3/12/70) that can restore expansion to the church in the 21st century. This book, *70: Jesus' Expansion Strategy*, presents the strategy concepts and steps necessary to complete the reformation of the church so that it can be the expansion instrument of God.
5. This quote is attributed to Carl Yung, Swiss psychiatrist and psychotherapist. However, a similar quote is attributed to Albert Einstein: "The consciousness that created the problem cannot solve the problem."

way of doing things. Nicodemus sincerely believed his information verified his world view and paradigm. Therefore, he was trapped in an existing system that he would never escape by gaining more knowledge. Jesus knew Nicodemus needed to be born again spiritually as a "little child" (Matt. 18:1-2). "The wisest keeps something of the vision of a child. Though he may understand a thousand things that a young child could not understand, he is always a beginner, close to the original meaning of life."[6]

God has something very special for pastors today who are willing to be learners. However, in most cases, a pastor does not become a learner by a deliberate mental process. God must jump start us with revelation before we will go back as a "little child" and be born again about the church. Jesus wants to say to us what He said to Peter. "This was not revealed to you by man, but by my Father in heaven" (Matt. 16:17).

Jim Putman, pastor of an impressive megachurch in Idaho, is looking beyond the success of his church model and considering a new disciple paradigm. He is an example of pastors today who are receiving a revelation word from God about the church. He believes pastors have "been handed a box historically, and we're just trying to live within that box, rather than ask if it was the right box to begin with. But the box doesn't make disciples."[7] Jim Putman has moved from being learned to being a learner open to new revelation.

LEARNERS MUST ALSO UNLEARN

The "learned" leaders of the traditional model are trapped in boxes within boxes: A Sunday worship and teaching box within

---

6. John Macy, civil servant under five presidents.
7. Jim Putman, "A Better Way to Make Disciples," Outreach Magazine, September 5, 2013; http://www.outreachmagazine.com/features/4838-jim-putman-needed-shifts-in-making-disciples.html?

a program ministry box within a professional leader box within an organization box within a consumer box, and all packaged in a building box. Now that is a box! The learning curve of the "learned" is restricted to what is known within the interrelated boxes. The only way out is to become a learner who looks outside of the boxes and begins to unlearn the old and learn a new paradigm.

God searches for us deep down within our boxes. Most of us are certainly no deeper into our traditional boxes than Paul was in his Judaism box. So there is hope that some of us will have eyes to see, ears to hear, and hearts to respond to God's revelation about the church. We can then learn about the organic and decentralized church outside traditional boxes. However, we also must unlearn, un-package, and un-box old concepts, values, paradigms, and methods. The problem is, unlearning an old strategy is painful because we are deeply invested in it.

Consequently, we need a strategy for unlearning old strategies. This is difficult because the traditional brick and mortar strategy is all we know and is our safe and secure box. Considering new concepts about the church feels threatening, negative, harsh, and even disloyal because the change is not just about concepts and methods. The necessary changes are about us. We must unlearn ideas and practices that have become integral to our very being, values, paradigm, and even theology.

Unlearning doesn't mean throwing out all of the old. Adding a mid-level group to the large group system doesn't mean the existing traditional system is completely abandoned. Once we escape the boxes there is much that God can use in the old traditional model that has brought us to this point in history. However, we must have faith to let God tear down the walls and to open up the old concepts to new interpretations and new methodologies.

My prayer is that God has brought you to a revelation place in your ministry; that you are now open to not only learning new concepts but to unlearning old ones that have trapped you in the boxes of programs, professional leaders, organization, budgets, and buildings.

As I begin this book on Jesus' strategy of 3/12/70, let me draw together the important events and conclusions in my personal journey. This is the second of two books about the expansion of the church through Jesus' 3/12/70 group strategy. These books are part of a trilogy that started with the publishing of my first book, *The Second Reformation*, in 1995.

> *The Second Reformation* (Theology)
>
> *The Second Reformation: Stage 2* (Structure)
>
> *70: Jesus' Expansion Strategy* (Expansion)

In spite of developing over two decades, the three books were born out of the same driving forces: My theological struggle to apply the New Testament church to the world today and my personal experience with the Cell Church Movement that gave me hope about the Church.

INTRODUCTION

DECENTRALIZING THE TOWER OF BABEL

We need to rediscover the power of a decentralized movement with power distributed to each part that can in turn generate new life.
• Neil Cole

The intriguing story of the Tower of Babel is about decentralizing: "The process of redistributing or dispersing functions, powers, people or things away from a central location or authority."

The time of the story is set between the flood and the call of Abraham. As Noah stepped off the Ark, God commanded him to "be fruitful and multiply and fill the earth" (Gen. 9:1,7). Several generations later, Noah's family, led by his great-grandson Nimrod, settled in one place and started building the building of all buildings, a "stairway to heaven." It was a monumental tower, a *ziggurat* built in receding tiers upon a rectangular, oval, or square platform, layer upon layer.

> *Now the whole world had one language and a common speech. As people moved eastward, they found a plain in Shinar and settled there. They said to each other, "Come, let's make bricks and bake them thoroughly." They used brick instead of stone, and tar for mortar. Then they said, "Come, let us build ourselves a city, with a tower that reaches to the heavens, so that*

we may make a name for ourselves; otherwise we will be scattered over the face of the whole earth." But the Lord came down to see the city and the tower the people were building. The Lord said, "If as one people speaking the same language they have begun to do this, then nothing they plan to do will be impossible for them. Come, let us go down and confuse their language so they will not understand each other." So the Lord scattered them from there over all the earth, and they stopped building the city. That is why it was called Babel — because there the Lord confused the language of the whole world. From there the Lord scattered them over the face of the whole earth (Genesis 11:1-8).

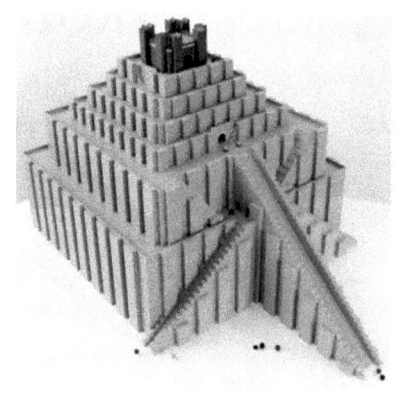

This was a fascinating story for me as a child. I could visualize captions over the heads of the people with Chinese, English, and Spanish words. They stood around their great building (ziggurat) in total confusion because they couldn't understand each other. However, even as a child I suspected there was more to the story than just a strange building and confused languages.

God saw in the actions of our ancient ancestors a dangerous spirit of pride and disobedience as they did what God said not to do: Centralize instead of decentralize. Throughout history humans have been drawn to Nimrods and Towers of Babel. Secular and spiritual centralization allows humans to feel safe in numbers and buildings, to be proud of a visible and measurable achievement, to have a sense of control over events and circumstances, and to idolize great leaders like Nimrod.

Decentralizing Versus Centralizing

"God has always intended for humankind to spread out and fill the earth with His glory."[8] To that end God has had to force decentralization over and over again because of the human tendency to try to centralize and control God's spontaneous expansion.

Judaism was formed in a decentralized process of hundreds of events, people, encounters, and revelations over thousands of years. God spoke to Abraham about leaving home for a new promised land out in the distant future that unborn generations would enjoy. At a simple handmade stone altar Abraham trusted his son Isaac to the will and goodness of God. Jacob's life was changed after a dream encounter in the desert that included angels going up and down a ladder between heaven and earth and a wrestling match with God. God met Moses on a mountaintop at a burning bush and later talked to Him face to face at that same mountain. God was in a lion's den with Daniel and walked with his friends, Shadrach, Meshach, and Abednego, in a fiery furnace. God revealed Himself through the spontaneous, and sometimes strange, utterances of prophets. For centuries the Ark of the Covenant, the place of the presence of God on earth, was carried along with the people in a movable tabernacle from one place to another.

By the time of Jesus, Judaism had been centralized in Jerusalem in a temple complex with special leaders, elaborate rituals, and thousands of rules. The temple as the center of religion became the vortex of a deadly dance between Jesus and the religious leaders that led to His death.

---

8. Neil Cole, *Organic Church* (San Francisco, CA: Jossey-Bass, 2005), 41.

Events in the New Testament show God taking direct action to decentralize. Jesus' response to Peter about the transfiguration (Matt. 17:1-6) was a statement about decentralization. Jesus did not intend for His followers to build a new temple on a central geographical or emotional mountaintop.

Jesus' commission to His followers cannot be fulfilled with a centralized paradigm. Each version of the commission suggests geographical (to the ends of the earth) and demographic (nations) expansion. "Therefore go and make disciples of all nations, baptizing them in the name of the Father and of the Son and of the Holy Spirit, and teaching them to obey everything I have commanded you. And surely I am with you always, to the very end of the age" (Matt. 28:18). "But you will receive power when the Holy Spirit comes on you; and you will be my witnesses in Jerusalem, and in all Judea and Samaria, and to the ends of the earth" (Acts 1:8). God forced decentralization because the Jerusalem church wanted to settle rather than to fill the earth.

Jesus designed the church for expansion. His followers were on the move and were called "the people of the Way" (Acts 9:2; 24:14), not the people of the building. The Early Church grew in space, not in place; it was going, expanding, multiplying, penetrating, and decentralizing. The church continued expansion during the first three hundred years of its existence and became the dominant religion of the Mediterranean world.

> *Jesus' plan was to decentralize, and He paid a dear price to make it possible. We need to rediscover the power of a decentralized movement with power distributed to each part that can in turn generate new life. Jesus' plan was ingenious. Do not disregard it and opt for another plan. Take another look at what He did and what He has given us to do.*[9]

---

9. Ibid., 44.

Introduction

Growth Versus Expansion

Organizational church growth and organic church expansion are different. Church growth is normally centralized in one area, controlled within one organization, and counted as one lump sum number. Church expansion penetrates many people groups, moves into wide geographical areas, crosses diverse social boundaries, and is hard to tally up as one number. Churches that use the traditional centralized model of growth lose the capacity to expand and instead grow "fatter" in one central location.

Donald McGavran, through his book *The Bridges of God*, and his church growth ministry, has influenced the church for decades and has blessed me personally. He, and the establishment of the School of World Mission at Fuller Theological Seminary in Pasadena, California in 1965, changed how the church views growth. McGavran and his followers have taught great theological and practical truths about the growth of the church.

Unfortunately, the great truths of the Church Growth Movement have been held captive by Constantine's centralized model. This is also true of the majority of church planting models that developed out of the church growth teachings. They use the same centralized large group that is building-centered, dependent on professional leaders, and focused inward on preaching and teaching programs.

Therefore, after several decades, I have concluded that church growth, as we do it through Constantine's centralized model, cannot produce an expansion movement. The theology, theories, technology, and impressive models built upon the Constantine model will reproduce a Constantine-kind of church. It will be stable, have impressive buildings, and produce extraordinary leaders. It will be accepted by society, will be at peace with surrounding political power, will blend into the prevailing culture, and will grow internally in a restricted geographical context. But the centralized traditional model will not produce the kind of pandemic people movement we see in the early years of the church and in periods of history when the church was forced to decentralize because of outside social or political pressure.

The building and services on Sunday act as a self-imposed quarantine that expose few to the Gospel during the week. Centralized churches reproduce in kind through new missions or satellite churches that carry the same brick and mortar come-structure genes. They lack the expansion gene we see in Jesus' church. Churches that use Jesus' expansion model have the capacity to grow internally and to expand externally.

Good church growth principles that are implemented through Constantine's traditional centralized structure may produce localized growth but will never produce a New Testament movement. Applying the same church growth principles through Jesus' organic decentralized model will produce expansion growth and movements.

I am convinced the church may grow on Sunday through large group ministries and programs but will only expand during the week through relationships and small groups.

Expansion and the Church Today

Today, extraordinary pastors of mega churches can grow the centralized church, sometimes to impressive sizes, with magnificent facilities, and professionally produced programs. More than 5 million people attend mega churches each Sunday. However, these extraordinary leaders do not expand the church as a dynamic people movement. These churches become giant religious ziggurats, one layer upon another layer, reaching higher

INTRODUCTION 29

and higher, and growing larger and larger. These are the churches featured at conventions and conferences and promoted as the growth model for smaller churches.

Placing the hope for expansion in this impressive mega church model is not backed up by empirical evidence. In his survey of 1000 churches in 32 countries, Christian Schwarz discovered that "the growth rate of churches decreased with increasing size"[10] and that "the evangelistic effectiveness of mini churches is statistically 1,600 percent greater than that of mega churches!"[11]

Schwarz's statistics clearly show that impressive brick and mortar churches led by extraordinarily gifted leaders, even when committed to church growth principles, do not result in expansion. In fact, these churches are part of the problem because they nurture the false hope that the existing centralized system, if done better on a grander scale, will generate New Testament-like expansion.

This brick and mortar ziggurat model cannot complete the Great Commission of expanding into all the earth (Matt. 28:18-20), the Great Command of loving (Matt. 22:36-40), the Great Mission of ministering (Luke 4:18-19), and the Great Example of sacrificially dying (John 12:24).

The reality of the centralized traditional model is: The leader's ability, gift mix, and expertise determine how many layers can be built on his/her ziggurat model and how high it will reach.

The spirit and mentality of the Tower of Babel is perpetuated by seventeen hundred years of group-think. Group-think about the structure and strategy of the traditional church is hundreds

---

10. Christian A. Schwarz, *Natural Church Development* (Carol Stream, IL: ChurchSmart Resources, 1996), 46.
11. Ibid, 48.

of years old and controls entire denominations and seminaries of learning. Some of the church's most charismatic and visionary leaders are isolated and insulated within the mega model and continue the delusion and the illusion of the centralized model.

Where does it stop? As these churches grow larger and larger, new classifications and categories are used to describe them. They were first classified as a "large church" and then a "mega church," a "super mega church," and the latest, a "super-ultra-mega church." They have grown into huge financial empires with facilities like a giant religious mall and diversified divisions for TV, book, and music CDs. Mega-churches require mega-stars.

The most successful centralized churches grow larger and larger on one campus or begin new campuses that are part of the mother campus. The fact that one of these churches forms another satellite church that does the same thing does not mean it is expanding. It is just forming another centralized church system.

Vacuum Cleaner Churches

The traditional centralized system is an organizational vacuum cleaner system that sucks members from other churches, primarily smaller churches that cannot compete with the impressive leaders and programs of the mega church. The criticism is that mega churches "steal sheep" from other churches, especially smaller churches. What are the facts?

Scott Thumma and Warren Bird conducted an extensive survey of mega churches in 2009.[12] Their survey shows how effective

---

12. "Not Who You Think They Are: A Profile of the People Who Attend America's Megachurches," Scott Thumma and Warren Bird, Copyright 2009 by Leadership Network and Hartford Seminary. Hartford Institute for Religious Research.

these churches are in attracting different segments of the population. Thumma and Bird divided growth in mega churches into five categories and give the following breakdown of where the members in mega churches come from:

4%	*Organic (Biological growth: Baptizing their children)*
6%	*Un-churched (Not part of any church)*
18%	*De-churched (Left another church, but its just been a while)*
28%	*Distant Transfer (From a church in another city)*
44%	*Local Transfer (From a church in the city)*

Small churches have more "un-churched" conversions as a percentage of members than large church but about the same statistical breakdown for the other categories in Thumma and Bird's survey. Church members (de-churched, distant transfer, and local transfer) are being shifted around between churches of all sizes, and have been for several decades. The game of shifting members is just more critical for a centralized church that is small because a church of 60 members that loses a family or two to a mega church has lost 10-20% of its membership and offerings.

This is nothing new. It always has been the rule of engagement with large churches and small churches in the traditional centralized system. The same centralized system and the same methods are used for a church of 100 members or 10,000 members: Preaching, teaching, and programs in a building with a professional leader. The shape is the same and the centralized come-structure nature is the same. This is what gives pastors of smaller churches the hope that they can duplicate the growth of a large church. It is the same model. Duplicate the methods of a large church, work harder, and the hope is that the system will produce the same results.

The only difference today is that megachurches are so powerful and effective. They are the centralized church on steroids. We should not fault them for doing the traditional centralized system better than other churches. I sympathize with the pastors of small churches but am surprised at their inability to see they are in a no win situation. In the ocean, the big fish always eat the little fish. However, pastors of small churches refuse to get out of this system in which they are severely disadvantaged.

The issue isn't the size of my ziggurat. A ziggurat is a ziggurat no matter its size. It is one layer upon another layer and upon another layer. Some of these churches suck members from surrounding smaller churches into their orb of ministry, or as one more layer on their great organizational ziggurat. The most successful vacuum cleaner churches become religious empires that grow larger and larger, all the time attracting more and more people into centralized ministries that must be sustained by attracting more and more people.

These large churches do many wonderful things. However, they are so successful that they reinforce the lie that bigger is better, the illusion that extraordinary leaders are Jesus' model of leadership, and the delusion that public worship, preaching, and teaching are Christ's primary purpose for His spiritual Body on earth. This system will not produce expansion!

So, are megachurches "stealing sheep?" Sure, just like all the other churches (large and small) that use this model have done for years. Megachurches just do it better!

Pastors of megachurches may not intend to be a vacuum cleaner church, may not realize they are damaging small churches, and may resent being called a vacuum cleaner church. However, this is the reality of the centralized system. This is not expansion growth no matter where it comes from. It is not a healthy expansion model. It is a growth model that for the most part shifts members around between churches. And the shift is almost always in the favor of the large church.

CAN GOD DECENTRALIZE TODAY?

Social, cultural, political, and religious factors contributed to the construction of the Tower of Babel. Nimrod wanted to centralize political power, of course into his hands. The people wanted to build something great with their own hands that would make them feel safe and important in the fortress and in their one culture. The religious factor was that they would be great, like God. They would not be turned from their mission by ordinary persuasion. Only some powerful force or factor would deter them. God used the cultural factor of language to stop centralization at the Tower of Babel.

Throughout history God has utilized internal and external factors and forces such as society, culture, and government to decentralize the church. A religious festival brought pilgrims to Jerusalem in the first century and a significant number became the first wave of Christians. After the festival they dispersed across the Roman Empire with the good news. A few years later the Roman government began to persecute the Church and scattered it across the Mediterranean world.

The Church in China in the 1950s is a more recent example of how God uses outside forces like the government to decentralize the church. The Communist government closed every church in China except a few showcase churches that they controlled. This forced the church to disperse as a decentralized people movement that was simple, inexpensive, low maintenance, contagious, and led by ordinary Christians. The decentralized church in China exploded in one of the greatest small group people movements in history.

I am not sure what social, cultural, or governmental force God can use to decentralize the church today. I can think of one government factor in the United States that can force the brick and mortar church to look beyond its centralized system. Churches (large and small) will find it difficult to exist in the current centralized building form without a tax-exempt status from the government. Imagine what is going to happen if the centralized brick and mortar churches are taxed in the United States. This will be a dispersal and decentralization of the church like the Tower of Babel. God can use the actions of government to do what leaders of brick and mortar churches have been unwilling to do: decentralize and disperse the church into the fields that are white unto harvest.

Depending on buildings, special leaders, and programs is not an expansion strategy. This is true of all the major church models regardless of their size: traditional (including Catholic), creative (small group, seeker, meta, and celebration), house church (simple church), revolutionary church, and cell church. It is also true of almost all church planting models that use a centralized building, worship, and program model as the strategy end game.

JESUS' DECENTRALIZING NUMBERS: 3/12/70

In his bestselling book, *The Tipping Point*, Malcolm Gladwell has a chapter titled: "The Magical Number of 150." In the chapter, he makes a case that 150 is the proper size for effective organization.

> *The figure of 150 seems to represent the maximum number of individuals with whom we can have genuinely social relationship, the kind of relationship that goes with knowing who*

INTRODUCTION

they are and how they relate to us. --- If we are interested in starting an epidemic---in reaching a Tipping Point --- what are the most effective kinds of groups? Is there a simple rule of thumb that distinguishes a group with real social authority from a group with little power at all? As it turns out, there is. It's called the Rule of 150, and it is a fascinating example of the stage and unexpected ways in which context affects the course of social epidemics.[13]

I also believe the group size of 150 is important. It corresponds to a small congregation in the church. (Most churches in the world operate at this size or smaller.) However, this number has been distorted by Constantine's centralized system to the point that it is an ineffective model for expansion. As it is used today, the public congregation is tied to a building, to professional leaders, and to preaching, teaching, and training programs. It can grow but cannot be Christ's group for expansion. Expansion in the 21st century depends on an even smaller church: Jesus' group of seventy is His expansion unit.

The mid-level number of 70 is Jesus' "magical" number because it contains the decentralizing forces of natural expansion (3), of organic community (12), and of supervision for the task and mission (70). It is necessary for leaders to think 70 (cluster) rather than 120 (congregation) in order to escape Constantine's congregational baggage of buildings, professional leaders, and preaching, teaching, and training programs.

The decentralized church will have some form of a large group public expression. The challenge is for the public large group to support the decentralized expansion of the 3/12/70 unit into the world. Today we have enough large group public churches.

---

13. Malcolm M. Gladwell, *The Tipping Point* (Boston: Back Bay Books, 2002), 174-175.

These churches need to use Jesus' mid-level unit of 3/12/70 to support an expansion people movement.

BE AWARE AND BEWARE

The lesson of the Tower of Babel is that dependence on a building, a great leader, and a central organization is a delusion, an illusion, and a lie. God will not share His glory with any person or organization. God's solution is to disperse and decentralize the church in a form that maximizes relationships, minimizes centralized programs, and multiplies ordinary leaders who can oversee Jesus' expansion system.

Pastor of a large church: Be aware and beware of the Tower of Babel temptation. The megachurch seems successful. It is large, powerful, influential, and growing with all the trappings of success. However, centralization of the church is dangerous. A church can become a Tower of Babel church that grows layer upon layer, higher and higher as a "stairway to heaven." The danger is that these mega models promote centralization of religion, no matter how spiritual the pastor, sincere the leaders, and wonderful the programs.

Pastor of a small church: Be aware and beware of the temptation to duplicate the centralized model. This is not Jesus' expansion model we see in the New Testament that created a pandemic people movement. It requires an extraordinary Nimrod leader to make it work. This model is no friend to your small church. It can suck your members into its grandeur and largeness and leave your church as a bare skeleton. Remember: small churches grow faster and win more people to Christ proportionally than the large vacuum cleaner church you may want to copy. You can grow and expand if you use Jesus' decentralized expansion system of 3/12/70.

INTRODUCTION

In this book I explain how pastors of churches of all sizes can be part of God's exponential expansion movement. Jesus' mid-level group of 70 represents three different types of groups that operate in concert as one unit: the contagious friendship group that naturally makes disciples and reaches the lost (3), the nurturing community group that maintains the health of the body (12), and the cluster of seventy that supervises expansion.

The 3/12/70 unit is able to expand because it moves through relationships and can exist underneath culture and government. It expands because it is contagious with the good news and is able to infect the maximum number of people with the maximum amount of the gospel for the maximum amount of time.

Your church can be God's instrument of expansion, whether a megachurch, a mini-church, or a size in between. Expansion in the 21st century depends on small churches and ordinary leaders. Jesus' mid-level unit of 3/12/70 operates as that small church and uses ordinary leaders.

Join me as we walk through the pages of this book and consider together Jesus' process of expansion.

Section 1

Factors in expansion

Chapter 1: Characteristics of Jesus' Strategy

Chapter 2: Where Are the Working Models?

Chapter 3: Jesus' Great Vision

Chapter 4: Decision Process and Values

Chapter 5: Challenges: The Dark Night of the Soul

Chapter 1

CHARACTERISTICS OF JESUS' STRATEGY

When Jesus' "plan is reflected on, the basic philosophy is so different from that of the modern church that its implications are nothing less than revolutionary."
• Robert Coleman

Jesus had a strategy to begin His church and to continue it. For some of us the thought of Jesus operating with a strategy doesn't seem spiritual. Nevertheless, the spontaneity we see in the gospels appeals to us. Jesus' strategy is unique because it is organic and relational rather than organizational. In fact, His life was and is the strategy.

> *At first glance it might even appear that Jesus had no plan. Another approach might discover some particular technique but miss the underlying pattern of it all. This is one of the marvels of his strategy. It is so unassuming and silent that it is unnoticed by the hurried churchman. But when the realization of his controlling method finally dawns on the open mind of the disciple, he will be amazed at its simplicity and will wonder how he could have ever failed to see it before. Nevertheless, when his plan is reflected on, the basic philosophy is so different from that of the modern church that its implications are nothing less than revolutionary.*[14]

---

14. Coleman, 19-20.

The Gospels are biographical, not books of strategy with a step-by-step process. Jesus lived out His strategy and from His life we can see the characteristics that guided what He did ... and what we should do.

So how do we make sure the vision we are following and the church we are serving is living out the expansion strategy Jesus modeled and taught in the New Testament? Consider 10 characteristics of Jesus' expansion strategy for the church:

1. Jesus' Strategy Is Not Constantine's Strategy

It is necessary to repeat a theme running through two previous books (*The Second Reformation* and *The Second Reformation: Stage 2*): Jesus' church strategy in the first century was not the same as Constantine's church strategy in the fourth century, or the traditional church today. The difference has nothing to do with the century or culture in which they developed. The difference is the nature of the church. Constantine saw the church as a static organization and Jesus saw the church as a living organism.

"Jesus' strategy is not Constantine's" must be repeated because Constantine's model has such a powerful grip on modern Christianity. Until pastors and church leaders dig deeper than the fourth century to find the true origin of the church, nothing will change. Why should it? If the traditional centralized model was Jesus' model for the church then we must make it work. However, Scripture, church history, my personal experience, and the prompting of the Holy Spirit convince me that Jesus' strategy of the church is not Constantine's strategy, and therefore cannot be ours today. My prayer is that God has brought you to the same conclusion, or is now speaking that into your spirit.

CHAPTER 1: CHARACTERISTICS OF JESUS' STRATEGY   43

I've gone so far as to state it like this: The greatest strategic hindrance to the expansion of the church in the 21st century is Constantine's model![15] Too often when we think and dream church, we are operating within Constantine's model: A come-structure, high-cost, high-maintenance, low-growth, labor intensive, immobile church, dependent on professional leaders, and isolated in buildings. This strategy appears to work for a few large churches and extraordinary leaders.

The mega church enterprises and empires that dominate the church world today are the best that Constantine's model can produce. However, they should not fool us. No matter how impressive these large churches, the traditional model is incapable of expansion. It survives by growing larger in a centralized building that is designed for preaching and teaching programs, and today increasingly for entertainment events. In fact, the massing of Christians in ever larger and imposing church fortresses proves the need for a new expansion strategy that will break the church out of its centralized paradigm.

One reaction to the traditional model has been to seek an organic way of being church and to form simple churches. My observation is that the organic or simple church just changes the size and place but not the nature of the traditional system. They form into small groups in houses but continue to use the preaching and teaching model on a smaller scale. The traditional mega church and new mini church are growth strategies, not expansion strategies.

---

15. William A. Beckham, "Small Churches and Ordinary Leaders," *The Second Reformation: Stage 2* (Moreno Valley, Ca: CCS Publishing, 2014), 15.

2. Jesus Focused His Strategy on People

The model of the Early Church was effective because it was based on people. To reach the generations in the 21st century, the church must be restructured as the organic body that we see in the New Testament. Jesus' model naturally cuts across social and cultural boundaries because it is built on relationships: a friendship relationship of two or three, a community relationship of twelve, and supervision relationships of seventy followers.

Dr. Philip Sell, professor at Trinity Evangelical Divinity School and a former pastor of a small group church, compares a "relationship-based church" to other models.

> This model of church life contrasts with the program-based church, where a church creates programs to meet needs, the entertainment-based church where people come to catch a spiritual high every week, and the content-based church, where the church is a 'teaching center' for people to attend every Sunday. Sadly, small groups will be forced to fit into the model of programs, entertainment or content, unless the core experience of the relational church is understood.[16]

The central focus of a church determines the end result. Focus on buildings and produce magnificent cathedrals and church buildings. Focus on preaching and teaching and produce great preachers and teachers. Focus on theology and produce theologians, theological institutions, and books. Focus on worship and produce great choirs, bands, and musicians. Focus on programs and produce slick and professional programs. Focus on a particular generation and produce sociological techniques and

---

16. M. Scott Boren, *How Do We Get There from Here?* (Houston, TX: Touch Publications, 2007), 15-16.

fads that attract that generation. Focus on relationships and the result is a people movement. From His people strategy, Jesus set into motion a pandemic people movement in the first century.

3. Jesus' Strategy Is to Form His Organic Body

Jesus created the church as a self-sustaining organism with the minimum amount of organization. "At Pentecost the new community now appears as a Church, a Church which can exist in thousands of local congregations dispersed throughout the entire world. The new humanity of God stretching from antiquity to the present is an organism."[17] In Colossians 1:27 Paul explains the factor that makes the church a living organism: "Christ in you, the hope of glory." The incarnate, indwelling, abiding, and manifest presence of Christ, through the Holy Spirit, is the great mystery that gives life and power to every physical expression of the church. This is the mystery of God in Trinity lived out in a spiritual/physical body on earth.

Dietrich Bonhoeffer shares an insightful interpretation of the scripture "My dear children, for whom I am again in the pains of childbirth until Christ is formed in you" (Gal. 4:19). Jesus forms Himself in the individual Christian and also forms the church into His body:

> *The Church is nothing but a section of humanity in which Christ has really taken form. What we have here is utterly and completely the form of Jesus Christ and not some other form side by side with Him. The Church is the man in Christ, incarnate, sentenced and awakened to new life. In the first instance, therefore, she has essentially nothing whatever to do with the so-called religious functions of man, but with the whole man*

---

17. Bernard Ramm, *Special Revelation and the Word of God* (Grand Rapids, MI: William B. Eerdmans, 1961), 101.

in his existence in the world with all its implications. What matters in the Church is not religion but the form of Christ, and its taking form amidst a band of men. If we allow ourselves to lose sight of this, even for an instant, we inevitably relapse into that programme planning for the ethical or religious shaping of the world, which was where we set out from.[18]

No model, no matter how biblical or successful, produces the life of Christ. Christ, through the creative will of the Father and the direction and intercession of the Holy Spirit, forms His life in the church in several different functioning groups that make up the life of the whole. These groups are the relational architecture of mankind in every generation. God is actively involved in history through the Holy Spirit, always moving the church toward the organic side of spiritual life.

When groups (3/12/70) operate as the organic body of Christ, they are the living body of Christ on earth. The friendship triad of two or three is Jesus' body in basic discipleship, special friendship, and contagious witness. The community group of twelve is Jesus' body living in nurturing family life. The cluster group of seventy is Jesus' body on mission moving into harvest and expansion. The "gathered" and "whole" group of one hundred and twenty is Jesus' body as a support unit. The Church of thousands is Jesus' body as the public expression of Christ in society, lifted up and proclaimed as Lord and Savior.

Whenever and wherever the biblical model has been implemented with the great mystery of Christ's presence, dynamic church movements have emerged.

---

18. Dietrich Bonhoeffer, *Ethics* (New York, NY: Touchstone by Simon & Schuster, 1995) 84–85.

Neil Cole uses an excellent illustration about skeleton systems to explain the structure of organizations such as the church.

> *The exoskeleton, found in insects as well as crustaceans such as lobsters and crabs, is outside---hard, inflexible, established at the start. This structure becomes a limitation for growth and development of the organism. The endoskeleton, however, is internal---not immediately visible, more flexible, and growing with the life of the organism. The exoskeleton is the first (and probably last) thing you see with the organism, while the endoskeleton is rarely seen at all, but its support of life is obvious. The Body of Christ should have an endoskeleton that can grow with the body to meet its need as it develops. The main purpose of the exoskeleton is protection, while the main reason for the endoskeleton is support and strengthening of the organism. Most churches today, more concerned with protection than expansion, have sought shelter in an exoskeleton structure.*[19]

The organic church Jesus created was an internal *endoskeleton* system with rigid bones on the inside like humans. The centralized organizational church developed an external *exoskeleton* system like a crab or lobster. The inability of the church today to operate effectively without the external skeleton structure of a building shows the endoskeleton nature of the traditional church. Some churches are like a tortoise with a combination of a thick shell surrounding a weak internal skeleton system.

Jesus' internal organic system gives the church the ability to support greater weight without becoming too heavy for the organism. It can grow with the organism and has greater mobility and flexibility. These structural systems (internal, external, and the combination of internal-external) are the options of all

---
19. Cole, *Organic Church*, 125.

churches, large and small. Most churches today are organized as a lobster or crab but some are tortoises. Jesus is restoring his organic church with its original internal spiritual structure.

4. Jesus' Strategy Mobilizes for Expansion

Jesus was always on the move, always going. Reading the Gospels, one has the sense of His freedom to go anywhere at anytime. He moved back and forth across Judea, Galilee, and Samaria in three short years of ministry. He was not tied down to a special building, to fund-raising, to a schedule of rituals, to seminary-trained ordained priests or pastors, or to the control of a hierarchy run by boards and committees. Jesus flowed with the people and the needs and was supremely and spiritually mobile and free.

In his critique on the church, Howard Snyder declares the church building to be a symbol of the church's immobility:

> *What is more immovable than a church building? And yet Christians are, supposedly, wayfaring pilgrims. Christians are to be a mobile people. In the Old Testament the portable tabernacle was the symbol of God's presence in community with his people ... The Old Testament did not find its fulfillment in impressive church buildings but in the fleshly temple, people. The gospel says, "Go," but our church buildings say, "Stay." The gospel says, "Seek the lost," but our churches say, "Let the lost seek the church." Architecture petrifies program.*[20]

Neil Cole suggests that dependence on buildings affects the expansion mission of the church. "Jesus paid a huge price to set His people free to take His presence everywhere. We need

---

20. Howard A. Snyder, *The Problem of Wineskins* (Downers Grove, Ill: Inter-varsity Press, 1975), 70.

to resist the seductive magnet of glamorous buildings and religious hierarchical systems that bind us to a place and form of church that cannot spread His glory across the planet."[21]

Coleman believes a mobile church is necessary because "the goal is world conquest. We dare not let a lesser concern capture our strategy of the moment...There can be no substitute for total victory, and our field is the world. We have not been called to hold the fort, but to storm the heights."[22]

Jesus was mobile and mobilized. The word "mobilize" means "to assemble or marshal (military forces) into readiness for active service; to marshal, bring together, prepare (power, force, wealth, etc.) for action, especially of a vigorous nature; to increase or bring to a full stage of development."[23] The expectation of the New Testament church was that every Christ-follower would be mobilized for witness, ministry, and the mission (expansion) of the Gospel.

Jesus mobilized a movement that "turned the world upside down." It was a spiritual revolution that changed the social, political, and economic landscape. Mobilization requires leaders who can lead others into the battle. Using any criteria, Jesus was the most effective leader the world has ever seen.

"The Church is the pilgrim people of God. It is on the move---hastening to the ends of the earth to beseech all men to be reconciled to God, and hastening to the end of time to meet its Lord who will gather all into one ... It cannot be understood

---

21. Cole, 45.
22. Coleman, 98.
23. Mobilize. Dictionary.com. Collins English Dictionary - Complete & Unabridged 10th Edition. HarperCollins Publishers. http://dictionary.reference.com/browse/mobilize (accessed: November 01, 2014).

rightly except in a perspective which is at once missionary and eschatological."[24]

5. Jesus Builds His Strategy around Leaders

Jesus' strategy was His "men." Robert Coleman believes "the time which Jesus invested in these few disciples was so much more by comparison than that given to others that it can only be regarded as a deliberate strategy."[25] Jesus "concentrated on those who were to be the beginning of His leadership. Though he did what he could to help the multitudes, he had to devote himself primarily to a few men rather than the masses, so that the masses could at last be saved. This was the genius of his strategy."[26] Greg Ogden calls Jesus' relationship to His men the "interpersonal environment" of the church.[27]

The traditional organizational model develops leaders of all kinds: Bible teachers, worship leaders, committee chairpersons, deacons, board members, counselors, and hospital visitors. Jesus designed His organic system to produce expansion leaders through on-the-job training in groups of 3/12/70.

The life and the systems of the church in the New Testament emerged out of the leadership strategy we see in Jesus' three-year ministry. We know this because of the final prayer report Jesus gave to the Father in John 17:1-26. Jesus confirmed to the Father that their strategy was going to be successful. At the time, He was still facing the cross, the betrayal of Judas, the falling away of the Disciples, and the turning away of the crowds.

---

24. Leslie Newbigin, *The Household of God* (London: SCM, 1953), 25.
25. Coleman, 43.
26. Ibid., 31.
27. Greg Ogden, *Transforming Discipleship* (Downers Grove, IL: InterVarsity Press, 2003), 75.

CHAPTER 1: CHARACTERISTICS OF JESUS' STRATEGY

Why such confidence? Consider three different strategy reports Jesus could have presented to the Father. "Our strategy is going to work because of:

1. The multitudes and early response
2. The large number of believers after Pentecost
3. Our leaders."

The first two reports look promising because of the numbers associated with the multitudes listening to Jesus and Peter's sermons. But it is strategy report 3 that Jesus gave to the Father. "Our strategy is going to be successful because of committed leaders empowered by the indwelling presence of the Holy Spirit." It is clear Jesus uses a leadership strategy.

An important characteristic of Jesus' leadership strategy is His emphasis on verb leaders (actions) instead of noun leaders (positions or titles). Jesus' organic church produces leaders who are verbs: elder-*ing*, pastor*ing*, teach*ing*, evangeliz*ing*, prophesiz*ing*, apostle-*ing*, and deacon-*ing*. A movement of God is always led by verbs. Verb leaders say, "Follow me" and "let me serve you."

However, noun leaders are important in the traditional church. This is the reason for the constant battle in the traditional church about clergy and laity. Positions and titles are created, sanctioned by other noun leaders, and then protected and perpetuated by the official system. Noun leaders say, "Obey me," "listen to me," "honor me," "serve me," and "support me."

When the most important task of the church is to do the work of ministry through small groups, then ordinary leaders are more important than leaders with titles and positions. Today, churches that operate with Jesus' system of 3/12/70 place a high value on verb leaders.

6. Jesus Provides the Power for His Strategy

Because Jesus' church is an organic body, power must come from a spiritual source because human power does not sustain a spiritual body. Jesus promised His authority and power to His followers and His church: "All authority in heaven and on earth has been given to me" (Matt. 19:20) and "you will receive power when the Holy Spirit comes on you" (Acts 1:7-8). Jesus' strategy for His organic church was predicated on His power.

It is futile to expect to do church through organizational structures and techniques. The activities of an organization cannot sustain the spiritual life of Christ's Body. Leaders must realize "the organizational realm of church ministry can be 'manufactured'---the organic level can't."[28] In the traditional system, buildings, professional leaders, and centralized programs must produce enough organizational energy to make the institution work. Consequently, Christians become institutionalized in the organization. Leaders work in the church organization and hope that what they do is the "work of ministry" that Paul talks about in Ephesians 4.

Human power can produce impressive results through organization. Look at the great buildings and structures of institutions and organizations. The New Testament church had none of these but produced an expansion people movement because of the power of God operating in a living spiritual organism. Jesus' strategy is designed for Him, through the Holy Spirit, to be the power source operating in each Christian, in triads of two or three Christians, in community groups of around twelve, in

---

28. Schwarz, *Natural Church Development*, 98.

churches that operate with Jesus' system of 3/12/70 mid-level supervising clusters of seventy, and in the gathered body of 120. These groups operate with His presence, power, and purpose.

> *The church is here on earth, not to do what other groups can do, but to do what no other group of human beings can probably do. It is here to manifest the life and power of Jesus Christ in fulfillment of the ministry which was given him by the Father, as he quoted it himself in the synagogue at Nazareth. "The Spirit of the Lord is upon me ... to preach good news to the poor ... to proclaim release to the captives and recovering of sight to the blind, to set at liberty those who are oppressed, to proclaim the acceptable year of the Lord (Luke 4:18-19).*[29]

7. JESUS' STRATEGY ACTIVATES ALL OF GOD'S PROVISIONS

Peter gives a blanket assurance to Christians. God provides everything!

> *His divine power has given us everything we need for life and godliness through our knowledge of him who called us by his own glory and goodness. Through these he has given us his very great and precious promises, so that through them you may participate in the divine nature and escape the corruption in the world caused by evil desires (2 Peter 1:3-4).*

God gives each Christian His divine power and this gives us "everything we need for life and godliness." The combination of His power, glory, and goodness allows each Christian to "participate in the divine nature and escape the corruption in the world caused by evil desires." The provision of His divine power and nature allows God to provide to the individual Christian and the

---

[29]. Ray C. Stedman, *Body Life* (Ventura, CA: Regal Books, 1972), 146.

corporate body the spiritual life and experiences we call doctrines.

As Christians participate in His divine power and nature in a friendship triad (3) God provides the experiences of Body life, confession, friendship fellowship, application of the Word, the presence of Christ, listening prayer, and encouraging edification. In a community cell (12), God provides the experiences of community, accountability, equipping, leadership, evangelism, Christ in the midst, and death.

In addition to these seven elements of a community cell, God supplies other necessary spiritual provisions. Prayer, the Word, and worship facilitate the relationship and communication between God and Christians as individuals and as a community. Redemption, sanctification, and edification are dynamic catalytic provisions that shape the life of a Christian and prepare for the Christian life.

God provides the Holy Spirit as personal helper and the Spirit supplies His gifts, such as serving, teaching, exhortation, giving, mercy, word of wisdom, word of knowledge, faith, gifts of healings, miracles, prophecy, tongues and interpretation of tongues. The Spirit produces spiritual fruit: love, joy, peace, forbearance, kindness, goodness, faithfulness, gentleness and self-control (Gal. 5:22-23). In addition, God also provides necessary leaders: apostles, prophets, evangelists, and pastors-teachers.

All of these provisions have their source in the provision of God's divine power: God "powerfully works in me" (Col. 1:29) and God's divine nature: God "conforms" (Rom. 8:29) and "transforms" me (2 Cor. 3:18). These provisions can be stated from the perspective of God's participation in the life of every Christian.

- *Prayer: God talks with me*
- *Word: God teaches me*
- *Worship: God inspires me*
- *Redemption: God redeems me*
- *Sanctification: God cleans me up for His use*
- *Edification: God builds up the Body (me also)*
- *Holiness: God sets me aside for His glory and use.*
- *Gifts: God invests Himself in me*
- *Fruit: God produces His fruit in and through me*
- *Leaders: God prepares the saints for the work of ministry*
- *Holy Spirit: God gives me a divine Helper*

These spiritual provisions are the work of God in the Christian and in the community of the church. The provisions are activated in different ways in the various groups of the church. However, most are experienced in the friendship triad, community cell, and mid-level supervising seventy. The Christian doesn't earn any of God's provisions and cannot produce them with human ability or effort. They are given as part of His love and grace and Christians have access to each of these provisions within the Body, individually and collectively.

All religions promise blessings and provisions, but God gives a helper along with the blessings and provisions. "The immanence of Christ promises presence and help. My behavior has a divine observer as well as a divine helper: the Holy Spirit."[30] The Holy Spirit empowers each Christian to participate in all of God's blessings and provisions that He entrusts to the Church.

---

30. E. Y. Mullins, The *Christian Religion in Doctrinal Expression*, (Philadelphia, PA: Roger Williams Press, 1917), 320.

8. Jesus' Strategy Produces Quantity and Quality

Luke, the historian of the New Testament Church, included periodic summaries of the state of the church in the book of Acts. The growth summaries were balanced between the numerical (quantity) and the spiritual (quality).

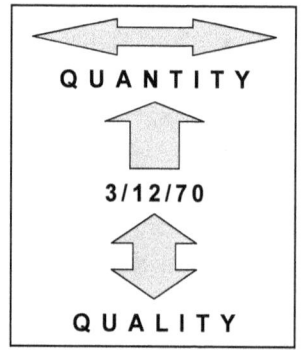

So the word of God (quality) spread (quantity). The number (quantity) of disciples (quality), in Jerusalem increased rapidly (quantity), and a large number of priests (quantity) became obedient to the faith (quality) (Acts 6:7).

Then the church throughout Judea, Galilee and Samaria (quantity) enjoyed a time of peace (quality). It was strengthened (quality); and encouraged by the Holy Spirit (quality), it grew in number (quantity), living in the fear of the Lord (quality) (Acts 9:31).

But the word of God (quality) continued to increase and spread" (quantity) (Acts 12:24). "So the churches were strengthened in the faith (quality) and grew daily in numbers (quantity)," (Acts 16:5). "In this way the word of the Lord (quality) spread widely (quantity in distance) and grew in power (quality) (Acts 19:20).

Jesus' commission to the church also has quantitative and qualitative balance. "Then Jesus came to them and said, "All authority in heaven and on earth has been given to me (quality). Therefore go and make disciples (quality) of all nations (quantity), baptizing them in the name of the Father and of the Son and of the

Holy Spirit (quality), and teaching them to obey (quality) everything (quantity) I have commanded you (quality). And surely I am with you (quality) always (quantity), to the very end of the age" (quantity) (Matt. 28:18-20).

"He said to them: "It is not for you to know the times or dates (quantity) the Father has set by his own authority (quality). But you will receive power when the Holy Spirit comes on you (quality); and you will be my witnesses (quality) in Jerusalem, and in all Judea and Samaria, and to the ends of the earth" (quantity) (Acts 1:7-8).

Jesus designed the church around relationship groups that produce quantity (external expansion) and also quality (internal spiritual growth). Through friendship triads, community cells, and supervision clusters of seventy, the quality of the church is increased. Through these same groups the church naturally expands and grows numerically. This is an important characteristic of Jesus' strategy.

9. Jesus' Strategy Requires Death/Resurrection

Death is a central characteristic of Jesus' strategy. The prophets foresaw His journey to the cross. Jesus told his followers that his end was the cross. The political powers and religious forces condemned Him to the cross. The Incarnation set into motion God's divine prototype for His plan for Mankind that was centered in the cross/resurrection event. Prototyping a strategy carries a cost. Jesus paid the price to prototype the Father's strategy of redemption with His life on the cross. Jesus was the strategy and His death/resurrection was the prototype.

We must count the cost of prototyping Jesus' organic church strategy. Living out a model of Jesus' church requires our death at each step of the process. Jesus' principle of death/

resurrection is necessary to develop a model of His church. "I tell you the truth, unless a kernel of wheat falls to the ground and dies, it remains only a single seed. But if it dies, it produces many seeds" (John 12:24).

The inclination of a leader is to develop a strategy to *do* something. Jesus' strategy is to lead us, through death, to *be* something. In order to become the strategy of the Father, Jesus had to surrender His will and life. Gethsemane is the climax of that surrender. God's strategy prototype is finalized at Gethsemane (Matt. 26:39-44).

> *Going a little farther, he fell with his face to the ground and prayed, "My Father, if it is possible, may this cup be taken from me. Yet not as I will, but as you will." Then he returned to his disciples and found them sleeping. "Could you men not keep watch with me for one hour?" he asked Peter. "Watch and pray so that you will not fall into temptation. The spirit is willing, but the body is weak." He went away a second time and prayed, "My Father, if it is not possible for this cup to be taken away unless I drink it, may your will be done." When he came back, he again found them sleeping, because their eyes were heavy. So he left them and went away once more and prayed the third time, saying the same thing.*

This passage reveals Jesus' emotional intensity and struggle as He came to the final act necessary to activate the Father's strategy of redemption. In Gethsemane Jesus died to His will (strategy) in order for the will (strategy) of the Father to be done. At Calvary Jesus died physically as the logical outcome of the decision finalized at Gethsemane. As long as it is my way and my will it is my strategy. Only when I die can God's will (strategy) be activated/resurrected. The leader who implements Jesus' strategy is well acquainted with Jesus' death/resurrection.

The door to God's strategy is submission death. We may consider that to be a negative but to God submission death is His power of salvation.

10. Jesus Began His Strategy with a Prototype

Jesus accomplished many things during His 3 ½ year ministry. Salvation was secured. The church as a body was formed and leaders were developed. One important accomplishment of Jesus' ministry may be missed: He lived out practical prototypes of His strategy. Remember, Jesus Christ was incarnated and became the "evidence of what He wanted practiced."

A church prototype integrates the working parts, process, and the dynamic life of a New Testament church. "Prototypes are essential to discovering and solving the key problems that stand between an idea and its full and successful implementation. Significant innovation cannot be achieved by talking about new ideas; you must build and test prototypes."[31] A prototype builds slowly toward a point where the different pieces, parts, and factors come together and it works. A prototype "takes a team from chaos to concept."[32]

A prototype is a practical working model of a strategy. A strategy visualizes an idea and proves the idea will actually work in a practical way. A prototype is simple, reproducible, and addresses both the mechanics and dynamics of a strategy. The mechanics include the working parts necessary for the process to be successful, such as groups, materials, procedures, and activities. The dynamics of a strategic prototype are the human factors and, in the case of the church, also the God factors.

---

31. Peter M. Senge, *The Fifth Discipline* (New York: Doubleday, 1990), 271.
32. Jim Collins, *Good to Great: Why Some Companies Make the Leap and Others Don't* (New York: HarperCollins, 2001), 12.

The next section shows how Jesus prototyped His expansion strategy. Only after successfully building and testing a prototype does a strategy on paper or in the mind become a valid working strategy.

Chapter 2

WHERE ARE THE WORKING MODELS?

> *"Those like myself whose imagination far exceeds their obedience are subject to a just penalty: we easily imagine conditions far higher than any we have really reached."*
>
> • C. S. Lewis

The church in the 21st century needs an expansion system with the organic dynamic of a New Testament house church, the supervision and expansion focus of Jesus' group of seventy, and the possibility of a streamlined forward operating base like the church at Antioch that sent out Paul, Barnabas, Mark, and Luke. This is the church without walls, programs, or professionals.

Is that kind of expansion system present today? Well, yes and no, because some ideas can only be validated in the future. This is what Roland Allen recognized about his radical concepts about the church in the 1930s.

> *I say what seems to me obviously true, but they do not know what to do about it. One day someone will see what action is demanded, and perhaps screw up their courage to take it. If I were out to organize and lead, that would be different, but as you well know I long ago determined that that was not the way of the Spirit for me. ... All I can say is "This is the way of Christ and His Apostles." If any man answers, "That is out of date," or "Times have changed"... I can only repeat "This*

is the way of Christ and His Apostles," and leave him to face that issue.[33]

With his revolutionary book, *Where Do We Go from Here?*, Ralph Neighbour introduced a new way of doing church in community cells in 1990. This book helped set into motion the small group part of the second reformation of structure. He explained his feelings about the process with a quote from C. S. Lewis, and followed the quote with a brutally honest confession and declaration about the small group model of the church he was introducing.

The quote from Lewis was: "Those like myself whose imagination far exceeds their obedience are subject to a just penalty: we easily imagine conditions far higher than any we have really reached. If we describe what we have imagined we may make others, and make ourselves, believe that we have really been there."[34]

Neighbour's confession was: "I confess that where I am going to take you in this chapter is a model of cell church life I have never fully experienced myself." His declaration was: "Of this I am certain: for those who won't settle for less, all we shall describe is possible.[35]

Twenty-five years after Neighbour's confession and declaration about the cell movement, it is obvious cell church life "is possible" and that Neighbour and many others "have really been there." In 2014, at the age of 85, God has Ralph Neighbour in

---

33. Roland Allen, *Missionary Methods: St. Paul's or Ours?* (Grand Rapids, MI: Wm. B. Eerdmans, 1962), i -ii.
34. C. S. Lewis, *The Four Loves* (New York: Harcourt, Brace & World, Inc., 1960), 192.
35. Ralph W. Neighbour, Jr., *Where Do We Go From Here?* (Houston, TX: Touch Publications, 1990), 172.

the middle of another New Testament type people movement in the Ukraine. However, in 1990 it was all just a vision and a venture of desperation and faith.

Roland Allen challenged the traditional church of his day with the New Testament expansion model of the church by analyzing its mission structure and church plants overseas. Ralph Neighbour helped reintroduce New Testament small groups back into the church. Both men confessed they were writing about concepts that had not been totally implemented, and yet they continued by faith. "We live by faith, not by sight" (2 Cor. 5:7) must be the attitude of visionaries who see what is yet to happen and innovators who quickly prototype what visionaries see.

A Confession about an Expansion Large Group

I must also make a confession about the expansion mid-level group (70) I am proposing in this book. I feel the same kind of desperation and venture of faith that accompanied stage one of the structural reformation in 1990. The idea of the seventy as a stand-alone and self-contained expansion group is not fully implemented as an intentional strategy in any model of the church that I know of today.

The words "expansion" and "intentional" are a caveat in my confession because the group of seventy does exist in churches that operate with cells. These churches organize around Jethro's system of 10, 50, 100, and 1000. Therefore, the supervision group of seventy naturally operates in the internal organization of these churches. (The supervision seventy corresponds to Jethro's fifty.) However, these churches have not *intentionally*, as a strategy, projected this same supervising seventy outward in external expansion.

The distinction between *internal* growth and *external* expansion is important. Cell churches organize *internally* around clusters of seventy that supervise community life under a large group umbrella. The unfortunate fact is cell churches do not use the seventy as the focal point of *external* church planting. Cell churches continue to use Constantine's preaching and teaching large group to start churches, just like the traditional model. This diverts the focus, time, energy, and resources of the church plant away from expansion through the cluster of seventy (3/12/70) to the traditional preaching and teaching model. New church plants from cell churches today generally grow at the same rate as other models. Once a church plant begins its own traditional preaching, teaching, and program large group with a building, expansion stops or is dramatically slowed.

Why do cell churches use the supervising large group in internal organization and not in expanding new churches externally beyond the mother church? The answer: The only stand-alone and self-contained large group in the minds of most pastors (even cell church pastors) is the one developed by Constantine in the fourth century and the one they use in the mother church. Constantine's model blinds leaders to other large group options.

Seeker and creative churches also use small groups for internal growth. They begin new satellite churches that can grow beyond the mother church campus, but cannot expand because they use the specialized seeker church large group model of the mother church. This requires a large number of members to maintain the excellence of the Sunday programs. Leaders of cell churches and seeker churches are the very people who could be expanding the church, if they catch the vision of the mid-level cluster of seventy.

I am not talking about size here but about function. The majority of churches in the world, regardless of the denomination or model, have 50 to 100 members. However, these small churches continue to function as a stand-alone preaching and teaching model just like their larger counterparts. The picture they have of themselves is not a supervision model of seventy or a forward base of 120. These mini churches see themselves as a preaching, teaching, and program headquarters. Small churches use such a high percentage of the time, energy, and focus of leaders in duplicating a preaching, teaching, and program large group that they never break the barrier of one hundred.

JESUS' MODEL OF THE SEVENTY

Where can a person go to observe a functioning group of seventy? First go to the New Testament. Look at Jesus' model. If you can't see the expansion model in scripture, you probably won't accept it as a model in your world today. Or, if you see it operating today, you will explain it away as just one more method. The same is true for the disciple triad of two or three and the community group of twelve. First, look for them in the New Testament.

Imagine you are with Jesus' seventy toward the end of His earthly ministry. The atmosphere is relaxed and relational, like a retreat. During the course of the activities of the day, Jesus gathers you and his other followers on a hillside in the shade of some old olive trees above a city in the distance. Jesus sits on a large rock and gives instructions for your next mission. He repeats the same basic instructions He shared with you and the seventy during an earlier period of His ministry (Luke 10). However, on this day Jesus is preparing you to replicate the task of the seventy after He is gone. Below is my interpretative account of His instructions. The Master speaks:

> *My plan is not for you to spend your energy and time gathering large crowds to preach and minister to them. I know you*

saw crowds in my public ministry, but a focus on crowds is a focus on growth and my plan is for expansion. Crowds will be the byproduct of my strategy as you implement it. You are going to support each other in the two or three unit, live together as a spiritual family in your homes, and supervise expansion in groups of seventy. You have experienced each of these groups several times now, so you should be able to naturally operate in them. Our group of seventy is ideal for supervising the other units of discipleship (two or three) and community (twelve). Operating at the level of seventy protects the organic nature of My body by limiting the type and amount of organization. This lets us be mobile and to move among the people. What we are doing today doesn't require a temple, synagogue, or special meeting place. Our place is among the people.

You know from my teaching and our experiences together that my numbers of 3/12/70 are not magical but organic and dynamic. The numbers are flexible categories that can increase and decrease by a few persons, but they always preserve the unique group purpose and focus of friendship (3), community (12), and supervision (70). The group of three begins with two persons and multiplies with four, the community group of twelve can be as small as four or five and as large as twelve to fifteen, and the group of seventy can be as small as thirty persons growing to a full cluster of seventy.

Remember, I integrate all ministry, teaching, and training through these growth and expansion groups. Make disciples of believers and contact seekers (persons of peace) through my friendship unit of two or three. I used this group in preparing Peter, James, and John and when I first sent you out two-by-two. This is where followers are nurtured, equipped, edified, and deployed to penetrate oikos relationships (households

Chapter 2: Where Are the Working Models?

of friends and relatives) and to harvest "persons of peace." Peter, Andrew, James, and John, you understand net fishing. Now, help all the followers become net fishers of men together. You won't catch a lot of fish with just one pole and one line.

A friendship group of two or three persons can survive on its own if necessary. However, with net fishing, a friendship group naturally grows into a community cell and participates in and experiences a fuller expression of My Body. Within community groups of ten to twelve, believers experience body life as a spiritual family: nurture, fellowship, equipping, edification, accountability, and working through conflicts. As the friendship triads grow, the community cells grow and naturally organize into clusters of thirty to seventy persons (as we are now). In a cluster of seventy, leaders will supervise, train, deploy, debrief, and pray for the harvest. The seventy will do everything to fulfill my mission to the church to expand as a people movement in Jerusalem, Judea, Samaria, and the world.

Let me walk you through my strategy in another way. I am organizing you as my spiritual army in units of 3/12/70. These units are the key for feeding my sheep and tending my lambs, for developing leaders, edifying the Body, contacting and cultivating the "person of peace," and supervising expansion. I will be with you in these groups in spiritual power. This is the way we are going to prepare leaders through on-the-job training. Each follower learns to watch out for another person in a friendship triad and is developed as a potential leader in the community cell.

When at least two or three full clusters of seventy are operational, you may want to form into a forward streamlined base (120). This will give you a logistical support base and allow you to coordinate the tactical expansion of the clusters of seventy out on the frontlines. These support congregations will develop naturally as the clusters of seventy grow. Don't forget: A cluster of seventy can stand on its own without a streamlined congregation of 120. In fact, it may expand more effectively without a congregation. However, two or more clusters may establish a forward base congregation when the support is needed to provide the spiritual and material logistics for expansion.

You will continue to attract large numbers of people. However, I have warned you that the crowds can and will turn on you as will happen shortly with me. My plan to expand into the whole world depends on organizing the large crowds into my mission expansion unit of 3/12/70. Therefore, be careful about your public congregations! Don't get tied down to buildings, crowds, or places as you see has happened at the Temple. Be mobile so you can take the message everywhere.

Now before you go down into the village where you will contact the "person of peace" in groups of two or three, let me summarize our strategy. In friendship triads: Be a friend; add a friend; add another friend; enter the oikos (households) of these "friends of peace." Be a spiritual family in groups of twelve as you have seen me do with the twelve. Organize in a tactical cluster of seventy in order to supervise expansion and growth (as we are now). This is simple. This is how I will build my church. Do what you have seen me do. The promised Spirit will help you do this. The Father will give increase. Now, go two-by-two into the village and we will meet back here in three days to debrief.

Chapter 2: Where Are the Working Models?

Personal Journey toward the Seventy

For years as a pastor and missionary, my only context for the church was the centralized preaching, teaching, and program traditional model. I grew up in that model in my home church. I studied about the brick and mortar church in seminary. By the time I was thirty-three, I had been pastor of three headquarters churches: the first with a membership of 100, the second with a membership of 300, and the last with a bragging membership of 1000.

In December of 1973, God spoke to Mary and me about becoming missionaries. Our call narrowed down to church planting, then to urban church planting, and finally to Bangkok, Thailand. I sensed the traditional model of which I had been pastor did not fit the vision God had placed in my heart.

My mind went to a Baptist pastor in Houston who was developing a different kind of church around small groups. The church was called West Memorial Baptist Church or Touch Community: Touching Others Under Christ's Hand. Their equally catchy logo also stuck with me: *The people who care!* I made a mental note to go to Houston before leaving the county and to spend some time with the pastor, Ralph Neighbour.

Three months later at a meeting with other missionary candidates, I was surprised to see the very same Ralph and Ruth Neighbour. They were being appointed to establish a model of a different kind of church in a major urban center. From that moment, we were connected in vision and ministry. They were assigned to Saigon, Viet Nam while waiting for a visa to begin work in Singapore. When Viet Nam fell to the North Vietnamese Communists they were in other Southeast Asian countries until they finally got their visa for Singapore.

We were assigned to Bangkok, Thailand and on January 1, 1975, our family flew into the Bangkok airport. Six weary and sweaty travelers, from 35 years of age to 3, began to think less harshly of Texas summers when we stepped out of the plane into the heat and humidity of Bangkok at the height of hot season.

Bangkok Model

God began to open my eyes to a different kind of church during our appointment process and our first missionary term in Bangkok. The traditional preaching, teaching, and program model dominated church planting across the world, including Thailand. A few pioneer church planters like Charles Brock in the Philippians were planting a simple and indigenous form of church.[36] However, most missionaries followed the preaching, teaching, and program model that required a building.

Mary and I were assigned to an existing church called Sala Christian Thonburi. A "sala" is a pavilion or arbor for teaching or resting.

On our first Sunday at the church (the second Sunday after our arrival), I did not yet speak the language, but I understood what was going on. The two-story concrete constructed building was filled with Thais and the Thai language, but organized just like a traditional church in the West with chairs in a row, attendance and financial boards at the front, hymnals, a pulpit, and an ordained pastor. We also had a fellowship hall on the bottom story and a parsonage nearby.

I not only had culture shock, language shock, and mission shock, but this experience also put me into church shock. Somehow I

---

36. Charles Brock, *Indigenous Church Planting: A Practical Journey* (Neosho, MO: Church Growth International).

had expected church in one of the least Christian major cities of the world would be different in nature from the one I left in Texas.

This church shock drove me back to the New Testament to examine the model. I began by studying the church in Acts and the Epistles, especially Paul's church planting methods. However, the promise by Jesus kept jumping into my mind: "I will build my church." The thought came to me: "Does Jesus know anything about planting churches?"

So I began a detailed, verse-by-verse study of the Gospels, listing on a yellow pad every situation that applied to the church from each of the Gospels. When I compared my lists I was frustrated because the writers approached Jesus' life and ministry from different perspectives and periods of ministry. I saw several common church planting principles but no organizing framework. However, I noticed something on my lists that was the same in each gospel: The numbers of 3, 12, 70, 120, and 1000 were used in each gospel. With the numbers, God gave me a way to conceptualize the church in an interrelated group system of 3/12/70. Some common principles began to coalesce around the numbers. It has taken almost forty years for me to work through the maze of Constantine's model in order to apply the numbers as an organizing framework to the church today.

For months a team of church planters in Bangkok met every Thursday morning at 6:00 to pray, research, brainstorm, and design an indigenous strategy that would penetrate the neighborhoods of Bangkok. The end product was Bangkok Urban Strategy (BUS): a 52-Week Neighborhood Strategy. Eventually five missionary families implemented the strategy in five geographical areas of Bangkok.

IMPLEMENTATION

Looking back I can see that Bangkok Urban Strategy was based on many of the principles of the seventy and was the beginning of my long journey to this book. We developed necessary materials and procedures to train a team of Thai Christians on how to choose a neighborhood, minister in it, and witness within it. The teams did this for 52 weeks.

Our goal was to (1) cultivate the lost in a neighborhood; (2) identify the person of peace; (3) begin a group in the home of a person of peace; (4) win as many people as possible in net fishing events; (5) begin a community cell; (6) raise up an indigenous leader; (7) multiply the cell; and (8) form a neighborhood church.

Every Sunday we trained, prayed, deployed, and debriefed. Several teams of Thai Christians ate lunch together after worship, were trained to implement a specific activity or assignment for that day, and prayed for God's presence, power, and purpose. The teams then formed into small groups of two or three and went into different sections of the same neighborhood. The assignment might be to acclimatize the neighborhood with tracts or to have a ministry activity such as teaching English, guitar, cooking, or showing a movie. The teams were always encouraged to go into the home of any person of peace who gave an invitation. After the activity or assignment, the teams returned to the church building, or an agreed upon place in the neighborhood. The teams debriefed and prayed together.

Looking back, I see that we operated with many of the characteristics of Jesus' cluster of seventy: deploy and debrief, focus on penetrating a neighborhood, work two-by-two, find the person of peace, establish a presence in the house of the person of peace, and form a community group around a local leader.

However, I missed two things: (1) the idea of the seventy as the expansion large group of the church and (2) the importance of the two or three friendship triad to establish contagious growth. I was blinded by the traditional preaching and teaching model and did not see the seventy as a mobile strategic methodology that could stand on its own. Even though we naturally operated through the 3/12/70 principles, the picture in my mind and the ultimate goal was still a place, a headquarters. That's the way success was measured: a headquarters church organized, constituted, and meeting regularly on Sunday with a trained, and preferably ordained, pastor.

We organized around Jesus' growth numbers of 3/12/70 but the preaching and teaching headquarters model was still in my mind and in the mind of the team. The emerging leaders fixated on the need to have a special meeting place in the neighborhood where the small group could duplicate what they saw happening on Sunday in the mother church. This physical place validated them as a leader and me as a missionary. With a set place and preacher we had tangible and measurable results that could be counted in the statistics.

My personal pilgrimage out of the traditional headquarters preaching, teaching, and program model has been slow and painful, almost forty years. This shows how ingrained the traditional headquarters model is in the church experience. If the church is to expand, it must refocus on Jesus' growth numbers and refuse to allow the traditional model to hinder expansion with buildings, services, programs, and professional leaders.

THE SEVENTY IN THE CELL CHURCH MODEL

If you want to see this seventy concept in operation today, go to a cell church and observe the mechanics and dynamics at work in an internal seventy cluster. These may be called sections or other names but are organized as clusters of cells. You will recognize a cluster because it will have a leader supervising three to seven cells (they may call the groups by different names).

Avoid studying two types of groups in a cell church. (1) Don't study the congregation (120) that is made up of two or three clusters of seventy. (You will recognize a congregation because a pastor will be assigned to oversee it.) In a large cell church, these will be internal congregations within the mother church. A typical congregation is not the unit you need to study or duplicate. The very word "congregation" or "church" has so much historical baggage that it is dangerous. A saying in Thailand applies here: "Be careful about the end of the rope you pick up. You don't know what kind of elephant is on the other end." The moment you pick up the congregation/church rope you are tied to the traditional program elephant that demands a place, a preacher, and programs to care for its members. It will dominate your thinking and your model. You will consume all your time feeding and caring for it.

(2) Don't study the church plant of a cell church because most cell churches use the traditional preaching, teaching, and program headquarters model to begin external growth, just like traditional churches. You want to observe the working of a mid-level group of seventy that operates internally in a cell church. If you go beyond that group, you will be tied to a set public formal worship service in a building, will have a preaching and teaching focus, and will depend on how many professional leaders with titles and positions (pastors) you can hire. These are the kiss of death for expansion.

The primary focus of the supervision mid-level group of seventy is not a public service. It is not a come structure built around preaching, formal worship, and teaching the Bible. The seventy is a go structure that is focused on training, deploying, and debriefing Christians in the work of expansion. The mid-level seventy cluster (in its smallest size of 30 and largest size of 70) is small enough to meet anywhere in natural venues and therefore does not require a building. The cluster of seventy also solves the professional leadership problem: There are many supervisors and coaches but few preachers, musicians, teachers, pastors, and motivators.

The closest example of the nature of the seventy is a retreat. The retreat is a unique meeting in the traditional church. We have given ourselves permission to do church differently at this one meeting. All other official meetings follow the preaching, teaching, praying, worshiping service pattern. In this one meeting the church doesn't have to feel guilty for operating in an informal way. The focus of retreats is not teaching and preaching in an assembled public service. A retreat atmosphere is dedicated to training and to practical tasks. Worship, teaching, and preaching may take place at a retreat, but the focus is on a task or mission. I have observed that a person's life is often changed more in a two-day retreat than in years of attending public church services, listening to sermons, and formally studying the Bible. A retreat setting provides a dynamic atmosphere for dramatic personal change.

Having a retreat setting does not mean physically meeting out in the woods near a lake and in cabins with a communal cafeteria. It is the atmosphere and agenda, tangible things that the cluster of seventy can duplicate, things that will change how we do church. A mid-level seventy may meet in a large house or a park. The point I am making is that the atmosphere and agenda of the seventy must strive to be more like a retreat than a formal preaching, teaching, praying, and worshiping service. The seventy must focus on the task and the mission.

A supervising coach of seventy emerges out of a community cell and will prepare the leaders of the cells of twelve to identify and win the person of peace, cultivate the *oikos* friends and relatives of members, and throw out evangelism nets. This friendship evangelism will begin through the friendship triads of two or three.

Brazil Model

Recently Robert Lay, the Director of the Cell Church Network in Brazil,[37] shared the report of a pastor who applied the supervising unit of seventy that he called a "simple church." The Maranatha Worship Cathedral is a network of churches in the area of São Luís, Maranhão in Northeast Brazil. The mother church began the transition to the cell model in 2004. Pastor Rafael Blume gave the following report about the process of the church from a traditional model, to a small group model, and then to a cell model that implemented a form of the principles of the seventy. The pastor explains that the church began to grow when it began to use small groups and then really grew when it installed the cell system. "We experienced such a powerful values change that we went through a special growth process: we soon were renting vans and buses from several locations in the city and surrounding cities to bring people to participate in our Sunday celebrations. Renting buses never was the best option

---

37. The Cell Church Network in Brazil is an excellent example of the kind of church movement God is developing in the 21st century. According to estimates from Cell Church Ministries in Brazil, in less than two decades, approximately sixteen thousand pastors and leaders have completed a special training called Acts (Advanced Cell Training), and five thousand churches, thirty-five thousand cells, six-hundred thousand Christians, representing seventy denominations or groups are part of the Network.

CHAPTER 2: WHERE ARE THE WORKING MODELS? 77

for us, since there was the intent to implement congregations in those locations, but we followed models we were observing in other churches."

> *In 2009, we were very impacted by the presence of Dr. Joel Comiskey and Dr. Bill Beckham in Brazil, speaking at the Cell Church National Conference on planting "simple churches." After that we took several actions:*
> - *We stopped renting vans*
> - *We planted new churches in the farthest locations of the city, led by supervisors and cell leaders;*
> - *We launched a local training school to equip the new workers, who went on to be mentored by the church pastors;*
> - *Workers were released from their cells with supervisors to begin new churches based on the cell vision.*
>
> *In two and a half years, through these simple churches, led by ordinary people, our church network grew from three large cell congregations at the mother church to eighteen churches, grew from 111 to 235 cells and from 1050 members to 2500. Some of these new plants went through an explosive growth process. Our growth index went from 25% to over 100% by implementing new "simple churches," led by supervisors or cell leaders. Ordinary people lead these small and simple churches. They meet in cells and in one-to-one discipleship. They meet on Sunday at house porches, in the district community's building, in the auditorium of community schools, and in locations in the community. These simple churches are led by ordinary people and are low investment and high return. The major characteristic of this missionary work is love demonstrated to the surrounding communities. Love mobilizes each cell member to take care of people and to shepherd them through concrete actions. These are simple churches, led by ordinary people, with a passion to serve God*

and the world He loves so much. This is a model that can be reproduced in any part of the world.[38]

This report is significant because the pastor developed strategy from concepts he heard. No one gave him a set strategy or a "how to" list. In fact, he combined Joel Comiskey's teaching about the simple church and my teaching on maximizing high-growth, low-maintenance, and relationship-centered ministry and minimizing high-maintenance, low-growth, and building-centered ministry.[39]

Of course the pastor and key leaders also had all of the cell training of the Cell Church Network in Brazil as a foundation. He developed a practical expansion strategy that used a mid-level expansion group. This pastor in Brazil took the following basic concepts about the New Testament Church for his church:

- The church is simple and small.
- God uses ordinary leaders to multiply His church.
- The two or three disciple unit is an important growth group.
- Holistic community cells are the basic unit of the church.
- A seventy cluster is a low maintenance, inexpensive, mobile, and high growth group for supervising the expansion growth of the church.
- Special buildings are not necessary for external expansion growth.

He applied the concepts of this book by planting low-maintenance, low-cost, and high-growth forward operating bases instead of bringing everyone to a central location or beginning

---

38. Rafael Blume, *Igreja: Movimento Mutiplicador* (Curitiba, PR: Cell Church Ministries, 2015).
39. William A. Beckham, "Expansion Analysis," in *The Second Reformation, Stage 2* (Moreno Valley, CA: CCS Publishing, 2014), 165.

mini headquarters.[40] This means the mid-level seventy model is not as heavily dependent on a set strategy and methodology of a traditional large group as some cell church approaches in the past. The steps in the strategy will naturally form, if a leader understands the basic group concepts of 3/12/70.

TOUCH RANCH

Ralph Neighbour took the dream of the church God placed within his heart and sought to make it a reality in an "experimental church" in Houston during the 1960s. The story of this church always includes warm memories about its retreat center that was called Touch Ranch. It was not a ranch in the Texas definition of a large piece of property and a herd of cattle. It was a rustic retreat center of a few acres conveniently located near Houston. When I first began to study the church, I sensed what happened "at the ranch" was important to the growth of the church and to the development of the cell church structure. I kept trying to understand where Touch Ranch fit into what happened.

Looking back through the prism of the 3/12/70 paradigm of the church, I now understand why Touch Ranch is such an important part of the early story of this experimental church. It was at Touch Ranch that the dynamic life of the seventy took place. In this mid-sized group form the church was released from the restraints of services, programs, and buildings. At the ranch, groups from the church experienced the qualities of Jesus' seventy: training for mission, debriefing, sending out, penetrating *oikos* households, and planning for expansion. In addition, individual Christians experienced personal growth and edification

---

40. William A. Beckham, "A Military Motif of the Church", in The Second Reformation: Stage 2, page 70. In the chapter I give an explanation of the church operating as a headquarters.

in special activities. Touch Ranch was a place to tactically prepare for the mission outside of a demanding preaching, teaching, and program atmosphere.

I can see Jesus at Touch Ranch sharing his Luke 10 discourse. It is more difficult to visualize Jesus sharing that discourse in the large group gathering on Sunday. The activities, atmosphere, agendas and focus I saw in the accounts about Touch Ranch are necessary to expand the church today.

The life of the cluster of seventy should be convenient and inexpensive with a relaxed retreat type atmosphere. This can be in a home that is large enough to accommodate thirty to seventy people. The danger in a home is that the members will default to the house church mentality and organize as a traditional preaching and teaching meeting in the house. The same is true of using the facilities of a church. Space is available in existing church buildings but the danger in the beginning of a strategy is the large group worship default mode that is inside the head of Christians: Plan a service that is focused on worship, ministry, and education that will motivate us, instead of a cluster of seventy focusing on the mission.

Creative venue options are available for the cluster of seventy once the idea is separated from the preaching, teaching, worshiping, and program activities. This is not about the place, although a retreat type place is an excellent venue for the meeting of a seventy group.

The pattern of tactical planning and preparation at Touch Ranch explains why West Memorial Baptist Church was also called Touch Family Church: The People Who Care. I wonder what would have happened if Touch Ranch had been the first model for expansion rather than the Touch Family that was organized as an innovative preaching and teaching congregation on Dairy Ashford Road.

DEFAULT SWITCH

The concept of the seventy supervising model as an alternative large group failed in my personal ministry because I was not yet clear about the concept. The concept of a preaching, teaching, and program congregation in a building always hangs over the cluster of seventy. The default or fall back pattern was so prevalent in my mind. The minute the clusters ran into trouble I automatically defaulted to the traditional Sunday model.

The seventy is an important concept for what God wants to do with the church in the 21st century. It has taken God more than half a century to get small groups back into the church. The mid-level group of seventy is so essential to God's way of doing church that I believe He will do whatever is necessary and spend whatever time is needed to form the church into these tactical expansion groups.

Church plants and missions must find a way to operate as a seventy rather than as a headquarters.

Expansion is built upon three structures: Friendship triads, community cells, and a supervising seventy. The friendship triad is the relationship chain of expansion. The community cell is the basic Christian family growing and living together. The cluster of seventy is the leadership and training group for expansion.

To see expansion, these three groups must operate as a holistic unit without a professional leader, a building, or programs whose only consistent fruit has been Christians trained to serve the system or sit as spectators in the pews.

Chapter 3

JESUS' GREAT VISION

"Vision without action is merely a dream. Action without vision just passes the time. Vision with action can change the world."
• Joel Barker, Futurist

Jim Collins and his research team set out to statistically prove or disprove the adage that "good is the enemy of the best" in Fortune 500 companies. Over a period of five years, the group researched hundreds of good companies and classified twenty-eight as "great" companies. They also identified the principles and actions that took the companies from "good to great." Collins published the findings in his bestseller of the same name, *Good to Great.*

The conclusions of the study are instructive for implementing Jesus' strategy. Collins discovered that companies go from just being good to becoming great by implementing simple concepts. He illustrates this important principle with the ancient fable about the fox and hedgehog. The wily fox knows many things and sees the world in its complexity. A hedgehog knows one big thing and simplifies a complex world into single organizing ideas: leave den in the morning, travel your path, eat along the way, return in the evening, and avoid predators like the wily fox. Collins conclusion: Hedgehog simplicity and focus is essential for success in a complex world.[41]

---

41. Collins, 90-92.

Great companies begin with a simple vision to be great. This vision is not defined in detail in the early stage of the process. Therefore, "great" companies are able to successfully identify and recruit leaders totally committed to the broad vision and not to every detail. This allows a company to focus on those committed to the vision rather than trying to explain the details while they are being worked out.

There are many "good" organizational churches today, but only Jesus' "great" organic church will produce expansion in the 21st century.

Good to Great in the Bible

The theme of the book of Hebrews is good to great. Jesus is the ultimate revelation and is superior to and greater than: the prophets (Heb. 1:2), angels (1:5-14), the Old Testament leaders (including Moses) (3:1-6), earthly priests, even Melchizedek (4:14-16), and religion (the old covenant and promise) (8:3-6). Jesus Christ is the new and living way (10:19). The writer sums up the book: "God had provided something better for us, so that apart from us they should not be made perfect (11:40).

The "good" in Jesus' time was the existing religious system that began two thousand years before with Abraham and ended in Jerusalem at the Temple (the same mountain where Abraham offered Isaac). Jesus moved Judaism from a good organized religion to the great: His organic, living Body that can expand from one sacred mountain throughout the earth. At the time of Jesus, Judaism was as good as a religion could be. However, Jesus was born to take Judaism to its supreme place: The spiritual Body of Christ in the world. Jesus' strategy was uniquely developed around a series of groups in order to establish the greatest possible expression of His spiritual life on earth.

Many strategies that are developed for the church today are "good" and help the church grow numerically as an organization. Jesus' "great" plan helps the church be the living and spiritual Body of Christ that will expand across the earth as a people movement. Good strategies are based on good, but partial visions, such as preaching, Bible study, ministry, gifts, worship, evangelism, prayer, discipleship, social causes, groups, or healing. Taken separately each of these are good visions, but no single one by itself will encompass the others. Only Jesus' organic community system will integrate all of the partial visions into one great vision. Many good visions are the greatest threat to Jesus' "great" church.

ONE VISION

Someone or some group in the beginning must verbalize a vision so that other leaders will be willing to join together around one basic strategy. This is necessary because the best prototypes are developed and implemented by leaders who have a clear and common vision. A prototype is the first (*protos*) impression (*typos*), an early sample or model built to test a concept or process that can be replicated or learned from. Prototyping provides specifications for a real working system rather than a theoretical one.[42]

Michael Gerber defines a prototype as "the working model of the dream, it is the dream in microcosm. The Prototype becomes the incubator and the nursery for all creative thought, the station where creativity is nursed by pragmatism to grow into an innovation that works."[43] "The prototype acts as a buffer between hypothesis and action."[44]

---

42. William A. Beckham, *The Second Reformation* (Houston, TX: Touch, 1999), 157-176.
43. Michael E. Gerber, 54.
44. Ibid., 55.

A leadership group with multiple visions will develop multiple prototypes, each prototype with its own agenda. Dion Robert expressed this with the statement: "Vision plus vision equals division."[45] One vision among many leaders is required for developing a successful prototype.

God's vision for Abraham demanded total commitment but provided precious few details. God gave Abraham a direction and a destination, but no map. "Leave this place." "Go to a place to which I will lead you." "I will be with you and will make you a great nation." The most important factor in the vision was Abraham's commitment to the vision, not his knowledge of the details of the vision.

The challenge of a catalytic church leader is to gather a group of leaders who will commit to the New Testament model when the only model they have known is the high-maintenance, high-cost, program-centered model with its buildings and professional leaders. This model has produced growth but not expansion. "In suggesting that vision deals with that which is preferable, we are insinuating that vision entails change. Vision is never about maintaining the status quo. Vision is about stretching reality to extend beyond the existing stage."[46]

THE RIGHT PEOPLE ON THE BUS

Jim Collins describes the process of building a leadership team as getting people on a bus. A vision must be able to draw leaders together and keep them together on a "vision bus" long enough to develop a working prototype of the vision. The

---

45. I heard Dion Robert (French pronunciation for "Robert" with the final "t" silent) first say this in French at a conference at Cornerstone Church in Harrisburg, Virginia in 1995. Since that time I have talked with him about the statement several times.
46. George Barna, *The Power of Vision* (Ventura, CA: Regal, 2009), 29.

primary issue in the beginning of a "great" company is not what are we going to do, but who is committed enough to get on the bus, and to stay on the bus?

"Getting the right people on the bus, the wrong people off the bus, and the right people in the right seat---these are all crucial steps in the early stages of buildup . . ."[47] This is a bus of commitment. The leader may not know every turn, but knows the direction, and knows the end destination is a great company. Therefore, those who board the bus go where the bus is going.

The driving force for implementing a vision isn't motivation but "brutal facts." "Expending energy trying to motivate people is largely a waste of time." "If you have the right people on the bus, they will be self-motivated."[48]

The bus analogy is instructive for an expansion church because it illustrates the importance of one vision. While experiencing the prototype pattern cells, leaders are committing to a special vision: a great church that expands across the world as the spiritual Body of Christ.

Everyone who gets on the bus goes the direction of the bus. Every detail of the trip may not be known, but the direction is fixed. That vision route must be the starting and ending point for every other vision and idea that comes along the journey. Catalytic vision leaders cannot afford to renegotiate the vision every time a new group of leaders board the bus.

---

47. Collins, 184.
48. Ibid., 73-74.

Invariably someone will get on the bus and say: "I want the bus to go down this agenda road." The leader replies: "Your agenda of Bible study, or discipleship, or evangelism, or political causes, or the gifts is good, but these good agendas are not our destination." "This bus is only going to the destination of a church living as the spiritual Body of Christ, carrying out His gospel mandate. Your agenda is a side road to us." "We will stop the bus and you can get off and get on another bus that is going on your agenda road."

RIGHT PEOPLE IN THE RIGHT SEATS

The details of Jesus' vision were discovered, owned, and shared by the Disciples while living together in the inner circle, the twelve, and the seventy. This is also true for leaders today: Com-mitment to Jesus' organic church is forged during the step-by-step group process of discipleship (3), community (12), and supervision (70), not in studying about the vision or the process.

The president of one of Collins' great companies admitted he "spent a lot of time thinking, and talking about who sits where on the bus." He called it "putting square pegs in square holes and round pegs in round holes."[49]

Moses and the Children of Israel came to a bus moment. "Then we turned and set out for the wilderness by the way to the Red Sea, as the LORD spoke to me, and circled Mount Seir for many days. It is eleven days' *journey* from Horeb by the way of Mount Seir to Kadesh-barnea. And it came about in the fortieth year, on the first day of the eleventh month, that Moses spoke to the children of Israel, according to all that the LORD had com-manded him *to give* to them (Deut. 1:2-5). "And the LORD spoke to me, saying, 'You have circled this mountain long enough. *Now* turn north" (Deut. 2:1-3).

49. Ibid., 57.

Joshua had a bus moment with the Children of Israel. "But if serving the LORD seems undesirable to you, then choose for yourselves this day whom you will serve, whether the gods your forefathers served beyond the River, or the gods of the Amorites, in whose land you are living. But as for me and my household, we will serve the LORD" (Joshua 24:15). Get on or get off!

Jesus was also concerned with who was on His bus. He challenged the loyalty and commitment of His followers. Those unwilling to forsake everything needed to get off His bus. We see that struggle with the rich young man who came to Jesus in Matthew 19:21. Even the disciples, who had left behind families and livelihoods, wrestled to remain committed to following Christ's vision. Perhaps the climax of that struggle occurs after the Feast of Dedication in Jerusalem, when the authorities tried to stone Him (John 10:3). Jesus took His disciples across the Jordan to the area where John the Baptist baptized (10:40).

Word came that Lazarus had died at Bethany, a suburb just outside the walls of Jerusalem, and Jesus is determined to go comfort Mary and Martha, and of course to raise Lazarus. The disciples try to discourage Him from going into danger ... and taking them with Him (11:8).

This is a revealing moment three years into Jesus' ministry. Who will stay on the bus and who will get off? Thomas finally responds "Let us also go, that we may die with Him" (11:16). For other "bus decisions" in Jesus' ministry see Luke 9:24-33; Luke: 17:33; Luke 14:26; John 8:31-32; John 13:34-35; John 10:10-17; John 12:25; Matthew 10:39; 16:25; 20:28; Mark 8:36. In each of these situations there was the option of exiting or staying on Jesus' bus.

Peter's commitment was severely tested on the night of Jesus' trial. The crow of the rooster woke Peter up just as he was about to get off Jesus' bus. After the resurrection, Jesus strongly reminded Peter of the importance of following the leader. Beside the Sea of Galilee, during one of the resurrection appearances, Peter was reconciled to Christ (John 21). While leaving the seaside Peter asked about John. Jesus replied, "What is that to you?" Then He said literally, "You! Here behind me!" "Get in your seat on my bus Peter, and stop worrying about where John is sitting!"

How does one know who should be on the bus and who is in the right seat? In the case of the strategy I am suggesting, the response of the initial followers to the friendship triads and the community cells will sort out the committed from those with personal agendas and reveal the proper seating for each person. Leaders reveal their heart, commitment, and level of submission while part of a friendship triad and when participating in a community cell. The friendship triad is especially helpful in revealing the commitment and humility of a potential leader. The triad is the door of commitment through which each person must enter the vision bus. A leader unwilling to participate in a basic friendship triad often wants to sit in the driver's seat. Every person on the vision bus must enter in through the door of a friendship triad and then sit in a community cell seat.

Collins' group observed: "The good-great companies showed the following bipolar pattern at the top management level. People either stayed on the bus for a long time or got off the bus in a hurry."[50]

THE SHAPE OF THE VISION

A young leader who was part of a church transition in the Washington DC area made a very astute observation to me about their transition: "Where the vision is unclear the cost is

---
50. Ibid., 12.

always too high." "A shared vision is not an idea. It is not even an important idea such as freedom. It is, rather, a force in people's hearts, a force of impressive power."[51]

Paul's statement about vision in Acts 26:19, "I was not disobedient to the heavenly vision," inspired Oswald Chambers to respond with a powerful word about vision:

> *We always have visions, before a thing is made real. When we realize that although the vision is real, it is not real in us, then is the time that Satan comes in with his temptations, and we are apt to say it is no use to go on. Instead of the vision becoming real, there has come the valley of humiliation.*
>
> *Life is not as idle ore,*
> *But iron dug from central gloom,*
> *And batter'd by the shocks of doom*
> *To shape and use.*
>
> *God gives us the vision, then He takes us down to the valley to batter us into the shape of the vision, and it is in the valley that so many of us faint and give way. Every vision will be made real if we will have patience. Think of the enormous leisure of God! He is never in a hurry. We are always in such a frantic hurry. In the light of the glory of the vision we go forth to do things, but the vision is not real in us yet; and God has to take us into the valley, and put us through fires and floods to batter us into shape, until we get to the place where He can trust us with the veritable reality. Ever since we had the vision God has been at work, getting us into the shape of the ideal, and over and over again we escape from His hand and try to batter ourselves into our own shape. The vision is not a castle in the air, but a vision of what God wants you to be. Let Him put you on His wheel and whirl you as He likes, and as sure as God is God and you are you, you will turn out exactly*

---
51. Senge, 206.

in accordance with the vision. Don't lose heart in the process. If you have ever had the vision of God, you may try as you like to be satisfied on a lower level, but God will never let you.[52]

The church that is the organic and living Body of Christ on earth is God's great vision. That vision is not received automatically or easily. God must mold ("batter") His followers into the shape of that great vision. Do not expect to go from good to great without God shaping you to the vision of His great organic church. "Beware of harking back to what you were once when God wants you to be something you have never been."[53]

The vision of Jesus' organic church is caught during the step-by-step process of discipleship, community, and supervision, not in studying about the vision or the process. The details of His vision are discovered, owned, and shared while living out His process.

Oswald Chambers recognized the importance and power of vision and the place that total commitment plays in living out a vision. "We cannot attain to a vision. We must live in the inspiration of it until it accomplishes itself."[54]

---

52. Oswald Chambers, *My Utmost for His Highest*, July 6.
53. Ibid., June 8.
54. Ibid., March 11.

Chapter 4

THE DECISION PROCESS AND VALUES

We do what we value and value what we do!

Pastors and leaders with a vision make a costly mistake by assuming that others, even friends, fellow workers, relatives, and dedicated members will easily or quickly decide to join the vision. The decision process for adopting change is far more difficult, complicated, and time consuming than perceived on the surface. Another mistake is to expect people to change their way of doing things because of sermons. Real change requires an experience.

The effectiveness in implementing Jesus' expansion model is determined by the commitment of the visionaries and leaders. Prayer is the path to spiritual commitment for Christians. However, even a lengthy period of sincere prayer does not guarantee a leader "owns" Jesus' approach and will actually implement it. A riddle illustrates this point.

Two frogs sit on a log. One decides to jump off. How many frogs remain on the log? The spontaneous answer is "one." However, the real answer is "two frogs remain on the log." The one frog just "decided" to jump. It did not actually jump. The point is, saying something is not ownership. Ownership is the result of a deep level of decision-making that acts upon a conviction or commitment. Leaders participating in the search for a strategy to implement Jesus model of expansion growth must own the vision and strategy. Ownership is actually jumping off the log.

A Model of Decision-making

Making decisions and adopting change have personal and group components. A model of decision-making developed by Ralph W. Neighbour, Jr. informs about how individuals make personal decisions about new concepts. Neighbour's instrument is an excellent tool for understanding personal ownership of important concepts and personal reaction to significant change. (Look at the pyramid in the chart.) This model is built upon Bloom's six levels of cognitive learning: knowledge, comprehension, application, analysis, synthesis, and evaluation. The process question associated with Bloom's Cognitive Scale asks what nuances of cognition take place in a learning process. Neighbour looks at the cognitive process from the standpoint of the person and the context rather than just the process and asks two other questions: What is happening with the person during a decision process? What forces or barriers in the context hinder the adoption and implementation of a decision?

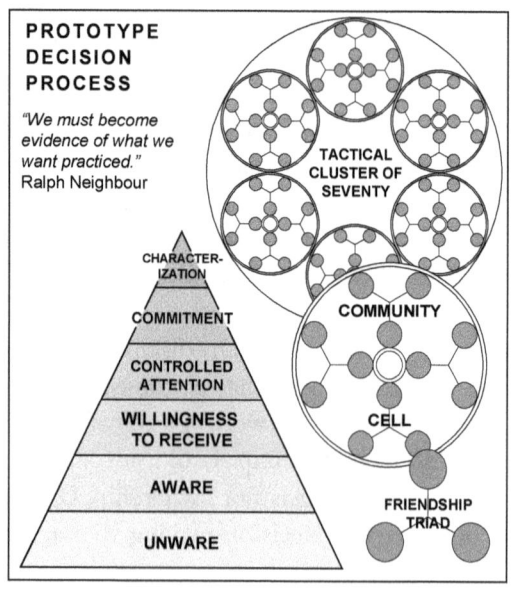

In Neighbour's decision process, a person goes from unaware, to aware, to willingness to receive, to controlled attention, to commitment to change, and then to characterization.[55] The biggest mistake of a change agent in evaluating personal ownership of a new idea is confusing "willingness to receive" (open to the new idea) and "controlled attention" (weighing the benefits and costs) with genuine "commitment."

At the stage of characterization, a new idea is no longer an outside theoretical concept. The idea is now inside the person who "owns" it, and in a real sense, the idea now "owns" the person. Ownership means stepping through old barriers and getting outside comfortable boxes. This internal and external struggle may take place at each stage of decision-making as a person moves through the process. The final stage of characterization applies the decision to life experience.

I have seen God transform Howard Partridge into a phenomenal Christian, husband, father, businessman, and motivational speaker. He lives out the principles of relationships in groups that we learned in cell life. Howard creatively adapted Neighbour's decision instrument to the business world and uses it as a theme in his recent book. He believes that we must *be* the different "levels"

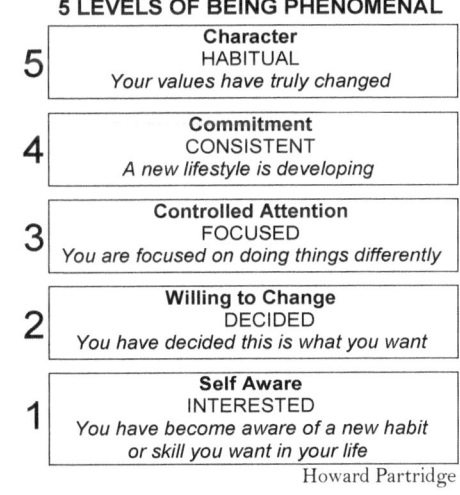

Howard Partridge

---

55. Ralph W. Neighbour, Jr., *Christ's Basic Bodies* (Houston: TOUCH, 2008), 26-43.

of this decision process and explains it in the chart, *5 Levels of Being Phenomenal.*[56]

This decision process operates during the prototype process of the friendship triad, the community cell, and the cluster of seventy.

ANOTHER HELPFUL DECISION INSTRUMENT

Peter M. Senge's commitment and compliance theory is also helpful in understanding the dynamics and nuances of personal decision-making.[57] Senge describes the personal dynamics going on in Neighbour's decision process. He lists seven possible reactions of a person considering a new vision. The nuances of commitment are critically important to a pastor or leader desiring to implement Jesus' growth expansion principles. A leader must be able to honestly evaluate his true personal commitment and the commitment of those who will be part of his leadership team. Who should be on the bus? Much of Jesus' ministry focused on the commitment/ownership of His followers to Him and to His kingdom principles.

1. *Commitment: Wants it. Will make it happen. Creates whatever "laws" (structures) are needed.*
2. *Enrollment: Wants it. Will do whatever can be done within the "spirit of the law."*
3. *Genuine compliance: Sees the benefits of the vision. Does everything expected and more. Follows the "letter of the law." "Good Soldiers."*
4. *Formal compliance: On the whole, sees the benefits of the vision. Does what's expected and no more. "Pretty good soldier."*

---

56. Howard Partridge, *Think and Be Phenomenal* (Melbourne, FL: Motivational Press, 2014), 47.
57. Senge, 219-220.

CHAPTER 4: THE DECISION PROCESS AND VALUES   97

5. Grudging compliance: Does not see the benefits of the vision. But also does not want to lose job. Does enough of what's expected because he has to, but lets it be known that he is not really on board.
6. Noncompliance: Does not see benefits of vision and will not do what's expected. "I won't do it; you can't make me."
7. Apathy: Neither for nor against vision. No interest. No energy. "Is it five o'clock yet?"[58]

ADOPTING CHANGE

After considering how a person decides in Neighbour's and Senge's instruments, it is helpful to look at the group component in adopting change. People make individual decisions within the context of a group or groups. "A group of people truly committed to a common vision is an awesome force. They can accomplish the seemingly impossible."[59] Shared commitment to one vision is absolutely essential during the preparation and prototype phases of a new strategy.

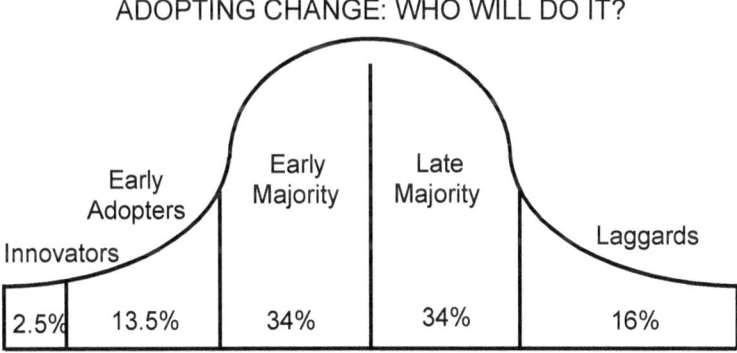

ADOPTING CHANGE: WHO WILL DO IT?

Innovators 2.5% | Early Adopters 13.5% | Early Majority 34% | Late Majority 34% | Laggards 16%

Innovation-Decision Period
Rodgers, *Communication of Innovation*, p. 281

---

58. Ibid., 219-220.
59. Ibid., 221.

Everett Rogers shows the "peer" group dynamic of decision-making in his "adoption of change model" and broader "diffusion of innovation" study. Rogers' model is based on a landmark case study conducted in the 1930s. Bruce Ryan and Neal Gross studied the response of 259 farmers in Greene County, Iowa, to the introduction of a new hybrid seed corn. Ryan and Gross identified five ideal types or adopter categories that are at work during the process of change. From this study Rogers identified universal adopter categories, the percentage of people in each category, and the time line for the adoption of change.[60]

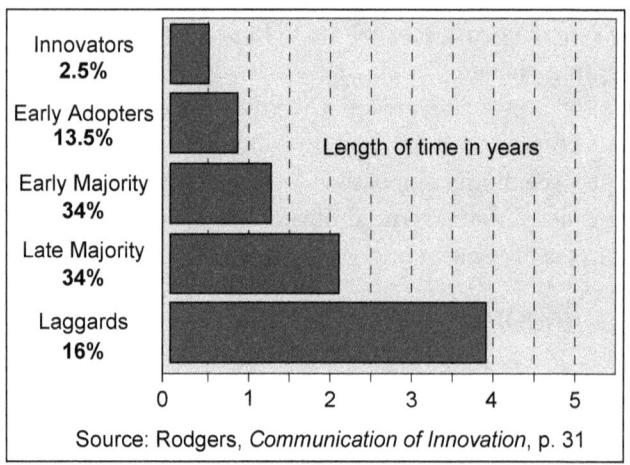

The Iowa farmers who first planted the hybrid seed corn were the Innovators. This small group of visionaries (2.5%) heard about the new experimental hybrid seed corn, acquired it, and immediately planted it. A slightly larger group (13.5%) of neighboring farmers (the Early Adopter category) was open to

---

60. Everett M. Rogers, *Diffusion of Innovations*, 5th ed. (New York, NY: Free Press, 2003), 22, 51, 215. For the length of the Innovation-Decision Period, Rogers explains Ryan's Bell Curve on page 281. An explanation of the S-Curve is given on page 273.

new ideas. These respected opinion leaders watched and analyzed what the Innovators were doing and then quickly planted the new hybrid seed corn at the end of the first growing season.

The Early Majority (34%) was more deliberate and cautious than the Early Adopters and carefully observed the Innovators and Early Adopters plant the new hybrid seed corn the first season. When they saw that the bushel per acre yield of the Innovators and Early Adopters was greater than the old corn, they bought the new hybrid seed and planted it the second growing season. The Late Majority (34%) approached the new seed corn with skepticism and was unwilling to use the new seed corn until the more "normal" Early Majority had tested it. After the harvest of the Early Majority, the Late Majority farmers planted the corn in the third planting season. The last group was the Laggards (16%), people who resist change as a first and last inclination. Someone described Laggards as people who "can't lead, won't follow and make wonderful roadblocks." The Iowa Laggard farmers planted the new hybrid seed when the local feed store stopped selling the old seed, and even then they complained about having to change.

This classic study indicates that one can expect people to respond to change within five categories and across general periods of time. A person may have a natural inclination toward one of the categories but can learn or be influenced to move to another category. For instance, the number and effectiveness of the Innovators influence the Early Adopters and the Early Adopters influence the Early Majority and Late Majority groups.

From Neighbour's decision process, Senge's commitment and compliance instrument, and Roger's diffusion of innovation study, we can conclude that leaders adopt new governing principles through a personal and group process. The more clearly the pastor and leaders understand the personal and group decision making process, the more effective will be the resulting adoption of change and the development of the prototype for an expansion church.

Check Your Values

A strategy is not developed in a vacuum but is shaped out of a basic value system that sets the parameters of a vision. The truth is: we do what we value and value what we do. Decisions are determined by values. If we value Jesus' organic model, we will do it. If we value Constantine's organizational model, we will do it. If we value maintenance we will have a maintenance strategy. If we value growth we will have a growth strategy. If we value expansion we will have an expansion strategy. All decisions are ultimately based on values.

The presupposition of this book is that Constantine's paradigm is a deeply flawed system that has shaped the core values of pastors and leaders. Therefore, pastors and leaders must return to the deepest roots of New Testament principles and revelation before they escape Constantine. Real change of the traditional way of being church only takes place at the point of values. Pastors and leaders today will not change because they have new methods, men (leaders), or models but only when they embrace Jesus' values.

Jesus and the religious authorities of His day played out this spiritual drama in their constant conflicts on the battlefields of semantics and concepts. However, the source of the conflict went to the deepest levels of life, to core values. Jesus' conflict with the religious leaders shows the difficulty of agreeing about values when those values are wrapped up in personal and group paradigms, views, perspectives, and history.

The core values of the Pharisee were in stark contrast to the values of Jesus. Dietrich Bonhoeffer saw the Pharisee as a universal type of spiritual legalism and rebellion. He used the Pharisee to contrast the two major approaches to values and ethics: judging good and evil and living the will of God.[61] The foundation of values for the Pharisees was the law that was based on right and wrong. Living out values from a perspective of right and wrong always leads to legalism.[62]

Jesus' values and ethical standards were not based on good and evil (judging) but upon the will of God (His nature and character).

MOVING THROUGH THE LEVELS

The chart, *Value Levels of Life*, helps explain the constant confrontations between Jesus and the Pharisees. Values are defined and lived out in layers or levels of life. These "levels" are reference points that all humans use in interpreting life. Decisions about every facet of life (personal, social, political, and religious) are made within these value structures.

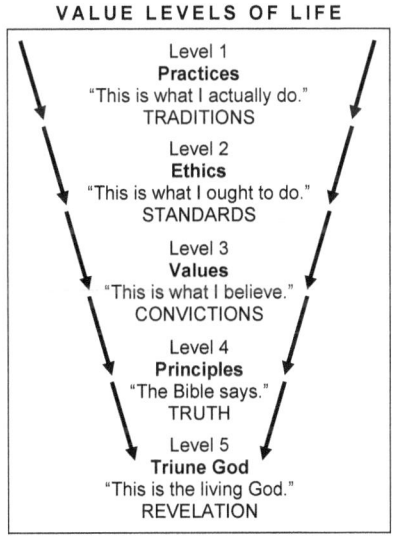

---

61. Bonhoeffer, *Ethics*, 30.
62. Scott Boren, Bill Beckham, Joel Comiskey, Ralph Neighbour, and Randall Neighbour, "Cell Group Church Values", in *The Navigation Guide* (Houston: TX: Cell Church Resources, 2003), 77-91. In this chapter I consider values in more depth.

Christian values must go down through all levels of life until resting upon the rock of the nature of the triune God in revelation.

Familiar practices (Level 1) are the most obvious way to determine how I am going to live and how the church is going to operate. These are the traditions I have learned from childhood. For instance, a family must establish some practices so that everyone gets to work and school on time in the morning. Some kind of regular routine is helpful. Over a period of time these "practices" become traditions and then are established as part of family culture.

Life can also be lived out in the paradigm of ethical behavior (Level 2) or standards that are learned from personal and group experiences. "We always do it this way" becomes "We ought to do it this way." At this level traditions are still important. However, precedents that have worked in the near past are included with traditions in making decisions. This is the level at which the basic structures of society, family, or village determine what is good and evil; proper and improper.

Life decisions can also be made from personal and group values (Level 3). "This is what I believe." Values are deeply held convictions that formed traditions and ethics in the first place. We don't have to consciously think about traditions. They are embedded in our paradigms that determine how we view life. They are forces that we don't question or that we don't know are influencing our paradigm of life. These values are handed down from generation to generation and internalized through subtle teaching and reinforced experiences that may or may not be stated in a written form. For instance, parents value (the third level) good teeth for themselves and their children. Therefore, parents set ethical (behavioral) priorities (second level) and develop traditions about how and when teeth are brushed (first level). At this third level of values, a person operates from convictions. These convictions form into paradigms that are not questioned and that direct life decisions and perspectives, but there is something we must learn to see behind and at a deeper level than our values and convictions: the Bible and God.

Principles are an important part of the process for making decisions (Level 4). For example, medical books contain the principles of hygiene and health from which the values about brushing teeth are developed. For a Christian, the principles of life are contained in the Bible. What the Bible says should be the primary consideration in making decisions and living life. These biblical principles are the truths that formed the values from which our priorities and practices evolved. In Classical Greek, "canon" means "a straight rule" or "a carpenter's rule." God gave the Biblical Canon in order for the apostles and prophets to continue to speak to every generation of Christians. The "rule" or "measuring line" for the Canon was the direct eyewitness accounts of those who had been with Jesus or those who were writing on behalf of the eyewitness accounts such as Mark and Luke.

However, even biblical principles do not go deep enough for Jesus. Jesus referred to Nicodemus as "the" teacher of Israel, implying that he understood biblical principles. Nicodemus knew truth and taught truth. However, Jesus told Nicodemus that he had not yet gone deep enough to understand the mystery of God or the secret of salvation. Nicodemus had to go to the source of God and be "born again." The most powerful force for good hygiene is Mother, not a hygiene chart on the wall.

Jesus is the only person whose every thought, every attitude, and every decision came out of the absolute: the presence of

God (Level 5). He interpreted every level of life out of His relationship with the Father. This was a natural process for Jesus and is God's expectation of every Christian. However, living in the presence of God is not natural for Christians because inward sin and outward culture entice Christians to make decisions from other levels of life.

The Holy Spirit takes every Christian individually by the hand and moves that person through these levels of life until he/she experiences God personally in divine revelation. This is the continuing process of abiding in Christ at the deepest level of life: relationship to the living God. This is the inward "Pilgrims Progress." The Holy Spirit "comes along side" and walks every Christian through traditions to priorities and then through priorities to deeply held convictions and values. From values the Holy Spirit moves a Christian through Biblical principles until the Christian stands in the presence of God Himself. At the point of God, the Christian has reached the deepest level of revelation, relationship, community, and ethical decision-making. The base for ethical and moral decision-making is God … His nature and character. From that point we experience the church as organic life and not as organization.

THE OTHER PART OF THE JOURNEY

When the Holy Spirit moves the Christian down through these layers of life values to the point of God, the journey is only half over. Once at the deepest level of God, the Holy Spirit focuses a Christian back to the presence of God Himself and then guides the Christian through the other layers of life. Out of the revelation relationship with God the Christian interprets and applies the truths of Scripture. The Christian then applies living Scripture to deeply held convictions and values. The deeply held values are applied in practical ethical behavior and traditions.

Because this journey begins with a relationship with God, the journey is not about good and evil but about a relationship with God. The laws are written on the heart of a Christian, not on tablets of stone.

Traditions, ethics, values, and beliefs are only safe for making decisions about life when they are driven out of a personal revelation and relationship with God. Terrible things happen when a culture or religion replaces God as the base reality of life and decision-making. People, including Christians, begin to live life on ethical autopilot.

Human culture and its systems of life are formed out of values and principles (Levels 3 and 4) and then the traditions and precedents (Levels 1 and 2) become the visible expression, the structure and the skin of culture. The danger is that traditions and precedents may eventually replace the original values and principles that formed the culture in the first place. Then a culture becomes rootless, cut away from the values and principles that produced it. Cultures, persons, and religions must be constantly renewed at the deeper root levels of life. Eventually, all human and religious cultures die or fall silent in the face of injustice unless they are born and reborn out of the presence of God at Level 5.

Jesus made decisions from the most basic level of life: God and His will (Level 5). Every decision He made and every value He lived out came from His relationship to the Father. The authorities made decisions from their own cultural paradigms that were mostly rooted in traditions (Levels 1) and standards (Level 2). Levels 1 through 3 are not bad but must be constantly interpreted out of Level 4 and 5. Christian organizations and movements usually begin at Level 4 or 5 but then almost always codify themselves at Level 1 & 2 (practices, traditions and standards) and then express their values and beliefs through their traditions, customs, and precedents. The Jewish authorities had done exactly that. The question for each Christian is "out of which level am I operating today in living out the church?"

Christians have access to the dynamic and powerful Level 5 of revelation and relationship with God through the Holy Spirit.

Church Values Inventory

Values determine the model a pastor or leader can and will use because we do what we value and value what we do. Remember that phrase. The questions and two-part answers below reveal values about nine important areas of the church: Sunday meeting type; meeting place; care of children; gift mix of leader; purpose of large group; timing of beginning public meeting; type of growth, and optimum size.

Answers to these questions will reveal if a leader and leadership team will be willing or able to use Jesus' decentralized expansion model or must use the traditional centralized headquarters model. This applies to pastors and leaders of all church models: cell church, small group church, traditional church, house church, and new church start.

Each of the following questions has two possible answers that can anticipate success or failure in implementing Jesus' expansion model of seventy. These values reveal your vision and determine your structures and strategy. In each question choose "a" or "b" that best states your approach to beginning a new church or in sending a team out from your church to begin a new church.

Question 1: What kind of large group experience is required during the early stages of the church plant or growth beginning?
    a. The team will begin with an intermediate large group meeting focused on training and expansion.
    b. The team will provide a permanent and set Sunday worship service with a teaching program.

Question 2: What kind of meeting place will be used in a new start?
    a. The start will use available and affordable places to meet, such as homes.
    b. The start will provide a special church facility that gives a public face.

Question 3: How will the team care for children and youth while establishing the new work?
    a. A family approach (children participate in community life) will be used to begin.
    b. A school approach (regular classes for teaching) will be used to begin.

Question 4: How will the team train leaders, equip the saints, and nurture believers?
    a. Relational on-the-job training will be the primary method of training, equipping and nurturing.
    b. Training, equipping, and nurturing will take place primarily in a classroom.

Question 5: What is the primary gift requirement and responsibility of the main leader?
    a. The leader must be able to supervise, coach, and pastor thirty-seventy Christians.
    b. The leader must be able to preach, teach, motivate, and administrate.

Question 6: What is the reason for gathering the initial people together in meetings?
  a. The purpose is to identify, train, and mobilize a committed core of leaders to build a prototype.
  b. The goal is to gather as large a crowd as possible for corporate worship, teaching and funding the program.

Question 7: In a new start, how soon should the leaders begin a public meeting?
  a. The plan is to move to a public meeting only after one or more clusters of seventy are functioning.
  b. The new start will become a public congregation as soon as possible and keep growing internally.

Question 8: Is the focus in an existing church on internal growth or external expansion?
  a. The base church will multiply growth units both inside and outside the base.
  b. The base church will primarily grow internally at one site.

Question 9: What is the optimum size of a church/congregation?
  a. The base church will grow to 100 to 200 and then use the seventy-growth model to hive off into natural growth areas.
  b. The church will grow as large as possible on one centralized campus: the bigger the better.

VALUES INTERPRETATION

If you selected the "b" answer for all or most of your responses for the above questions, then your values are more traditional. The "b" answers suggest you will be very frustrated trying to implement an organic expansion model. If you fall into this category, you should use the traditional approach to try to begin a new work or to reproduce your existing church. You will not change unless you see another biblical way to do church and if God reveals it to you. Seed expansion values into your church by beginning friendship triads.

On the other hand, the "a" answers suggest you are thinking outside the box about the nature and structure of the church. Your "a" answers show you value a more New Testament model that is inexpensive, mobile, and organic and can operate outside of buildings on the frontlines of the battle.

This is why the leaders of every church that will move from good to great must experience the process of 3/12/70. The process sorts out the committed and the uncommitted. The process reveals vision and the level of commitment to the vision. Life in the disciple triad and community cell will reveal who should be on the bus and will expose who should be off the bus.

Chapter 5

THE DARK NIGHT OF THE SOUL

"After years of lurching back and forth, the companion companies failed to build sustained momentum and fell instead into what we came to call the doom loop."

•Jim Collins

A "backlash" is the ultimate frustration for a fisherman. Just when a fisherman sees the perfect moment to catch the big one, throwing the line with the perfect lure toward the perfect place ... then the line backlashes. He must stop, get into the spool, and try to unravel the tangled mess. Backlashes can be so bad that the line is snarled in multiple places and must be cut. The perfect moment is lost.

My son Jimmy dreams of fixing this and has developed a patent for a backlash-free fishing reel. He recently showed me the prototype, set up in his garage workroom. A short rod with an attached reel and fishing line sat on the waist-high workbench. Nearby was a notebook with all of the formulas, diagrams, and procedures germane to the project. The prototype is hooked up to two computers, one monitoring a tiny camera and one a special microchip. Jimmy explains the prototype this way:

> This technology is based on a closed-loop control system of the spool braking system, which derives feedback from a high-speed camera. The camera "looks" at the backlash condition

60 times per second. The micro-controller (computer) processes each image by passing it through an edge-detection algorithm, reducing the image to only edges. When the pixel count exceeds a pre-determined amount (where backlash begins to occur) a brake is applied proportionate to the amount above the minimum backlash threshold and a maximum quantification, at which point the brake is applied 100%. As backlash begins, a brake slows the spool. As backlash reduces, the brake force decreases.

As impressive as the prototype is, it is not the final product. If it is, it will not sell. No fisherman wants a reel hooked up to two computers, tied to electrical wires for power, dependent on a detailed notebook to program the various formulas and algorithms, and restricted to a garage workshop. Fishermen like to fish in lakes and oceans, not garages. The prototype requires elements, procedures, and an environment not necessary or even desired in the final product. Additionally the process from the beginning of the aspirational phase of a backlash-free reel to the operational phase when it is actually on a production line takes several years. Nevertheless, the prototype is essential to the working model, even though it requires more time, computers, investors, and an inventor to do it. And when the finished model is ready, production will be an effective and streamlined process of mere days.

The prototype is necessary to test out the concept, and to produce a working model with the intended result: backlash-free and problem-free fishing. After observing the prototype, I can see myself on a tributary of the Amazon casting the reel with no worry about the cursed backlash. A huge peacock bass dances on the water with my lure in its mouth. Prototypes test out, produce and make possible practical dreams.

CHAPTER 5: THE DARK NIGHT OF THE SOUL

PROTOTYPE DEFINITION & ILLUSTRATION

Developing a prototype takes time and is accompanied by frustration. The presuppositions and vision of leaders are tested while developing a working model. This is especially true when developing a prototype that depends on people. Prototyping a fishing reel does not have the same dynamic forces at play as prototyping an expansion model of the church. The fishing reel prototype is made up of material, the church prototype of people.

A crucial concept in understanding the process of a prototype is "critical mass." "The critical mass occurs at the point at which enough individuals in a system have adopted an innovation so that the innovation's further rate of adoption becomes self-sustaining."[63]

The concept of the j-curve explains the point of critical mass or critical action. It is applied to several fields, including economics, social science, political science, population studies, and studies about change. The j-curve shows something beginning slowly, increasing momentum, and then breaking though with rapid acceleration or growth. When placed on a graft, the curve looks like a slanted "j" and is therefore called "j-curve." An airplane's take off is a good example of the j-curve. A plane taxis down the runway. It barely moves in the beginning. Then it picks up speed until it reaches between 140 to 160 MPH. At that point, an aeronautical engineer explained to me, "It will fly!" The speed and the configuration of the wings mean that it has reached the point of no return (critical mass). It will not remain on the ground.

---

63. Rogers, 343-346.

Small Deliberate Actions Produce a Prototype

Success in developing a prototype doesn't happen all at once with a single effort. A prototype is the result of a process that increases in efficiency and momentum as it moves forward toward a predetermined point. Jim Collins illustrates the principle of critical mass 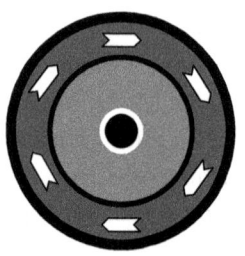 or the tipping point with the picture of a flywheel: a rotating mechanical device that is used to store rotational energy.

> *Picture a huge, heavy flywheel---a massive metal disk mounted horizontally on an axle, almost 30 feet in diameter, 2 feet thick, and weighing about 5,000 pounds. Now imagine that your task is to get the flywheel rotating on the axle as fast and long as possible. Pushing with great effort, you get the flywheel to complete one entire turn. You keep pushing, and the flywheel begins to move a little bit faster, and with continued great effort, you move it around a second rotation. You keep pushing in a consistent direction. Three turns ... four ... five ... six ... the flywheel builds up speed ... seven ... eight ... nine ... ten ... it builds up momentum ... eleven ... twelve ... moving faster with each turn ... twenty ... thirty ... fifty ... a hundred. Then, at some point --- breakthrough! The momentum of the thing kicks in your favor, hurling the flywheel forward, turn after turn ... whoosh! ... its own heavy weight working for you. You're pushing no harder than during the first rotation, but the flywheel goes faster and faster. Each turn of the flywheel builds upon work done earlier, compounding your investment of effort. A thousand times faster, then ten thousand, then a hundred thousand. The huge heavy disk flies forward, with almost unstoppable momentum. Now suppose someone came along and asked, "What was the one big push that caused this thing to go so fast?"*[64]

---

64. Collins, 164–165.

Momentum in a prototype is caused by a series of efforts that finally reach a "tipping point."[65] The pieces and parts come together and the process consolidates into one focus and entity. Consolidation is a normal phase of life. "When people begin to feel the magic of momentum --- when they begin to see tangible results, when they can feel the flywheel beginning to build speed --- that's when the bulk of people line up to throw their shoulders against the wheel and push."[66]

PROTOTYPE FATIGUE . . . THE DOOM LOOP

Collin's research group saw a different pattern when comparing the "good" companion companies to the "great" companies. They called the phenomenon the "doom loop," what I call prototype fatigue.

> *Instead of a quiet, deliberate process of figuring out what needed to be done and then simply doing it, the companion companies frequently launched new programs --- often with great fanfare and hoopla aimed at 'motivating the troops' --- only to see the programs fail to produce sustained results. They sought the single defining action, the grand program, the one killer innovation, the miracle moment that would allow them to skip the arduous buildup stage and jump right to breakthrough. They would push the flywheel in one direction, then stop, change course, and throw it in a new direction --- and then they would stop, change course, and throw it into yet another direction. After years of lurching back and forth, the companion companies failed to build sustained momentum and fell instead into what we came to call the doom loop.[67]*

---

65. Gladwell, 9.
66. Collins, 178.
67. Ibid., 178-179.

Strategy fatigue is the condition that a leader (or a group of leaders) experiences while trying to introduce change and innovation. In fact, it now appears to me that sometime during the process of becoming an expansion church, prototype fatigue is probable, if not inevitable. The devil makes sure of it! This phenomenon usually takes place after leaders attempt to implement the practical systems during the prototype stage.

Prototype fatigue is characterized by disorientation, discouragement, and disintegration and is the final barrier that must be overcome before reaching critical mass. During this period, failure seems to be at its highest probability and success seems to be at its lowest point. Jesus sought to avoid two extremes with His disciples. One scenario was the mount of inspiration without the valley of difficult ministry. The other was the valley of difficult ministry without the mount of inspiration. The job of the visionary is to maintain this balance and a good prototype helps do that.

Prototype fatigue equally affects leaders of a transition, a new start, and everything between. A team starting from scratch faces a daunting task: beginning from nothing. Of course, the larger the core team, the better the chance to be successful. However, prototype fatigue will at some point be part of every new start. Unlike a new start, an existing church transitioning to organic and holistic community groups begins with something. However, a pastor and team in an existing church face the challenging task of dealing with the traditional structure, historical programs, and old value systems while developing a prototype of a more organic church. Few pastors and teams of existing churches escape prototype fatigue when transitioning to a church of holistic community cells that will grow internally and expand externally.

The Dark Night & the Point of Quitting

Everett M. Rodgers discovered in his extensive research of innovations that even innovators have their ups and downs in the midst of change. The chart below, *The Anatomy of Innovation*, shows a graft of this process. I first saw this chart in a presentation by Jim Egli in 1993. In content the chart is related to Rogers teaching on innovation. However, I have not found the chart in any of his materials.[68]

Follow the line in the chart from "skepticism" to "it works!" Leaders of innovation normally reach a point of great euphoria very early in the process but many innovators gradually sink down into the "dark night of the soul" that we see in the *Anatomy of Innovation* chart.[69] Only commitment to an overarching vision will carry an innovator through this darkness of discouragement and despair.

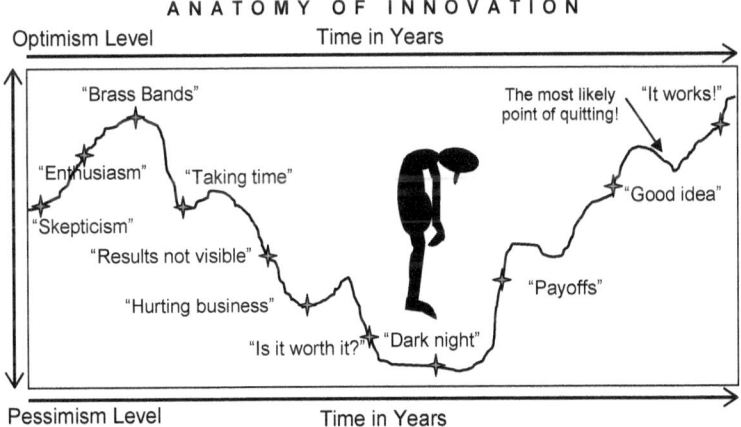

---

68. See Rodgers, *The Diffusion of Innovations*.
69. Jim Egli says he found the diagram in an old library book at Regent University but failed to write down the source at the time. He has repeatedly tried to find the original source without success. The book Jim Egli coauthored with Paul M. Zehr, *Alternative Models of Mennonite Pastoral Formation*, is an excellent study of pastoral leadership. It can be found in Occasional Papers No. 15 (Elkhart: Institute of Mennonite Studies, 1999).

Leaders who experience the dark night of the soul are deeply affected by the experience and are always in danger of being sucked into a spiral of perceived failure and suffocating discouragement. One common reaction is to over-react to future downturns and bail out just before a project is about to succeed. Look at the chart. The most likely point of quitting is just before the project is about to work when there is another downturn. The leader is afraid the downturn is another free fall into the dark night of the soul, and the leader cannot face that experience again.

In May of 1867, John Wesley Powell guided an expedition of three months and 930 miles down the Colorado River that made it the first documented group to pass through the Grand Canyon from beginning to end. After three months, the group became discouraged and three of his men chose to try to walk out. As it turned out they left just two days before the group got out of the canyon. They were never seen again. They left just before success.

The Face of Prototype Fatigue

In Psalm 55 David describes leadership fatigue as he speaks of his restless and distracted heart that is full of anguish. Fear, trembling, and horror overwhelm him. David longs to have "wings like a dove" so he "can fly away and be at rest." King David is experiencing the dark night of the soul.

Who caused David's anguish? "It is not an enemy who reproaches me. Then I could bear it. Nor is it one who hates me who has exalted himself against me, then I could hide myself from him. But it is you, a man my equal, my companion and my familiar friend. We who had sweet fellowship together, walked in the house of God in the throng." It is a friend who has turned away from David and has turned upon him! Trusted friends who bail out of the vision are some of the greatest causes of prototype fatigue among the leaders who remain.

Prototype fatigue shares some of the same common characteristics as battle fatigue in war. During the development of a prototype, leaders can become shell shocked from a constant bombardment of criticism from those who are unconvinced and uncommitted. Physical, spiritual, and emotional weariness may flood over the catalytic leaders who are responsible for implementing the vision. Leaders often face disorientation. Like a fatigued pilot, leaders during the prototype may lose their sense of orientation or direction. They begin to question which way is up and down, which way is forward and backward, and which way is out of the mess.

Prototype fatigue isolates people from each other. Conflict and misunderstanding among leaders often develops during the prototype. Discouragement and even depression are characteristics of prototype fatigue. Courage is tested at every step. Leaders become homesick and like the Children of Israel in the desert long for the old life in Egypt. After the triumph over the prophets of Baal on Mt. Carmel, Elijah experienced spiritual fatigue underneath the juniper tree in the desert. Only God can give the spiritual energy necessary to break prototype fatigue.

Some are unable to handle the pressure of the battle and go AWOL during the stress of the prototype. Jesus' disciples experienced prototype fatigue during the last year of His ministry. They manifested this symptom when they were fighting among themselves on the road to Jerusalem. The disintegration of the disciples was painfully evident when Christ was arrested, tried, and crucified. Only the women remained with Him. Jesus' men scattered because their expectations were dashed, their hopes were destroyed, and their lives were endangered.

In 1513 Niccolo Machiavelli recognized the forces that come against change and innovation. "There is nothing more difficult to plan, more doubtful of success, nor more dangerous to manage than the creation of a new order of things. ...Whenever the enemies have the ability to attack the innovation, they do so with the passion of partisans, while the others defend him sluggishly, so that the innovator and his party alike are vulnerable."

THE CAUSE OF PROTOTYPE FATIGUE

Several factors that contribute to prototype fatigue are inherent in the very nature of a prototype. This is why fatigue shows up during the prototype period. The prototype period is not only a time for testing systems but also a time for testing the commitment and vision of leaders; testing the dynamics as well as the mechanics; and testing the values as well as the actions.

The first factor is *time*. It is difficult to develop and maintain momentum during a church prototype because of the length of time required to become an organic cell church. The "big bang" theory doesn't work for beginning an organic church. The reason "instant cell church" does not work is because this is not a new program or the latest fad. Becoming an organic church is a new way of life, a new culture, and a new value system. Jesus used 3 1/2 years in this initial stage of the first church. Most of this time was required to change the values of His leadership base.

Therefore, it takes time to become an organic church of holistic cells. The length of time it takes to complete a prototype is an important factor in prototype fatigue because leaders wear down in the grind.

The second factor is *life itself*. Failure is a principle of life. Babe Ruth is considered the greatest home run hitter in baseball. Hank

Aaron eventually erased his total number of home runs (715) and Roger Maris broke his record of 60 home runs in a season. Later, in 1999, Mark McGuire and Sammy Sosa set new high marks for home runs in a season with 70 and 65 home runs respectively. But Babe Ruth and all these home run hitters had one thing in common. They struck out more often than other players. Even the best baseball players will hit the ball successfully only 1/3 of their time at bat. This means they "fail" 2/3 of the time.

The third factor is *the nature of the learning process*. Trial and error is an important element in growth. A baby spends a lot of time on the seat of its pants on the floor trying to learn to walk. A child learns to talk by speaking, making mistakes and learning from the mistakes. Research follows a pattern of "trial and error." Many of our greatest medical and scientific advances have only come after years of trial and error. In some cases it is as important to know what will not work as what will work.

This is also true of a church learning to be an expansion church of holistic cells. Failures that accumulate during the normal learning process are a contributing factor in prototype fatigue. Scattered across the church trying to develop holistic community cells is the wreckage of all the failures that have been experienced in learning how to do the individual systems. Often, the failures loom largest upon the landscape. Of course, the team has also been successful in many elements and has learned much about how to do things correctly. However, it is to the benefit of the enemy if the team sees the glass as half empty rather than half full. Therefore, it is the failures that often cast the largest shadow upon the process of a church becoming a church of holistic community cells.

The fourth factor is *the Second Law of Thermodynamics*. The natural law of life is that all things are in a state of chaos and it takes great energy to bring about order out of chaos. My British friend, Lawrence Singlehurst, gives his Mother's version of this law: "Left alone all things tend to swerve to rot." A prototype is always in danger of coming apart at the seams. Added to the physical Law of Thermodynamics is the spiritual Law of Thermo-discouragement. The evil one has a stake in causing discouragement in every attempt to become an organic expansion church. The natural order of things will cause a certain amount of failure. But it is Satan who sows the seeds of discouragement that can destroy a new church start or transition.

Factor number five is *the relationship between the parts and the whole*. The process must focus on the pieces and parts in order to make the process work. The danger is fixation on the parts instead of on the vision of the whole. Some of the individual parts of an automobile will "work" on their own to some degree. However, it is not the individual parts that cause a car to operate as a car. All of the parts are fitted together so that the car functions as a whole car. A set of brand new tires sitting in our driveway will not take us anywhere and have little other practical use. Tires are only useful when attached to the whole car. All the practical elements necessary to become a New Testament Church with holistic community cells must be tested out. Not any one element can be implemented with 100% efficiency in the early phases of the process. Some failure will be associated with each and every system that is learned. Perceived failures that focus on the individual parts of the process can abort the project before leaders can apply the lessons they have learned about the individual elements to the total project.

Therefore, we must understand from the beginning that the process will often feel like fragmentation. But we cannot stop there. Fragmentation is the lie of the Devil. God will eventually bring the different parts together. Therefore, innovators and visionaries must have faith that God can integrate all that is learned in the separate parts into a whole.

The sixth factor in prototype fatigue is *fuzzy vision and vague values*. Leaders who begin with a fuzzy vision and vague values are very susceptible to prototype fatigue. Several years ago a young leader in a church summed up the importance of a vision: "Where the vision is unclear, the cost is always too high."

A vision, by its very nature, is often perceived in its totality and completeness. The vision is seen in its final state when everything is working perfectly. The vision is long-term victory. This vision picture helps innovators know the end result and gives a target at which to aim. However, when vision is seen in its totality as a long-term victory, discouragement and despair often result. Visionaries "oversell" the vision to the point that success is measured if the entire vision is working. This means the step-by-step process always feels like failure because the entire vision is not yet a reality. Because of this, failure is an almost inevitable consequence. Short-term wins are needed to overcome vision totality and to build hope for long-term victory. A short-term win celebrates incremental success and builds a sense of accomplishment even though the total vision is not yet achieved.

The seventh factor in prototype fatigue is *the dynamic of gathering leaders* who are tested and prepared in the process crucible. Finding a stable core of leaders who won't "bail out on you" contributes to vision fatigue. It is during the prototype phase that leaders must count the cost and internalize the values because the practical application of the systems puts the values of a leader to the test. Some leaders who enter into the vision with great enthusiasm do not survive the process of setting up the systems that will live out the vision. Leaders begin lobbying for their favorite agenda as a way to speed up the prototype.

Nothing fatigues leaders more than having to defend a vision against good agendas. Collins suggests successful leaders view a vision like a bus.[70]

Every time a leader gets off the bus a certain amount of prototype fatigue sets in. This affects the momentum of the prototype. Desertion is so dangerous to the morale of an army that execution during wartime is the penalty. This is why the preparation phase is so important in a church strategy. Leaders must be gathered, identified, chosen, and trained who will not abandon the vision at the most critical points during the establishment of the prototype.

A catalytic leader finds encouragement and hope during the development of a prototype by experiencing the presence of Christ, by entering into a new depth of prayer, and by participating in edification in the prototype process.

Winston Churchill exhibits the spirit and resolve that must motivate the leaders God calls to develop an organic model of the church.

> *Never give in, ever give in, never, never, never, never – in nothing, great or small, large or petty – never give in except to convictions of honor and good sense. Never yield to force. Never yield to the apparently overwhelming might of the enemy.*

---

70. Collins, 13.

Section II

The dynamics & mechanics of a prototype

Chapter 6: Prototype Presence

Chapter 7: Prototype Prayer

Chapter 8: Prototype Edification

Chapter 9: Prototype Friendship (2–3)

Chapter 10: Prototype Community (12)

Chapter 11: Prototype Supervision (70)

Chapter 6

PROTOTYPE THE PRESENCE

> "*Earth's crammed with Heaven, and every common bush afire with God; but only he who sees takes off his shoes. The rest sit round it and pluck blackberries.*"[71]
> • Elizabeth Barrett Browning

Pastors generally feel comfortable with procedures and protocols because for years they have been implementing new programs for evangelism, discipleship, prayer, stewardship, and Bible study. Denominations provide these programs, ministries sell them, authors of best-selling books explain them, and consultants teach them. These programs come with instruction kits, materials, procedures, and schedules that promise to help a church grow. Therefore, implementing the procedures and protocols of small groups is part of the skill set of most church leaders. However, procedures and protocols cannot reproduce the dynamic life of Christ we see in the New Testament church, and that is what we need today. We desperately need to experience and live in God's presence.

In his comments on John 14:16-18, Francis Schaeffer explains how Christ will be present with the Church through the agency of the Holy Spirit between the ascension and the second coming.

---

71. Elizabeth Barrett Browning, "Aurora Leigh," The Poetical Works of Elizabeth Barrett Browning (New York: Thomas Y. Crowell & Co., 1882), 134.

> *Notice the words "I will not leave you orphans, I will come to you." The promise of Christ ---crucified, risen, ascended, glorified --- is that he will be with his Church, between the ascension and his second coming, through the agency of the indwelling Holy Spirit. These are universal promises, made to the Church for our entire era. These are the things that the world should see when they look upon the Church --- something that they cannot possibly explain away. The Church should be committed to the practical reality of these things, not merely assenting to them.*[72]

His presence was God's plan from the very beginning. The creation reveals the presence of God in His glory and power. It was the presence that consumed Abraham and the Patriarchs, King David, and the Prophets. The incarnation was the ultimate revelation of presence (Spirit became flesh) and this presence continued after the cross, death, and tomb in Jesus' post resurrection appearances. The presence continued through the ministry of the Holy Spirit in a new way, more powerful and fruitful than all previous manifestations of presence.

> *Jesus Christ is active in the here and now. He's not off in some remote corner of the universe, not viewing the world through a telescope from heaven. He has not left His people here to struggle and flounder until He comes back again. Christ is alive and has been at work in human society for twenty centuries, just as He said He would be: "Lo, I am with you always, to the close of the age" (Matthew. 28:20).*[73]

This is a promise of omnipresence: God's presence in every place and situation. God promised to be present in each individual and

---

72. Francis Schaeffer, *True Spirituality* (Wheaton, IL: Tyndale Publishers, 1971), 172.
73. Stedman, 100-101.

in groups, especially groups of two or three and small community groups. Learning to abide in the presence is the challenging part of becoming a New Testament church. Leaders must experience (prototype) the presence of God in friendship triads of two or three and community cells of twelve because these groups cannot work in a New Testament way without the presence.

God's Presence as I AM

God's name is the essence of His nature. This is why Moses asked God to identify Himself by name so he could validate his God-given role to Israel. God did not only use the common name that ancient cultures used for deity. God revealed His name as "presence" or "being." Tell them I AM --- first person, present tense --- has sent you. God's Self-identification is the name that could not be spoken in Israel, *ehyeh-asher-ehyeh*. Jesus used this unique name in the book of John in a grammatical technique that allowed Him to claim deity.

- *John 6:35:* "**I am** *the bread of life.*"
- *John 8:12:* "**I am** *the light of the world.*"
- *John 8:24* "*If you do not believe that* **I am** *(He), you will die in your sins.*"
- *John 8:58:* "*Before Abraham was,* **I am**.*"
- *John 10:9:* "**I am** *the door.*"
- *John 10:11:* "**I am** *the good shepherd.*"
- *John 11:25:* "**I am** *the resurrection and the life.*"
- *John 14:6:* "**I am** *the way, the truth, and the life.*"
- *John 15:1:* "**I am** *the true vine.*"

It is obvious Jesus is not just using the first person-present tense subject and verb in the above statements in a grammatical way. He is using "I am" to identify Himself with the special name that

God revealed to the Patriarchs. In one of my favorite poems, *My Name Is I AM*, poet Helen Mallicoat captures the practical implications of God's name:

> *I was regretting the past, and fearing the future.*
> *Suddenly my Lord was speaking: "My name is I AM."*
> *He paused. I waited. He continued,*
> *"When you live in the past,*
> *With its mistakes and regrets, it is hard.*
> *I am not there.*
> *My name is not I WAS.*
> *When you live in the future,*
> *With its problems and fears, it is hard.*
> *I am not there.*
> *My name is not I WILL BE.*
> *When you live in this moment it is not hard.*
> *I am here. My name is I AM."*

JESUS PROMISED TRINITARIAN PRESENCE

God is present with His people in every age in the fullness of His nature: Father, Son, and Spirit. "And what God is, essentially, is presence --- the doctrine of the Trinity says God is three persons who are present to each other in perfect knowledge and perfect love."[74] This relationship between a Christian and the Trinitarian God separates authentic God-indwelled Christianity from organized religion. The promised Spirit is the administrator of the Godhead and the advocate of the Christian.

In John 14, Jesus promised His followers that, after He returned to heaven, He (Jesus), the Holy Spirit, and the Father would be with them in a continuing presence.

---

74. Lee Strobel, *The Case for Faith* (Grand Rapids, Mich.: Zondervan, 2000), 53.

> *John 14:17: "But you know him (the Spirit of truth), for he lives with you and will be in you."*
>
> *John 14:18: "I will not leave you as orphans; I (Jesus) will come to you."*
>
> *John 14:23: "We (Father and Jesus) will come to him and make our home with him."*

Paul gives an account of a person who encountered the presence of God in a community cell meeting in 1 Corinthians 14:24-25:

> *But if an unbeliever or someone who does not understand comes in while everybody is prophesying, he will be convinced by all that he is a sinner and will be judged by all, and the secrets of his heart will be laid bare. So he will fall down and worship God, exclaiming, "God is really among you!"*

The observer of basic Christian community did not say, "This is a great meeting." "This is wonderful worship." "This is powerful healing." "This is a deep Bible study." "This is the best fellowship I have ever experienced." "Praise God for the working of the spiritual gifts." All of these may be meaningful but they are secondary experiences. The visitor in Paul's group described the primary experience of the Christian and the church in all of its group expressions: "God is really among you."

We have lived with the secondary experiences in church groups long enough. It is time to live in the primary experience. God is really with us! The presence of God in Christ through the promised Spirit in friendship triads of two or three, community cells, and a mid-level group of seventy must be real, not magical, not secondary learned manifestations, or new age wishful thinking. Pastors and church leaders must experience God-reality (presence) in friendship triads and community cells if they are to successfully introduce them to the church.

Leaders must be evidence of the presence so that followers will experience the presence.

Organizations Don't Produce the Presence

The presence is not produced by church practices, conjured up in ceremonial formulas, hyped up in human emotions through the gifts, or produced by a special flavor of worship (traditional or contemporary). Denominations and churches, no matter their historical significance or size, do not, of themselves, produce the presence. All of these are expressions of the presence, not the presence. The presence produces genuine expressions, manifestations, and organizations; otherwise all we do in church is just human learned behavior.

The Christian experience with God in New Testament groups is not about the manifestations but about Christ, the source of the manifestations. If my wife leaves the room and I smell her perfume, the perfume is not my wife but a manifestation of my wife. Physical manifestations of buildings, ceremonies, or programs, along with the spiritual manifestations of gifts, healings, and tongues are not the foundation experience or expression of the church. Christ is!

The presence has always been the foundation of the church. Without the presence of Christ in resurrection there would be no church. It was not the empty tomb that convinced the early Christians, but the presence of Christ among them for seven weeks before the ascension. Then afterwards, His presence, through the Holy Spirit, was poured out upon them at Pentecost. Jesus promised to be present in each individual Christian, in small groups of Christians, and in large groups … and that is what happens.

Small groups are the place of the continuing presence of Christ in the world through the Holy Spirit. They are more important to God's plan than large crowds, beautiful buildings, religious ceremonies, and impressive programs. The nature and power of friendship triads and community cells is found in Christ's presence: "Where two or three are gathered together in my name, there I am in their midst." His power is in the triad and cell: "Greater works shall you do" (because I am going away and the Spirit will come and be in you and with you). His purpose is fulfilled through the triad and cell: Again Jesus said, "Peace be with you! As the Father has sent me, I am sending you" (John 20:21).

Satan hoped that if he could destroy the Son incarnated in the flesh, he would destroy God's divine work and change the order of the universe: Satan would be equal or greater than God. "Let us kill the heir, and the kingdom is ours" (Matt. 21:33-46; Mark 12:1-12; Luke 20:9-19). Satan's scheme failed at the mouth of the open tomb. The presence could not be destroyed, defeated, denied, deterred, detained, or delayed.

Today, Satan's strategy is once again to attack the manifest presence of Christ and Satan has chosen the vulnerable and exposed point of the small friendship triad and community cell. Satan believes he will win the battle here on earth that he has already lost in Heaven. Destroy Christ at the point where He manifests His presence, power, and purpose in His new Body. If Satan cannot keep friendship triads and community cells from forming, then He will distort their nature, confuse their focus, get them to rely upon human techniques, neutralize their spiritual power, or water down the wine of the Spirit in the wineskin. Satan will do anything to get Christ out of friendship triads and community cells and make them just good Christian fellowship groups and Bible studies.

GOD'S PRESENCE IS THE ANSWER TO LIFE

While trying to prove or disprove God, reporter and skeptic Lee Strobel investigated eight of the most common objections about God. The first objection was, "Since evil and suffering exist, a loving God cannot." His interview with Professor Peter John Kreeft ended with a surprising discussion about the importance of God's presence. In conversational dialogue, Kreeft explains how God's presence is the answer to life:

> At the end of the book of Job, the all-time classic on the problem of suffering, God finally shows up with the answer --- and the answer is a question. He says to Job, 'Who are you? Are you God? Did you write this script? Were you there when I laid the foundations of the earth?" And Job realizes the answer is no. Then he's satisfied. Why? Because he sees God! God doesn't write him a book. He could have written the best book on the problem of evil ever written. Instead, he shows himself to Job. "And that satisfies him ---" Yes! It has to --- that's what's going to satisfy us forever in heaven. I think Job gets a foretaste of heaven at the end of the book of Job, because he meets God. If it were only words that God gave him, that would mean that Job could dialogue and ask God another question and God would give a good answer and Job would ask another question the next day and the next day, because Job was a very demanding philosopher. This would go on and on and never end. What could make it end? God's presence! God didn't let Job suffer because he lacked love, but because he did love, in order to bring Job to the point of encountering God face-to-face, which is humanity's supreme happiness. Job's suffering hollowed out a big space in him so that God and joy could fill it. As we look at human relationships, what we see is that lovers don't want explanations but presence. And what God is, essentially, is presence --- the doctrine of

> *the Trinity says God is three persons who are present to each other in perfect knowledge and perfect love. That's why God is perfect joy. And insofar as we can participate in that presence, we too have infinite joy. So that's what Job has --- even on the dung heap, even before he gets any of his worldly goods back --- once he sees God face to face.*[75]

The conversation above gives insights about God's presence as the foundation experience and all-encompassing truth of the Christian here on earth and in heaven: (1) God is present in the midst of suffering, (2) God's presence is a "foretaste of heaven," (3) "We can participate in God's presence," and (4) God provides His Trinitarian presence for all of life.

Present to the Presence of God

Presence is the key to the organic church (the Body of Christ) and is the great miracle of the Christian life. It is the meaning of the incarnation: God wrapped up in human flesh. Jesus begins the presence in each individual Christian at the moment of salvation when relationship with the eternal God in the fullness of the Father, Son, and Spirit is experienced personally through the indwelling Spirit. Jesus promised this in John 7:37-39 and it was fulfilled at Pentecost:

> *Now on the last day, the great day of the feast, Jesus stood and cried out, saying, "If anyone is thirsty, let him come to Me and drink. He who believes in Me, as the Scripture said, 'From his innermost being will flow rivers of living water.'" But this He spoke of the Spirit, whom those who believed in Him were to receive; for the Spirit was not yet given, because Jesus was not yet glorified."*

---

75. Strobel, 53.

Christians also experience the presence in its fullness in community. "Where two or three gather in my name, there I am in their midst."

It is possible to be present without being present. We "tune people out" all the time and go into relational neutrality. We may talk to someone at a convention while looking through him/her for the next person. We can go into automatic pilot with our spouse, boss, or even God.

Think of restaurants that still have free seating. That means you sit wherever there is an open space even if someone else is already at the table. Crowded noddle shops in Thailand have open seating and in Brazil some restaurants use free seating. Rudy's BBQ Restaurant in Texas has long tables and benches in the middle of its large interior room. It is free seating, not private tables that are in the surrounding rooms. You may have someone sitting beside or in front of you that you don't know. They are present but not present unless there is acknowledgment through a word or gesture. Presence requires relationship and that means acknowledgment and interaction with each other. Once someone nods, speaks, makes a gesture of acknowledgment, or just asks for the saltshaker or BBQ sauce, you are then present to each other. Until then you are present but not present to each other in relationship. In a free seating restaurant we might talk about the strangers around us without them hearing us. We whisper "he looks like Santa Claus with his white beard." Or, we carry on a conversation as if they aren't right there, even though they can hear us.

Too often our group meetings can be like free seating. Christ is present in our groups because he promised to be present when two or three join together in His name. However, many small groups talk *at* Jesus Christ and a lot *about* Him instead of talking *to* Him. He is present but not present to those present. Presence is a personal and a communal experience and it requires acknowledgment.

The post resurrection relationship of Jesus with His followers is instructive about how we relate to Him today. After His resurrection, Jesus was present with His disciples in a different spiritual way, even more real than just the physical. However, only eyes of faith could see His spiritual but real manifest presence.

THE ROAD TO EMMAUS

Two disciples, one named Cleopas and one unnamed (were they husband and wife?), were walking home to Emmaus on the evening of the resurrection of Christ. "And after that, He appeared in a different form to two of them, while they were walking along on their way to the country. And they went away and reported it to the others, but they did not believe them either" (Mark 16:212-13). See Luke 24:13-35 for a more detailed account of this fascinating story.

The Two Disciples are heartbroken by the death of Christ and are talking about Him and remembering all the events of the past few days. Tears are in their eyes as they walk westward into the setting sun. Sorrow, sadness and despair are written on their faces. They had hoped that He was the Messiah but He had died on the cross. They talk about the rumors that someone stole His body. They try to piece together all the accounts of the Women who reported that some of them had seen Christ alive. They attempt to make sense out of the claims of ten of the Disciples that Christ had been among them and had talked to them.

Cleopas and his companion finally notice a stranger who has appeared and is walking along with them. The Two Disciples are surprised that he seems to know nothing about the events in Jerusalem. They quickly bring him up to date during their seven-mile journey home. At a certain point the stranger begins to teach them. But they still don't recognize that this is Jesus.

The Two Disciples invite their travel companion for supper. As was the custom, He, as the guest, is given the honor of breaking the bread for the meal. As He breaks bread and hands it to the Two Disciples they see the nail-prints in His wrist and "their eyes are opened and they recognize Him." The scripture then says that Jesus "vanished from their sight."

They now try to make sense out of this latest event that has happened to them (probably as they are hurrying back to Jerusalem to report the incident). They think back to the time they spent with the resurrected Christ in a different form on their journey home. (The seven-mile walk plus the brief time Jesus was in the home must have taken at least two hours, the amount of time for a small group cell meeting.) They remember that their hearts had "burned within" them as they walked on the road with Him.

PRESENT, BUT NOT RECOGNIZED

Is it possible for Christ to have a manifest presence in a group and the members not recognize Him and relate to Him? The post-resurrection appearance of Jesus on the Road to Emmaus is an instance where Christians who knew Christ did not recognize Him even though He was with them for at least two hours, teaching them during part of that time.

Christ promised to be in the midst of every group that gathers in His name. However, we must have our eyes of faith open. We must expect Him! We must acknowledge His presence! We must keep an appointment with Him instead of attending a meeting about Him. Otherwise, we do what the two Disciples did. We talk about Him. We even explain things to Him. We recite Scriptures referring to Him. And, we even receive teaching from Him. But all the time we do not recognize Him and acknowledge Him as Christ with us. Like the two Disciples we have a "burning in our hearts" about Him. But, that was not the intention of Christ when He began to walk with them. He wanted them to know Him, to talk with Him, and to experience Him.

Think of the tragedy of that seven-mile walk. These two Disciples could have been with the Resurrected Lord for those seven miles, worshiping Him, learning from Him, and having fellowship with Him. But all they experienced was a stimulating conversation, some good teaching, and a "burning in their hearts."

Think about the modern day tragedy! Christ has been showing up in every one of the small group meetings wherever and whenever Christians gather together in His name. Yet, for the most part those Christians study about Christ, or talk about Christ, or do something in His name. But they do not experience the reality of His living presence.

In a God-made cell Christ will certainly be present in power, purpose, and passion. However, we must expect Him, prepare for Him, acknowledge Him, and listen and talk to Him. We must be present to His presence!

How to Prototype the Presence in Community

What can pastors and church leaders do to restore the presence to friendship triads and community cells?

One, understand that the most important aspect of a triad or a community cell is not the cell leader, a good worship leader, a good meeting agenda, or small group techniques that facilitate Christian community. The most important aspect of a triad or community cell is whether or not those in the groups acknowledge and experience the promised presence of Christ.

Two, personally live in the presence and abide in Christ. "He is not far from each of us: for in him we live, and move, and have our being" (Acts 17:28).

Three, stop just "meeting!" Come together in Christ's presence! Live out Matthew 18:20: "For where two or three come together in my name, there am I with them." This applies to the two or three friendship triad but also to the community cell because triads are sub groups of the community cell.

Four, welcome Christ at the beginning of every group meeting and acknowledge His presence. Just as you welcome each member into the group, it is appropriate to welcome the honored guest: Christ.

Five, believe that Jesus does what He promised: He is present in every group that meets in His name. In a community cell the presence of Christ is multiplied, the power of Christ is intensified, and the purpose of Christ is focused through the Holy Spirit toward harvest. The gates of hell cannot prevail against the risen and present Christ in a triad and cell.

Six, release Christ through the Holy Spirit to lead the triad and cell. Experience His presence through listening prayer. Trust Christ to be powerful and loving enough to deal with the real problems and situations the community faces. Apply the Word to practical life problems. Participate in practical prayer prophecy so Christ can edify the body. Experience His presence in real time and life: "Surely God is in this place."

Seven, daily practice the presence of God and you will discover with Frank Laubach that "the most wonderful discovery of all is, to use the words of St. Paul, 'Christ liveth in me.' He dwells in us, walks in our minds, reaches out through our hands, speaks with our voices, if we respond to His every whisper."[76]

> *The one condition that precedes every kind of prayer is being present to God with conscious awareness. God is always present with us, whether or not we can feel this reality. In a very real sense, then, the foundation of all prayer is being present to the presence of God.*[77]

Pastors and church leaders must prototype (experience) "being present to the presence of God." The next chapter considers the dynamics of prayer in His presence.

---

76. Frank C. Laubach, "The Game with Minutes"; a pamphlet about the virtues of a life lived with unceasing focus on God. In it, Laubach, a Christian Evangelical missionary, urged Christians to attempt keeping God in mind for at least one second of every minute of the day. In this way Christians can attempt the attitude of constant prayer spoken of in Colossians 4:2-3.
77. Marjorie J. Thompson, *Soul Feast: An Invitation to the Christian Spiritual Life*, (Louisville, KY: Westminster Press), 35.

Chapter 7

PROTOTYPE PRAYER

*"Prayer is not monologue, but dialogue.
Gods voice in response to mine is its most essential part."*
• Andrew Murray

In his classic book *Practicing His Presence*, Brother Lawrence, 17th century Carmelite lay brother, tied God's presence and prayer together.

> *My prayers are nothing other than a sense of the presence of God.*[78] *I have given up all forms of devotion and set prayers other than those to which my state obliges me. My only business now is to persevere in His holy presence. I do so by a simple and loving attention to the Lord. Then I have the experience of the actual presence of God. To use another term I will call it a secret conversation between my soul and the Lord.*[79]

The Disciples saw this kind of presence/praying in Jesus' life. "One day Jesus was praying in a certain place. When he finished, one of his disciples said to him, 'Lord, teach us to pray, just as John taught his disciples'" (Luke 11:1).

The followers of Jesus quickly realized that prayer was the key to His life and that they could not be His disciples unless they

---

78. Brother Lawrence & Frank Laubach, *Practicing His Presence* (Sargent, GA: The SeedSower, MCMLXXIII), 56.
79. Ibid., 77.

learned His kind of praying. As Jews, they had been praying all their lives but they recognized a difference in how Jesus, and evidently John, prayed. The Disciples understood from watching Jesus that "spiritual people are not those who engage in certain spiritual practices; they are those who draw their life from a conversational relationship with God."[80]

Prayer is the lifeblood of Jesus' spiritual Body on earth, the oxygen of its life, and the catalytic force for the ministry of the church. Prayer is an amazing resource that God provides for those who follow Him. Prayer within small group community activates the presence of Christ in the midst, the power of Christ in edification, and the purpose of Christ to preach good news to the poor; to proclaim freedom for the prisoners and recovery of sight for the blind, to release the oppressed, and to proclaim the year of the Lord's favor" (Luke 4:18-19). Dietrich Bonhoeffer believed that "where a people prays, there is the church; and where the church is; there is never loneliness."[81]

The church that will expand as a pandemic people movement requires a special kind of prayer. Will you join me in asking what the Disciples asked? "Lord, teach us to pray like you and the Christians in the Early Church prayed."

JESUS' PRAYING IS SIMPLE

Jesus' praying is characterized by simplicity. One of His stories illustrates the desire of God for simple and sincere prayers rather than long public prayers (Luke 18:10-14).

> *Two men went up to the temple to pray, one a Pharisee and the other a tax collector. The Pharisee stood up and prayed about*

---

80. Dallas Willard, *Hearing God* (Drovers Grove, Ill: InterVarsity Press, 2012), 288.
81. Eric Metaas, *Bonhoeffer: Pastor, Martyr, Prophet, Spy* (Nashville, TN: Thomas Nelson, 2010), 69.

himself: "God, I thank you that I am not like other men – robbers, evildoers, adulterers – or even like this tax collector. I fast twice a week and give a tenth of all I get." But the tax collector stood at a distance. He would not even look up to heaven, but beat his breast and said, "God, have mercy on me, a sinner." I tell you that this man, rather than the other, went home justified before God. For everyone who exalts himself will be humbled, and he who humbles himself will be exalted.*

Christians in the institutional church have fallen into a harmful habit about prayer that Rosalind Rinker calls "prayer-speeches." Several decades ago she introduced prayer as a simple conversation with God, both as an individual and as a group.[82] Jesus' kind of prayer is natural: not religious, not formal, and not rehearsed. It is childlike in simplicity. The chart, *One Hundred Thirty-three Simply Prayers*, shows simple spontaneous prayers that are different from elaborate "prayer speeches."

Each line of prayer in the chart represents seven simple prayers. For example, one could pray the first line: "God fill me; God fill him; God fill her; God fill them; I repent; we repent; and You are kind." These are simple prayers that can be thought, whispered, or declared aloud in personal intimacy with God, in times of public prayer and gathering in the presence of God, or

SIMPLE PRAYERS

PRAYERS ABOUT GOD	PRAYERS TO GOD	PRAYERS FOR PEOPLE	
You Are Kind!	I Repent!	Fill	Me/Others!
You Are King!	I Submit!	Use	Me/Others!
You Are Lord!	I Confess!	Help	Me/Others!
You Are Love!	I Love You!	Save	Me/Others!
You Are Holy!	I Obey You!	Give	Me/Others!
You Are Good!	I Am Sorry!	Make	Me/Others!
You Are Creator!	I Serve You!	Bless	Me/Others!
You Are Eternal!	I Surrender!	Show	Me/Others!
You Are Merciful!	I Trust You!	Guide	Me/Others!
You Are Redeemer!	I Thank You!	Teach	Me/Others!
You Are Gracious!	I Praise You!	Touch	Me/Others!
You Are All Wise!	I Crown You!	Receive	Me/Others!
You Are Majestic!	I Believe You!	Forgive	Me/Others!
You Are Righteous!	I Receive You!	Change	Me/Others!
You Are Everlasting!	I Follow You!	Protect	Me/Others!
You Are Omnipresent!	I Rest In You!	Prepare	Me/Others!
You Are All Powerful!	I Glorify You!	Indwell	Me/Others!
You Are Alpha & Omega!	I Abide In You!	Abide In	Me/Others!
You Are Compassionate!	I Worship You!!	Empower	Me/

---

82. Rosalind Rinker, *Prayer: Conversing with God* (Grand Rapids: Zondervan, 1959), 17.

just as a Christian seeking to see and respond to God in the normal events of the day.

C. S. Lewis describes a simple act of prayer from the perspective of a Christian but reveals the multi-dimensional spiritual elements of that simple prayer from God's Trinitarian perspective.

> *An ordinary simple Christian kneels down to say his prayers. He is trying to get into touch with God. But, if he is a Christian he knows that what is prompting him to pray is also God: God, so to speak, inside him. But he also knows that all his real knowledge of God comes through Christ, the Man who was God---that Christ is standing beside him, helping him to pray, praying for him. You see what is happening. God is the thing to which he is praying---the goal he is trying to reach. God is also the thing inside him which is pushing him on---the motive power. God is also the road or bridge along which he is being pushed to that goal. So that the whole threefold life of the three-personal Being is actually going on in the ordinary little bedroom where an ordinary man is saying his prayers. The man is being caught up into the higher kind of life ... he is being pulled into God, by God, while still remaining himself.*[83]

Every sincere prayer has the element of revelation as God speaks and reveals Himself. Therefore, every prayer is a miracle of the presence of God.

Prayer Lists

Marjorie Thompson suggests there are "two primary expressions of prayer as communication: listening to God and speaking

---

83. C. S. Lewis, *Mere Christianity*, (New York: The Macmillan Company, 1965), 127.

to God."[84] She also observes that, "it is the listening side of the communication loop that has been given inadequate attention in most Protestant church teachings on prayer."[85]

The writers of the Bible encourage Christians to speak to God and to ask for things from God. God encouraged the prophet Jeremiah to "call to Me, and I will answer you, and I will tell you great and mighty things, which you do not know" (Jer. 33:3). Jesus taught his disciples to "ask, and it shall be given you; seek, and ye shall find; knock, and it shall be opened unto you" (Matt. 7:7). Paul told the Christians in Philippi: "Do not be anxious about anything, but in everything by prayer and supplication with thanksgiving let your requests be made known to God. And the peace of God, which surpasses all understanding, will guard your hearts and your minds in Christ Jesus" (Phil. 4:6-7). James encouraged his readers: "If any of you lacks wisdom, he should ask God, who gives generously to all without finding fault, and it will be given to him" (James 1:5-8).[86]

Unfortunately, human nature has led Christians to abuse the open invitation to ask God for things. "For many of us prayer ... seems to be a quite one-sided affair, prayer simply means talking

---

84. Thompson, 35.
85. Ibid.
86. Other scriptures about asking in prayer are: John 14:13: "And I will do whatever you ask in my name, so that the Son may bring glory to the Father. You may ask me for anything in my name, and I will do it." John 16:24: "Until now you have not asked for anything in my name. Ask and you will receive, and your joy will be complete." John 15:7: "If you remain in me and my words remain in you, ask whatever you wish, and it will be given you." Eph. 6:18: "Pray in the Spirit on all occasions with all kinds of prayers and requests. With this in mind, be alert and always keep on praying for all the saints."

1 John 5:14-15: "This is the confidence we have in approaching God: that if we ask anything according to his will, he hears us. And if we know that he hears us—whatever we ask—we know that we have what we asked of him."

to God. This may be stated as talking "at" God."[87] Asking has become an obsessive habit in the traditional church. We have formulated asking into a prayer list.

Wednesday night was at one time devoted to a prayer meeting in most churches. These prayer meetings spent more time listening to a mini sermon and developing a prayer list than in actually praying. The prayer time went like this: "Does anyone have a prayer need?" People's problems and needs were shared and written on a list. Then the group prayed down the list. More time was devoted to making the list than for actually praying for the people and items on the list, and only a limited number of regular prayers prayed.

Wednesday night prayer meeting is almost extinct today. However, prayer-list praying is alive and well. I found the same prayer habit in Thailand as a missionary. At one point, I told my Thai Christian small groups that they could not ask God for anything until they thanked Him for something. Because God speaks to me, I naturally feel free as a child to ask God to help me with my needs, and often for my wants, but a prayer list bypasses listening and goes directly to asking. Asking without listening gives little opportunity for God's input and often has little relationship to what God knows we need.

Imagine a child going to a parent with a list of wants! That might work for a time or two, if it is a very short list, or is addressed to Santa. However, using a list is not the normal form of communication between child and parent. God's desire is that I ask for what God wants for me. That also requires listening to God so I will know what He wants for me. This requires trust, humility, and submission and I believe that is the point. I don't

---

87. Henri J. M. Nouwen, *The Way of the Heart* (New York: Ballantine Books, 1981), 68.

trust God to give me what I want. I think I know what is best for me. True prayer always begins with a submissive heart.

LISTENING PRAYER

Listening precedes speaking in the development of a child's language skills. The same order applies to the development of our prayer life. The Divine Spirit touches something in our spirit before we are drawn to speak. As we grow in maturity we understand that "in listening prayer, spoken prayer is born."[88] Therefore, we must personally learn to listen, and we must practice listening in order to live in Christian community. Jesus shows us a beautiful picture of our prayer relationship. "My sheep listen to my voice; I know them, and they follow me" (John 10:27). We know Jesus, listen to His voice, and follow Him. Listening is an important part of our relationship with Jesus.

We take a step toward spiritual maturity when we realize "that the listening mode of prayer has been neglected" and that "we are good at making requests of God, but not so good at hearing God speak to us."[89] Effective praying will have a healthy balance of God speaking and the Christian listening, and the Christian speaking and God listening. "Call to me and I will answer you and tell you great and unsearchable things you do not know" (Jer. 33:3). Søren Kierkegaard suggests we must pray until we are silent so we can then enter into the other side of prayer: hearing God.

The earthly-minded person thinks and imagines that when he prays, the important thing, the thing he must concentrate

---

88. Jennifer Kennedy Dean, *Listening Prayer*, www.prayinglife.org; The Praying Life Foundation.
89. Marlene Kropf and Eddy Hall, *Praying with the Anabaptists* (Newton, Kansas: Faith and Life Press, 1994), 7.

upon, is that God should hear what he is praying for. And yet in the true, eternal sense it is just the reverse: the true relation in prayer is not when God hears what is prayed for, but when the person praying continues to pray until he is the one who hears, who hears what God is asking for. In proportion as one becomes more and more earnest in prayer, one has less and less to say, and in the end one becomes quite silent. Indeed, one becomes quite a hearer. And so it is; to pray is not to hear oneself speak, but it is to be silent, and to remain silent, to wait, until the one who prays hears God.[90]

The key to God transforming us is not found in what we say as we pray but in what we hear as we listen. As God speaks to us we cannot remain unchanged. Listening to God is essential for living in community together. Edification will not happen until and unless a group of believers learn to listen to God for each other. Listening is the language of wellness for the Christian and the Church because we are able to hear God's diagnosis of our condition and His prescription for our spiritual health.

Something special happens when we listen to God. He often speaks the name of someone and shows us a face. People are in God's heart and He wants to put them in our hearts. When we listen to Him we are able to see the faces of those around us. This is a key step in edification.

Frank Laubach observed, "The trouble with nearly everybody who prays is that he says "Amen" and runs away before God has a chance to reply. Listening to God is far more important than giving Him your ideas."[91] Dietrich Bonhoeffer understood the

---

90. Søren Kierkegaard, *Provocations: Spiritual Writings of Kierkegaard*, Compiled and Edited by Charles E. Moore (Rifton, NY: The Plough Publishing House, 2010), 347.
91. Laubach, "The Game with Minutes."

importance of listening prayer for living in community together and warned about the tendency of Christians to give attention to God "with half an ear." He believed Christians have a "ministry of listening."

> *There is a kind of listening with half an ear that presumes already to know what the other person has to say. It is an impatient, inattentive listening, that despises the brother and is only waiting for a chance to speak and thus get rid of the other person. This is no fulfillment of our obligation, and it is certain that here too our attitude toward our brother only reflects our relationship to God. It is little wonder that we are no longer capable of the greatest service of listening that God has committed to us, that of hearing our brother's confession, if we refuse to give ear to our brother on lesser subjects. Secular education today is aware that often a person can be helped merely by having someone who will listen to him seriously, and upon this insight it has constructed its own soul therapy, which has attracted great numbers of people, including Christians. But Christians have forgotten that the ministry of listening has been committed to them by Him who is Himself the great listener and whose work they should share. We should listen with the ears of God that we may speak the Word of God.*[92]

LISTENING ROOM

Early in his journey into community life, Ralph Neighbour realized that listening to God was important for New Testament community to work properly. He built the Listening Room into his community and discipleship system.

---

92. Dietrich Bonhoeffer, *Life Together: The Classic Exploration of Christian Community* (New York, NY: HarperCollins, 1954), 98-99.

> *Before spiritual gifts can be properly manifested in cell groups for building up one another, believers must have a Listening Room and must know how to hear the voice of God. The physical location is not as significant as the event. The believer must not only talk to the Lord Jesus in prayer, but also hear from Him in the process. Christ must provide edification before the believer can use it. Otherwise, the 'building up' in the cell meeting is nothing more than the activity of the flesh.*[93]

A listening room is more than a physical place. It is a spiritual space in our mind and spirit. The door to the listening room is opened when I am more interested in what God has to say than what I want to say to God. Then this kind of listening prayer becomes the door to identify genuine needs from God's perspective. Therefore, we must listen, hear, and understand His solutions and guidance.

Too often our prayers are driven by a wish list or a bucket list made up of our wants and desires. "In communicating with God, therefore, (we should) not demand what we want or think we need; rather, we should discuss with God what he wants for us."[94] Jesus listened. He did not present a list to the Father. We experience and prototype prayer from the listening room, not from a list.

Prayer lists must be accompanied with prayer listening. This is both a provision and requirement for God's people. Leaders must experience this kind of prayer listening in community life so that followers have a prototype of how to listen to God and how to listen to God for each other.

---

93. Neighbour, *Where Do We Go from Here?*, 172-178.
94. Bruce B. Barton, Philip W. Comfort, Linda Chaffee Taylor, David R. Veerman, Len Woods, *Life Application Commentary 1,2, & 3 John* (Carol Stream, IL: Tyndale, 1998) 116.

Cultivating the proper listening attitude in prayer will help us pray for the right things. James warns: "When you ask, you do not receive, because you ask with wrong motives, that you may spend what you get on your pleasures" (James 4:3). The King James Version uses the phrase "you ask amiss." We most often "ask amiss" because we are so busy asking that we have not listened to God about the right motives and right things.

Asking according to God's will focuses a Christian and community of Christians on God's priorities. When we don't know God's priorities we will naturally pray for our own priorities that usually center around getting more pleasant circumstances, having others treat us the way we want to be treated, and getting relief from painful conditions or irritating people. If this is what dominates our prayer requests, our batting average of answered prayers is going to be pretty low, and our motivation to pray is going to diminish.

Entering the listening room takes the Christian out of the arena of asking and places him/her in a position to listen to and hear God at a deeper heart/spirit level of spiritual communication. This is the reason listening to God is a key ingredient in edification. (See the next chapter on edification.)

JESUS PRAYED AT THE HEART LEVEL

At a certain point in the prayer process we must move "from head to heart" and that "means moving from a limited and partial dimension of our lives to the center of our whole being."[95] Prayer that results in the edification of a Christian and the church is a heart encounter that comes from a deep work of the Holy Spirit. Heart prayer happens in the total experience of listening, speaking, and abiding. "The crisis of our prayer life is

---
95. Thompson, Ibid., 50.

that our mind may be filled with ideas of God while our heart remains far from him. Real prayer comes from the heart."[96]

A Russian mystic stated it well: "To pray is to descend with the mind into the heart, and there to stand before the face of the Lord, ever-present, all-seeing, with you."[97] As we learn to pray as Jesus prayed, we descend with our mind into our heart and experience the "mystery that the heart, which is the center of our being, is transformed by God into his own heart" and "God's heart has become one with ours."[98]

We see heart praying in Gethsemane. Facing the might of Rome, the anger of Jewish religious leaders, and the power of Satan, Jesus desperately needed the Father's guidance and affirmation of the plan. But more than knowledge about the plan, Jesus needed the touch of the Father, heart to heart. This heart connection took Jesus to the next step after Gethsemane: Placing His will with His heart in the Father's hands at His trial and at the cross.

Life (and prayer) always comes to a choice of wills. In His Gethsemane prayer, we see in Jesus the deepest dimension of trust and obedience at the heart level of abiding. Jesus accepted the Father's will and guidance even though it required the extreme commitment of suffering and death. The critical moment in prayer is when we pray the Gethsemane prayer from our heart: "Not my will but your will be done" (Luke 22:42). C. S. Lewis observes that in those Gethsemane moments, "We're not necessarily doubting that God will do the best for us: we are wondering how painful the best will turn out to be."[99]

---

96. Nouwen, 71.
97. Ibid., 73.
98. Ibid., 86.
99. C. S. Lewis, *Letters of C. S. Lewis*, ed. W. H. Lewis, (USA: Harvest Original, 1966), 457.

"Prayer is not a convenient device for imposing our will on God, or for bending his will to ours, but the prescribed way of subordinating our will to his. It is by prayer that we seek God's will, embrace it and align ourselves with it. Every true prayer is a variation on the theme 'your will be done.'"[100] "It is only when we know that we are powerless that we are prepared to listen to Jesus Christ and to do what He says."[101]

Being silent and listening to God leads to a deeper relationship that transcends the mind and rests in the deepest part of a person's heart/spirit. At that moment, God has a Christian's attention and the Christian's attention is given to God. External distractions are minimized at the point of the heart and spirit.

SPIRIT PRAYER

Leaders must experience and prototype simple prayer, listening prayer, and heart prayer. These are essential for developing spiritually mature Christians and a healthy church. In friendship triads Christians learn to listen to God for personal needs as Scripture is applied to life. In holistic community Christians learn to listen to God for others through the Word and Spirit. In the mid-level cluster of seventy, Christians learn to listen to God about the task of witness, evangelism, mission, and expansion. The church today must learn to listen in order to function as the Body of Christ. Only in this way can edification and community life take place.

In Romans 8:26-27, Paul suggests another aspect of prayer. The Holy Spirit "helps" ("lends a hand together with") and intercedes for me when I pray.

---

100. John R. W. Stott, *Tyndale New Testament Commentaries, The Letters of John* (Grand Rapids: Eerdmans Publishing Co., 1996), 188.
101. Oswald Chambers, *If You Will Ask* (USA: Dodd, Mead and Company, Inc, 1938), 5.

> *In the same way, the Spirit helps us in our weakness. We do not know what we ought to pray for, but the Spirit himself intercedes for us with groans that words cannot express. And he who searches our hearts knows the mind of the Spirit, because the Spirit intercedes for the saints in accordance with God's will.*

Greek scholar, Kenneth Wuest, gives an interpretation of the Greek text of this intriguing prayer. "God the Father who searches the hearts of His saints for their prayers, uttered and unexpressed, interprets those inarticulate sighings of the Spirit in us by reason of the fact that the Spirit pleads for us and in us and through us according to the will of God."[102] In his commentary on Romans, Douglas Moo summarizes Paul's thought in these verses:

> *Paul is saying ... that our failure to know God's will and consequent inability to petition God specifically and assuredly is met by God's Spirit, who himself expresses to God those intercessory petitions that perfectly match the will of God. When we do not know what to pray for – yes, even when we pray for things that are not best for us – we need not despair, for we can depend on the Spirit's ministry of perfect intercession 'on our behalf.'*[103]

French mystic Jeanne Guyon sees this as another depth of prayer: The Spirit prays within the Christian. The key to this experience is giving up our wills, desires, and requests for "His prayers."

---

102. Kenneth S. Wuest, *Golden Nuggets from the Greek New Testament* (Grand Rapids, MI: Wm. B. Eerdmans, 1940), 100.
103. Douglas Moo, *The Epistle to the Romans* (Grand Rapids, MI: Eerdmans, 1996), 526.

> As you continue in this venture with Christ---this venture that began as a simple way of prayer---yet another experience may await you. It is this: Do not be too surprised if you find you are no longer able to offer up prayers of petition. You may find that prayers of request become more difficult. Yes, it is true that in the past you offered up petitions and requests with complete ease. Until now, praying this way was never difficult. But in this new relationship with your Lord, it is the Spirit who prays! And as the Spirit prays, He helps your weakness. He is making intercession for you. And He is praying according to the will of God. "For we don't know how to pray as we should; but the Spirit Himself intercedes for us with groanings too deep for words." (Romans 8:26)
>
> There is your will; there is God's will. There is your plan; there is God's plan. There is your prayer; there is His prayer. You must agree to His plans. He takes from you all your own workings so that His may be substituted in their place. Therefore, yield. Let God do in you what He will. In His prayers, which He prays, there is also His will. Let Him pray. Give up your own prayers; give up your own desires and your own requests. Yes, you have a will; yes, you have desires and requests. Nevertheless, let Him have the will, the desire, that is in the prayers He prays.[104]

While beginning a prototype the leader must experience (become evidence of) simple prayer, listening prayer, heart prayer, and Spirit prayer so that followers can practice Jesus' kind of praying together in community.

---

104. Jeanne Guyon, *Experiencing the Depths of Jesus Christ* (Sargent, GA: SeedSowers, 1975/MCMLXXV), 81-82.

Chapter 8

PROTOTYPE EDIFICATION

*"But everyone who prophesies speaks to men
for their strengthening, encouragement and comfort."*
• 1 Corinthians 14:3

The word "wellness" is defined as "the quality or state of being healthy." The medical field uses the word to explain its multidimensional mission to provide health care.

Wellness is also God's mission statement for the Church: "Cleansing her by the washing with water through the word, and to present her to himself as a radiant church, without stain or wrinkle or any other blemish, but holy and blameless" (Eph. 5:26-27).

The traditional church system devotes millions of dollars and thousand of man-hours to the health of the church. It provides church services, seminaries to train leaders, programs of all kinds to prepare Christians for ministry, staff positions for counseling, and various wholesome activities. All are part of the wellness program of the church dedicated to developing emotionally and spiritually mature and healthy Christians, with the residual effect of promoting the spiritual health of society.

The church appears to be in good health when evaluated from its physical appearance: large buildings, impressive crowds, mega churches, and exposure on the airwaves. However, the state of society and the church tells another story. Mental, emotional, and spiritual illnesses are on the rise at an alarming rate in society and in the church. It appears that in spite of all the effort, society (and the church) is sicker than it has ever been. Church programs, the sermons and teaching of pastors, and the work of Christian counselors touch only a small portion of the hurts and needs inside and outside of the church.

The Emotional State of America and the Church

The statistics of the moral decline of the United States over the last generation (50 to 60 years) are well known. "The divorce rate has doubled, teen suicide has tripled, reported violent crime has quadrupled, the prison population has quintupled, the percentage of babies born out of wedlock has risen six-fold, couples living together out of wedlock have increased sevenfold."[105]

Sigmund Freud, in the fading years of his life, observed that humans are threatened with suffering from three directions. First, our bodies are doomed and its aches and pains remind us even now that we will die. Second, the structures of society can rage against us. And, third, our relations with one another can hurt us. "The suffering," he added, "which comes from this last source is perhaps more painful than any other."[106]

---

105. Bert Farias, "The Great Deception in the American Church"; *The Flaming Herald*, 700AM EDT 5/19/2014; @Bertarias 1 on Twitter. Farias sums up George Barna's statistics about the state of US society.
106. Sigmund Freud, *Civilization and its Discontents* (New York: W. W. Norton & Company, 1962), 24.

Daniel Wisneski and a team of colleagues conducted a research project that focused on "the science of morality."[107] They "assessed moral or immoral acts in a large sample using ecological momentary assessment." Using Craigslist, Facebook, Twitter, and other outlets they recruited 1252 adults ages 18 to 68 throughout the United States and Canada. Participants downloaded an app to their smart phones that allowed researchers to buzz them via text five times a day between 9 a.m. and 9 p.m. When they opened the texts, participants were prompted to open a link where they could confidentially report whether they had witnessed, heard about, or performed any moral or immoral acts within the past hour, and jot down a description. They also entered details about how intensely they felt about the event, rating emotions such as disgust on a 0 to 5 scale.

The research team received 13,240 messages over the course of the 3-day study. One statement about their conclusions speaks to the health of the church. The team reported that "overall, people who had identified themselves as religious or nonreligious when they registered for the study committed both moral and immoral deeds with 'comparable frequency.'" This finding corresponds to other studies over the years that show morality is almost the same among religious and nonreligious people.

The modern Church is ineffective in delivering wellness to its members much less to society. I am not talking about spiritual wellness as perfection: the absence of all sin and sin related diseases. By wellness I mean a person who is, with God's help, able to cope with life in forgiveness and self worth, to walk in integrity with God, others, and society, and consequently to live in

---

107. Daniel Wisneski, Ph.D., "Morality in Everyday Life" published in the journal Science (September 2014, Vol. 345, No. 6202, pp. 1340-1343). The research work was profiled in an article in The New York Times (September 11, 2014) entitled "In a Study, Text Messages Add Up to a Balance Sheet of Everyday Morality."

joy, peace, and happiness. The church needs a way to multiply spiritual wellness and wholeness.

Where is the place of healing and restoration of feelings, hurts, spirits, and bodies in our world? Christian counselors are too few to turn even the dysfunctional Christians around much less dysfunctional pagans who are being reproduced at an alarming rate.

Today we desperately need an economy of healing in order to deal with the epidemic of emotional and spiritual sickness. In order to make a significant difference in the emotional state of society, healing on couches and chairs must be supplemented with spiritual edification in Christian groups. The community of faith does not take the place of Christian counseling and therapy but can significantly increase the emotional and spiritual health of the hurting.

Jesus made provision for the continuing healing of His people through the work of the Holy Spirit in spiritual community. God's place of spiritual healing is the New Testament family: the community of faith. This community is designed so that emotional, spiritual, mental, and physical healing takes place within it. In a nurturing small group community God is able to re-parent us. God is able to bind up wounds, apply a balm, remove cancerous feelings and past experiences, restore spiritual health, and heal both physical and spiritual aches, pains and hurts.

God's Wellness Program

When Jeremiah received the word from God about what Babylon would do to Judah, he lamented, "Is there no balm in Gilead" (Jer. 8:22)? The "balm of Gilead" was an expensive and costly ointment with healing properties. The Bible uses the term "balm of Gilead" metaphorically as an example of something with healing or soothing powers.

This is the way the term is used in the African-American spiritual, *"There is a balm in Gilead to make the wounded whole; There is a balm in Gilead to heal the sin sick soul."* The healing balm is the saving power of Jesus. He is the one true treatment that never fails to heal our spiritual wounds.

Jesus' death on the cross and resurrection from the grave is the healing balm of salvation for the sin sick soul. Jesus' life in His community Body on earth is the healing balm for the sanctifying and edifying process of the individual Christian and the church. Edification within community is God's basic wellness program for the church: His balm of Gilead for the individual Christian and the Church.

Edification does not replace Christian counseling or psychiatry but it contributes at a level that makes a substantial difference in the emotional, spiritual, and physical wellness of Christians. God's basic wellness program requires no offices, no buildings, no salaries, no academic degrees, no insurance policies, and no professional healers.

He edifies His church through revelation (His presence), intercessory prayer, and practical prophecy. God's wellness system is built into His holistic cell community design of the church. God, speaking to and through a community, can be a balm in Gilead for emotional, spiritual, and physical hurts.

Holistic community cells are God's wellness centers through which He can touch the hurts of His people and facilitate substantial wellness. The health of the church in turn impacts the health of surrounding society. After Wesley and his circuit-riding preachers entered the coal-mining region of England, the miners had to retrain the mules that were used to haul the coal out of the mines. The mules no longer understood the commands of the miners because most had become Christians and no longer used curse words in their commands. A healthy church has a residual effect on society.

New Testament edification is one of the most important experiences for the modern church. It is the means by which God builds up the Body so that both the individual Christian and the church are healthy. Edification is the spiritual vortex where the presence, power, and purpose of Christ come together. These aspects of the nature of Christ then activate community revelation, prayer, and prophecy like a laser so that Christ through the Holy Spirit can bring God's power and eliminate the diseased and cancerous elements in the body. God's power is manifested in practical prophecy and His purpose of forming every Christian into the image of His Son is accomplished as spiritual, emotional, and physical healing take place.

Modern Substitutes for Edification

In describing an impending judgment on Egypt to the prophet Jeremiah, God points out the futility of their cures (Jer. 46:11): "Go up to Gilead and obtain balm, O virgin daughter of Egypt! In vain have you multiplied remedies; there is no healing for you!" The modern church is trying multiple remedies for its own illness and for the sickness of society. However, there is no ultimate healing in human remedies for the individual, the church, or society. The "balm of Gilead" that God has provided for His church is New Testament edification.

New Testament edification is one of the most neglected and misunderstood experiences in the church because edification cannot be understood or applied apart from Jesus' community relationship groups. Unfortunately, that community framework has been replaced by Constantine's institutional system. In trying to meet the spiritual needs of its members, the church has substituted human solutions for New Testament edification. Constantine's church took edification out of its New Testament community setting and placed it in a confessional box, attached it to beautiful ceremonies, and entrusted it to holy men authorized to shake holy water over the problems and needs of members.

Protestant churches have taken divergent courses in trying to build up the church. Some rely on Bible study to maintain the health of the church. They believe that knowledge of the Word is sufficient to edify the individuals studying the Word and sermons from the pulpit are sufficient to build up the church body. Another approach substitutes spiritual gifts for community edification: Special leaders take care of the edification needs of individual Christians and the church in healing actions and prophetic words. Other mainline denominational churches depend on counseling and the ministry of pastors to edify the church and make it spiritually healthy. Prayer ministries are used as spiritual therapy for emotional weaknesses and moral failures.

The hope behind this chapter is that God's biblical wellness plan of edification can be restored. We will look at the spiritual elements that contribute to the wellness of the Christian and the Church: The presence of Christ, intercessory prayer, practical prophecy, and holistic community. Edification is always a work of God but He uses ordinary Christians as His instruments to build up and heal His Body, one person at a time within community.

In holistic community, a group of Christians can experience the presence, power, and purpose of Christ as they listen to God for each other, and speak His words of edification into each other's lives. Community life, where each person can experience edification, produces a church that is healthy and well. It is essential for internal growth and external expansion.

Definition & Nature of Edification

Edification in Greek is *oikodomeo* and in English is translated "build up." Paul says: "Love builds up" (1 Cor. 8:1). The one rule of cell life: Everything must build up the community (1 Cor. 14:12).[108] I have learned the following core truths about edification:

- *Only Christ through the Spirit edifies. My personal opinions and counseling are not edification.*
- *Christ's death and my death are necessary to experience New Testament edification. I must die to my solutions.*
- *Revelation, prayer, and practical prophecy are spiritual elements in edification.*
- *New Testament community is the primary context for New Testament edification.*
- *Identifying the root problem is key to edification, not listening to the circumstances.*

---

108. The centrality of edification can also be seen in the following scriptures. "Knowledge makes arrogant, but love edifies (builds up) (1 Cor. 8:1). "So also you, since you are zealous of spiritual gifts, seek to abound for the edification of the church" (1 Cor. 14:12). "Therefore encourage one another and build each other up, just as in fact you are doing" (1 Thess. 5:11). "Do not let any unwholesome talk come out of your mouths, but only what is helpful for building others up according to their needs, that it may benefit those who listen" (Eph. 4:29). "To prepare God's people for works of service, so that the body of Christ may be built up until we all reach unity in the faith and in the knowledge of the Son of God and become mature, attaining to the whole measure of the fullness of Christ" (Eph. 4:12).

- *The key question that leads to New Testament edification is "why," not what happened or who did it.*
- *Edifying gifts are for the benefit of the community, not for an individual Christian.*
- *Edification is activated out of a specific personal need.*
- *Edification heals the individual Christian and the Body of Christ.*
- *Edification (and its related elements of revelation, prayer, practical prophecy, and community) is God's way of providing wellness to Christians and the Church.*

It is important to be clear about the part the different roles play in edification. I do not edify! You do not edify! Christ, through the love of the Father, redemptive work of the Son, and resurrection power of the Spirit, is the one who edifies (builds up, heals, and strengthens). This is holistic healing: emotional, spiritual, and physical healing of individual Christians and the church.

Edification is a work of Christ through the Holy Spirit. Therefore, edification flows out of the spiritual reality of the presence of Christ in cell community. Prayer is the conduit through which Christ through the Holy Spirit edifies His Body.

An important truth often stated about salvation is that humans have a primary "sin" (nature) problem and a secondary "sins" problem (actions). The same applies to edification. The work of edification is first in the sin nature and then changes the specific actions. Edification does not begin nor end with the specific sin but penetrates down into my sin nature.

However, in edification today a specific sin is often unsuccessfully addressed as the problem. A specific sin is like a sore on the skin that is caused by an internal virus or infection. The internal infection must be treated in order to heal the external sore. God, through the work of Christ on the cross and the power of the Holy Spirit, edifies at the deepest part of my sin nature and does not just stop with the specific sin I commit. Focusing on specific sins is behavioral modification, not New Testament edification. When edification takes place within my sin nature, the specific sin that is the outward manifestation of that sin nature is revealed in its true nature. Healing can then take place at the root.

Christian community is the context of edification and Christians are the channels of edification. Christ ministers to you through me, and ministers to me through you.

God edifies through the gifts and fruits of the Spirit that He shares with Christians. "There are different kinds of gifts, but the same Spirit. There are different kinds of service, but the same Lord. There are different kinds of working, but the same God works all of them in all men. Now to each one the manifestation of the Spirit is given for the common good" (1 Cor. 12:4-7).

This means edification is a multiple blessing from God---for the recipient of edification and for the channel of edification. The person being edified is blessed and the persons doing the edifying are blessed. Edification is the wellness factor in the Church, the healing balm that God applies to every aspect of the spiritual health of the individual Christian and the church as a whole.

Edification is Intercession

Edification is a priestly function (1 Pet. 2:5, 9) of intercession. A Christian stands between God and another person (intercession) among God's people (community), listens to God (revelation) for that person who has a need, and speaks what God speaks (practical prophecy) to the need.

Jesus was constantly in intersession for His followers (present and future) and for the world. Luke records one of these intercession events: "Simon, Simon, Satan has asked to sift you as wheat. But I have prayed for you, Simon that your faith may not fail. And when you have turned back, strengthen your brothers" (Luke 22:31-32). In order to live together in community and to participate in New Testament edification, Christians must learn to intercede for each other. This means hearing what God is saying to them personally and hearing what God is saying for another person. That is intercessory edification.

The relationship of Eli and Samuel is a good example of the special ministry of intercessory edification. God uses Eli to interpret His word for Samuel (1 Sam. 3:3-18). The incident took place early in the life of the young boy Samuel, during troubled days when "the word of the Lord was rare and there were not many visions." Samuel had been dedicated to God by his mother Hannah and placed in the temple to serve Eli, the high priest. The boy Samuel wakes up three times one night when he hears a voice calling him. Each time he thinks it is Eli and each time he goes to Eli. Each time Eli sends him back to bed. After the third visit, Eli realizes the Lord is calling Samuel and the old priest interprets what is happening. "Go and lie down, and if he calls you, say, 'Speak, Lord, for your servant is listening.'" The next morning Eli again guided Samuel about what to do with the communication from God: "Do not hide it from me." As it turned out, the word was not good for Eli because of his corrupt sons.

The intercessory ministry of Eli is needed today to help others identify God's voice, to interpret communication from God for another person, and to encourage the hearer to personally listen to God. The friendship triad of two or three and the community cell are the places where the ministry of Eli operates for new and immature followers of Christ.

Intercessory edification is a special work of the Holy Spirit. In Romans 8:26, Paul assures us that the Spirit "helps us in our weakness" and "intercedes with sighs too deep for words." The intercessory work of the Holy Spirit takes place at both ends of edification. He intercedes for the intercessor and He intercedes within the spirit of the one who has the need for intercession. Intercessory edification must be experienced and prototyped by each leader who wants the church to operate in a New Testament way.

Practical Prophecy

As the followers of Jesus lived together in community, a special kind of prayer emerged: The followers of Christ focused prayer on edification that was channeled through practical prophecy. We looked at listening prayer in the previous chapter and will now consider a key ingredient in edification that builds on listening prayer: practical prayer prophecy.

Prophecy is the second ministry of Christ mentioned in Paul's list of leaders that are given to the church. "And He gave some as apostles, and some as *prophets*, and some as evangelists, and some as pastors and teachers" (Eph. 4:11). "Worship God! For the testimony of Jesus is the spirit of prophecy" (Rev. 19:10).

The word "prophecy" is constructed out of *pro* as in the word "pronoun" or "in the place of" and "phecy" or *phemi* ... to speak. A prophet is one who speaks in place of another. God said to Moses: "Aaron thy brother shall be thy prophet (Ex. 4:16), or literally "mouthpiece." The Hebrew word for a prophet is *nabi* that comes from a word meaning to boil up or boil forth, like some hot spring or fountain. The phrase *N'um* Yahweh ("thus says the Lord") was often used to introduce Old Testament prophecy.

Mount Sinai is the prophetic model used in the Old Testament. Moses alone went into God's presence on the mountain and brought God's Word down to the people. In the Old Testament, prophecy was from above down to man. In the New Testament, prophecy was from above but was also from within. The indwelling Holy Spirit spoke to and through all Christians in practical prophetic words.

In the predictive sense, biblical prophecy is foretelling the future out of a special revelation from God that is beyond human knowledge. In the non-predictive sense, prophecy is forth telling, making public the present will and message of God because of a specific inspiration from God. This brings exhortation, consolation, and comfort.

Prophesy in Greek is *propheteuein* (προφητεύ) and is used in four ways in the New Testament. The first three are found in both the Old and New Testaments in some form, but the fourth is uniquely New Testament: (1) to announce a revelation from God (Mt. 7:22; Acts 19:6; 21:9); (2) to reveal what has been hidden (Mt. 26:68); (3) to foretell the future (Mt. 11:13; 15:7; 1 Pet. 1:10); and (4) to edify within community (Acts 2:17-18; 1 Cor. 11:4f; 13:9; 14:1, 3).

The focus of this chapter is number four: community practical prophecy. It is prophecy incarnated within the context of community life and therefore could only be experienced after Christ established His spiritual community on earth. We must understand and use this fourth kind of community prophecy because God uses it to build up the church. Paul admonished the Corinthian Christians to "pursue love, yet desire earnestly spiritual gifts, but especially that you may (all) prophesy" (1 Cor. 14:1). Later in the same chapter Paul again emphasized the word "all." "For you can *all* prophesy one by one so that all may learn and all may be exhorted" (1 Cor. 14:31).[109]

This kind of prophecy is so important Paul said: "I would that you *all* prophesy." Someone stated Paul's point in this way: "All means all and that is all that all means!" Two things must happen for all to prophesy: (1) Prophecy must be seen as a verb or action and not just as a noun (a person or position) and (2) the context must be small group community because "all" limits the number of people who can prophesy at any given time in a large group. Therefore, the church today should focus on the verb "prophesying" rather than the nouns "prophecy" or "prophet."

The New Testament teaches that every Christian is to prophesy but that every Christian is *not* a prophet! Only a few are nouns with the position, title, and office of prophet. Do you understand the difference? Christ, through the Holy Spirit, speaks words (prophecy) through each Christian in the context of community in order to bring wellness into the lives of individual Christians and the church as a whole. This is the work of prophecy as an active verb.

The message and messenger in practical prophecy may change with the situation. However, the source of prophecy is always the same: God through special revelation, the redemptive work of Christ, and the administration of the Holy Spirit.

---

109. Other scriptures that refer to practical prophecy are: "Pursue love, yet desire earnestly spiritual gifts, but especially that you may prophesy" (1 Cor. 14:1). "But one who prophesies speaks to men for edification and exhortation and consolation" (1 Cor. 14:3). "One who prophesies edifies the church" (1 Cor. 14:4). "I wish that even more you all would prophesy" (1 Cor.14: 5).

> *Special revelation is special in that it comes to specific persons but not to humanity in general. It is special also in the second sense that it comes to resolve a particular difficulty: the loss of the knowledge of God through sin. Special revelation, then, comes to particular men. It must also be observed that when revelation comes to a particular man he is living in a concrete situation, and relation meets him in his concrete situation.*[110]

God decides which situation will be addressed and how, when, and where. Lest you protest that God cannot speak through you, remember that God spoke through Balaam's donkey in Numbers 22:12. Interpret that event any way you like. I don't put much theological importance on the donkey prophesying. However, the picture does make me think: If God can use a donkey to give a word, He may be able to give a word through me ... and through you.

Through revelation and prayer, Christians who listen together in community receive prophetic words from God that result in edification.

EDIFICATION & PRACTICAL PROPHECY: APPLIED IN COMMUNITY

Edification is an essential catalytic encounter in the church because of the powerful doctrines that converge in the experience: Christ's presence, God's revelation, and prayer prophecy begin in the friendship triad and meet at the point of nurturing community. Christians today must be retrained to experience God's presence in community, to hear His edifying words in prayer, and to faithfully speak the words of practical prophecy to a real need in a person's life. This kind of edification explains the reaction of the person in 1 Corinthians 14:24-25:

---

110. Bernard Ramm, *Special Revelation and the Word of God*, 32.

> But if an unbeliever or an inquirer comes in while everyone is prophesying, they are convicted of sin and are brought under judgment by all, as the secrets of their hearts are laid bare. So they will fall down and worship God, exclaiming, "God is really among you!"

Friendship triads and holistic community cells are Christ's training and implementing centers for practical prophecy and edification. Edification prayer is the intercessory lifeline from God through which He identifies and heals the hurts and needs of individuals in the Body. God applies the Word to real needs in the lives of individuals. Grateful praise and worship flow out of the hearts of all who participate in edification: the one being edified and those who are God's instruments of edification. Christ applies His gifts through individual Christians to specific needs. God touches spiritual, emotional, and physical needs and genuine healing takes place. Observers are filled with awe at such a genuine expression of the presence of God. Christians in a community cell, who are instruments of edification and those who have experienced edification, witness and evangelize out of an overflow of the presence, power, and purpose of God that they have experienced.

Spiritual edification penetrates every level of human awareness. This is why it is so powerful. Joe Luft and Harry Ingham developed the Johari Window in the 1950s to show the different levels of relationships and self-awareness.[111] The chart gives insights into some of the dynamics at work in a person experiencing New Testament edification. Truth, transparency, openness, and honesty are required for the healing of the wounded spirit of humans. This ideally begins in the smaller triad of two or three but eventually becomes part of a community cell.

---

111. Joseph Luft, *Of Human Interaction* (Palo Alto, CA: National Press, 1969), 177.

JOHARI WINDOW

	Known to self	Not known to self
Known to others	**OPEN SELF** Information about yourself that you and others know.	**BLIND SELF** Information you don't know but others know about you.
Not known to others	**HIDDEN SELF** Information you know about yourself but others don't.	**UNKNOWN SELF** Information about yourself that you and others don't know.

Edification may take place at any square in the chart: Open Self, Blind Self, Hidden Self, and Unknown Self. However, it is in the levels of information that I know about myself and am not about to share with others (Hidden Self) that God may open up for edification. Or, information that only God knows about me (Unknown Self) may be revealed to someone listening to God in the group for me. Through practical prophecy God can reveal what I hide from others, and what only he knows about me. God can lead a Christian in a group to speak the truth in edifying love about what they know about me that I don't know. These are the places of practical prophecy that lead to edification.

What can a Christian do personally to participate in edification: either to be a channel of edification or to be a recipient of edification?

- *Listen to God! Listen to God for yourself. Listen to God for another person.*
- *Remember: God has prepared every Christian to be His instrument of grace and edification.*
- *Don't speak personal opinions. Discern what is from God and what is from you.*
- *Don't use prophecy props: loud pronouncements, vague and flowery images, and spiritual formulas.*

- *Give and receive correction with humility. Be teachable. Journal God's word to you and to others.*
- *In faith, share what you hear God saying.*
- *Package personal words from the Spirit in Scripture and short simple sentences.*
- *Confirm the interpretation of prophecy in your cell.*
- *Test and verify words of edification!*

Because encouragement and healing of the soul and the spirit is the central purpose of edification, words of prophecy never feel judgmental, embarrassing, unkind, or condemning. Edification through practical prophecy must always be judged by factors outside the situation and solution. This eliminates weird and immature actions that can be passed off as the genuine work of the Holy Spirit. The seven questions in the chart can help us test the spirit of practical prophecy.

TEST THE SPIRIT OF PRACTICL PROPHECY BY:	
SCRIPTURE:	Is it validated by God's word?
COMMUNITY:	Do others think it is from God?
REALNESS:	Is the language genuine or copied?
FOCUS:	Does it glorify Jesus Christ alone?
MATURITY:	Do mature Christians agree?
VERIFICATION:	Is it verified in actual events?
EDIFICATION:	Does it build up and encourage?

A Story of Edification

Joy had been struggling since childhood with deep anger, fear and resentment of her father.[112] As a small child she would sit at the dinner table and try to become invisible so she would not

---

112. "Joy" praises God that her experience can be a witness to the power of His edification. She likes the pseudonym "Joy" that I gave her in her story because it reflects how God edified her and changed her life. Tom, also a pseudonym, praises God that he was the channel of practical prophecy in edification for his sister.

displease her father. She built a place within her inner being where she retreated and felt safe to hold on to her hate for her father. A root of intimidation and fear controlled her life and took away her confidence. Her only place of safety and refuge as a child was the stronghold deep within her inner being. As an adult, instead of giving her confidence, the place perpetuated the feelings of intimidation and fear. A trained and gifted artist, many of her paintings looked like the dark womb of death with shades of greys and blacks that reflected how she saw her outside and inside worlds. She was a gentle and sensitive person who had obviously experienced deep trauma in her inner being.

God started to reveal the root of her fear within our community cell. Tom, her brother, was part of the cell and understood her situation. He regularly talked with Joy before and after cell meetings as God revealed pieces and parts of her inward withdrawal. Others in the cell prayed with her and spoke into her life. One night as the cell came to a conclusion she asked to sit in the edification chair so we could pray for her. She shared briefly about her need, as she understood it.

The group gathered around her and began to listen to God. Someone shared a word and another shared a scripture. Both words seemed to speak to her need. Then Tom walked over beside the chair, knelled down beside his sister and began to read 1 Corinthians 13 from his large Bible. This kind of bold action was not characteristic of him. Joy's eyes were closed and her hands were open in her lap.

When Tom came to the verse "love is" he substituted "God" for "love" and read all the verses that contained the word love as: "*God* is patient," "*God* is kind." "*God* does not envy," "*God* does not boast," "*God* is not proud," "*God* is not rude," "*God* is not self-seeking," "*God* is not easily angered," "*God* keeps no record of wrongs," "*God* does not delight in evil but rejoices with the truth," "*God* always protects," "*God* always trusts," "*God* always hopes," "*God* always perseveres," "*God* never fails."

As he read, a soft groan came from deep within Joy's inner being, as if something was being torn out or separated from within her. She explained later that her image of God had come from her experience with her father that was buried deep down in her earliest memories and deepest feelings. As Tom substituted the word God for the wonderful attributes of love, God touched Joy with His edifying healing. The lie that held her hostage to the past was broken and she began the healing process of walking in truth and freedom.

Everyone knew, along with Tom, that what happened did not come from him but from God. This was a prophetic word and act from God for Joy that God delivered through her brother within the community.

THE CONTINUING EDIFICATION PROCESS

God, personally, and through the community, continued to help Joy understand what happened in that moment of edification so she could walk it out in life. At least four Christians were part of Joy's edification in an Eli ministry role (listening to God for her). Much of my own Eli dialogue with Joy was through emails. Her explanation of what happened reveals the genuineness of her edification experience.

> *As I have shared with you about when Mary and I had coffee, she had mentioned about the unforgiveness I have for my father being the root of my fear. I knew at that time that God had spoken a word through Mary to me. Tears from within me started to come up when I realized the scope of what I was*

> *forgiving him for, even though I had a hard time feeling at all. So much has been uncovered this past month, I feel now I am able to understand that word far better.*
>
> *Recognizing this hatred inside is enormous for my healing. As Tom and I spoke tonight, our conversation somehow turned to my father and his behavior. I confessed to Tom what I have come to realize about what has been in my heart about our Father. I knew I needed to share it with him at some point because he knows what life was like with him as a child. I told him about the hate. His response was very compassionate. He knew this was very important to uncover.*
>
> *I wanted to share this with you because this is such a pivotal discovery. I know this. I believe this is the Sin. I don't fully understand about how it works in keeping me shrouded or enfolded, but I just sense it's at the center of the bondage.*

God continued the edification process in Joy for several months, both within the cell and in personal moments with cell members. She wrote to me about this continuing edification process that God revealed through Mary and others.

> *What I have come to understand is that I have held in my heart an unforgiveness for my father. What felt like a rock inside of my inner self, was actually Hate. When I was a child, I hated my father. (This was not an easy thing to uncover and then confess). I can feel it now when I go back to that child within. As an adult I don't feel that (hate), but as a child I do. I felt guilt as I realized what was in my heart. As I prayed for understanding about what this sin was, I believe God spoke through a book that I've been reading about the Wounded Spirit.*[113]

---

113. John Sandford, *"Healing the Wounded Spirit"* (Tulsa, OK: Victory House, Inc, 1985).

> "In the victim's helplessness, his hate, anger and resentment may have seemed to be his only means of retaliation. That anger, hate and resentment held in our hearts work inside us like a poisonous substance. If allowed to remain, they sicken not only our hearts, minds and spirits, but affect our physical health as well because of the tension they create." "When I kept silent about my sin, my body wasted away through my groaning all day long" (Psalm 32:3).

> The book speaks about forgiveness. "Forgiveness is not easy. It is not something we can accomplish by an act of our will. But we can choose to be made willing. We probably will need to make that choice again and again; in our hearts because we are no longer willfully hanging on to the "right" to hate. The wounded child in the heart of an adult finds forgiving more difficult. He has practiced his feelings for so long or has suppressed them, covering them over with a façade of forgiveness." (This is me).

I hope Joy's story helps you see the value of community edification and also helps you understand what practical prophecy looks like within a cell meeting and in the process that continues outside of the meeting. Edification is an essential prototype that must be experienced by the pastor and leaders who are developing a New Testament paradigm of church.

Chapter 9

PROTOTYPE FRIENDSHIP

"Greater love has no one than this, that he lay down his life for his friends ... I no longer call you servants ... instead, I have called you friends."
• Jesus (John 15:13-15)

During a conference in Sydney, Australia in 2001, a young pastor invited me to take a flight with him over the city. Others at the conference assured me he was a sane and safe pilot. For some reason, the fact that his father flew for Qantas Airlines gave me some added confidence in his ability.

After the conference finished, the pilot, another pastor and his six-year old daughter and I drove through the eucalyptus landscape to a small airport on the outskirts of Sydney. A beautiful little four-seat Cessna was gassed up and waiting for us. The pastor and his daughter squeezed into the two back seats and I strapped myself into the copilot seat with the dual controls in front of me. Take off was smooth and the view was spectacular as we climbed into the beautiful clear sky to our assigned 6000 feet altitude.

Our flight plan permitted us to fly over the Sydney Harbor at 3,000 feet where we saw the Sydney Opera House at the mouth of the harbor. (It was the year after the Summer Olympics and the Opera House was a landmark recognized around the world.)

After circling the harbor twice with battleships and large ocean liners moving slowly beneath us, we turned south over the Tasman Sea and began our ascent back to 6,000 feet. We flew up the coast for several miles parallel to scenic cliffs on our right. Then we turned right and headed west over the Blue Mountains toward our small home airport. I realized we were flying a complete clockwise circle around Sydney.

The pilot had asked me at the beginning of our flight if I wanted to fly the plane. I gave a joking response and declined. However, when we headed home he again urged me to take the controls. I didn't want to be a wimp and so agreed. He gave me simple instructions about what to do: how to keep the wings of the plane level, how to determine the pitch (up and down), and how to bank (turn). He assured me one more time, with more confidence than I thought was warranted, that I could do it. "The plane wants to fly if you will just let it." He turned loose of the controls to demonstrate that the plane would not immediately go into a nosedive. However, I was still relieved that he had a set of controls in front of him.

I reluctantly took my controls and experienced an incredible thrill that seemed very brief but was probably about twenty minutes. I flew the plane from 6,000 feet to 3,000 feet, keeping the wings level and gradually pushing down on the yoke so the plane would descend. The plane was designed to fly and even an amateur could keep it in the air. However, it was not designed to take off and land with an amateur pilot. Certainly no one in that plane (most of all me) wanted me to land the plane. When we approached the airport I gladly turned the controls over to the trained pilot. As we approached our landing, a sudden crosswind tilted the plane sideways and the nose of the plane went up. I thought we were going into a stall and would crash. The pilot expertly made a correction and we landed safely. Maybe the landing moment was not as dangerous as it felt to a novice but it certainly colored my attitude about future flying: "I would love to fly airplanes if I had someone to take off and land for me."

This personal experience reminds me of a friendship triad for two reasons. (1) The triad is simple and is designed to work naturally with ordinary Christians. This is why the friendship triad (and also the community cell) is the greatest ministry done by the greatest number of people. (2) In this important ministry, Jesus is beside us to do what we are not able to do. He promised something very special for a friendship triad and a community cell: "For where two or three gather in my name, there am I with them" (Matt. 18:20). The Christian life, for an individual Christian and for Christians in community, has dual controls. Jesus is the experienced pilot who sits beside us, encouraging us and doing the tasks that are beyond our abilities. He assures us "You can do it!"

The First Prototype

Leaders who want to be part of expansion growth must prototype the dynamics and mechanics of three groups: the friendship triad, community cell, and supervising cluster.

If a pastor or catalytic leader were to say to me: "I can only prototype the triad or the cell, which should I do?" I would suggest: "Prototype the friendship triad!" It is better to learn the simple and basic and then go to the more complex. For example, learn simple arithmetic and then algebra. The triad is the microcosm of the cell. Prototyping the dynamics and mechanics of a friendship triad prepares a leader to experience community in a cell and expansion in the cluster of seventy.

The triad is practical, simple, and the most basic unit in the church; even more basic than the community small group. A triad is a natural organic entity that is designed to function in fellowship, to promote wellness, and to expand. "By reducing multiplication to the simplest level, reproduction can be part of the genetic fabric of the entire body of Christ."[114]

Throughout history groups of two or three have been an informal part of most church movements. The two or three relationship has been central in the one-on-one discipleship strategies of the Navigators, Campus Crusade, and ministries such as Promise Keepers. In addition, in cell meetings in cell churches smaller sub groups are often formed for prayer and edification. In large meetings, triads are used to connect the crowd to one another, to apply the message, and to share in prayer. In addition, the two or three principle is often used to train leaders.

Whereas triads have been used in the cell church movement, they have been more of an attachment to a cell than an essential separate sub group. They have not been given the same biblical and strategic weight as the community cell. I am convinced triads are too important to float around the edges of the church as an option. They must be intentionally factored into the DNA of the church today. The triad of two or three is a key for church expansion because it is the building block for community, edification, equipping, and evangelism.

The Friendship Triad chart shows the different elements (disciplines or experiences) at work in a friendship triad of two or three: Presence (worship), the Lordship of Christ, application of the Word, confession of sins, prayer listening, body life in friendship, following and obeying the Spirit (exercising the gifts and producing spiritual fruit), accountability to and for each other, edification and encouragement, and friendship evangelism. These elements continue in a community cell.

Neil Cole correctly observed the importance of the friendship triad to the cell leader. "Though the evangelical church seems to

---
114. Cole, *Organic Church*, 103.

be taking strategic steps toward a cell-based ministry, we must go further at lowering the bar of ministry beyond the cell leader to every Christian. Too much is still placed on the shoulders of the cell leader." Cole believes the triad of two or three (what he calls a LTG: Life Transformation Group) "releases the cell leader and pastor from being the chief caregiver."[115]

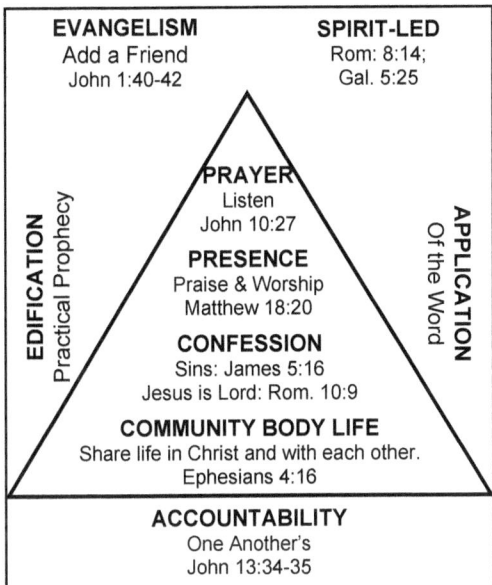

BASIC CHRISTIAN FRIENDSHIP

I call the two or three unit a friendship triad rather than a disciple triad. Discipleship is one function of a triad but the name carries a lot of historical baggage and methodology. Friendship is one of the most basic relationships between Christ and a Christian. It encompasses the core meaning of a two or three group.

God had a friendship relationship with Abraham. "O our God, did you not drive out the inhabitants of this land before your people Israel and give it forever to the descendants of Abraham your friend?" (2 Chron. 20:7). "But you, O Israel, my servant, Jacob, whom I have chosen, you descendants of Abraham my friend" (Isa. 41:8) "And the scripture was fulfilled that says, 'Abraham believed God, and it was credited to him as righteousness,' and

---

115. Cole, *Cultivating a Life for God*, 90.

he was called God's friend" (James 2:23). Abraham believed God and trusted God, and God trusted Abraham as a friend. Friends believe in and trust each other.

Jesus continues this relationship of friendship with His followers and explains it in His discourse in John 15:13-17.

> *Greater love has no one than this, that he lay down his life for his friends. You are my friends if you do what I command. I no longer call you servants, because a servant does not know his master's business. Instead, I have called you friends, for everything that I learned from my Father I have made known to you. You did not choose me, but I chose you and appointed you to go and bear fruit — fruit that will last. Then the Father will give you whatever you ask in my name. This is my command: Love each other.*

The theological concept of friendship found in 2 Corinthians 5:17-20 instructs us about the two or three group.[116] In this passage, the Good News Translation uses the root meaning of the word "reconciliation" rather than a more literal word-by-word translation: Through Christ we have become the "friends of God rather than enemies."

> *When anyone is joined to Christ he is a new being; the old is gone, the new has come. All this is done by God, who through Christ changed us from enemies into his friends, and gave us the task of making others his friends also. Our message is that God was making friends of all men through Christ. God did not keep an account of their sins against them, and he has given us the message of how he makes them his friends. Here we are, then, speaking for Christ, as*

---

116. William A. Beckham, "The Disciple Dimension of the Church," in *The Second Reformation: Stage 2* (Moreno Valley, CA: CCS Publishing, 2014), 236.

if God himself were appealing to you through us: on Christ's behalf, we beg you, let Christ change you from enemies to friends! (GNT)

God has given us the *"task* of making others his friends" and has given us the *"message* of how He makes them his friend." Christians are *"speaking for Christ,* as if God himself" were begging unbelievers to, "let Christ change you from enemies to friends!" In Colossians 1:15-22, Paul explains our friendship with God from the nature of Christ and the Church.

The Son is the image of the invisible God, the firstborn over all creation. For in him all things were created: things in heaven and on earth, visible and invisible, whether thrones or powers or rulers or authorities; all things have been created through him and for him. He is before all things, and in him all things hold together. And he is the head of the body, the church; he is the beginning and the firstborn from among the dead, so that in everything he might have the supremacy. For God was pleased to have all his fullness dwell in him, and through him to reconcile to himself all things, whether things on earth or things in heaven, by making peace through his blood, shed on the cross. Once you were alienated from God and were enemies in your minds because of your evil behavior. But now he has reconciled you by Christ's physical body through death to present you holy in his sight ...

Friendship is the greatest ministry in the sense that it is the ministry of every Christian, and it has the greatest impact on the mission God gave to the church to expand the gospel throughout all the earth through relationships. This is why the pastor and/or catalytic leader/s of the church must experience a friendship triad. As a leader you must become evidence of what you want practiced and that begins with the friendship triad.

Friendship Triad Mainframe

A mainframe is a structural system that supports other components of a physical construction. This concept helps explain Jesus' integrated church system. The people in a friendship triad are built upon an intentional and spiritual mainframe that holds the church together as the Body of Christ.

That framework holds the life and nature of a triad and the triad in turn is the embryo of a community cell and the community cell integrates leadership and expansion. I view the mainframe as a yoke that provides the structure upon which is placed the basic elements of the Body of Christ.

The simple mainframe of the church (Christ, believer, and others) begins at the most basic unit of the church with the friendship triad and then is filled out and applied in each relationship unit of the community cell of twelve and the expansion supervision unit of seventy. This mainframe integrates the entire church from the inside out, from the most basic unit to the more complex. The eleven disciplines within the mainframe are lived out as a personal rule of life.

Without the basic mainframe the church has no binding force to hold the different pieces of the church in a unified whole. Without this mainframe, the church so often seems like a disintegrated organization with separate ministries and programs.

Triad Definition

The friendship triad is the first experience of a seeker or new Christian into spiritual community. In fact, the friendship triad is community cell life in embryo. Therefore, pastors and leaders must experience the presence and Lordship of Christ, application of the Word, confession, prayer, edification, following the Spirit, accountability, confession of sins, edification, friendship body life, and natural *oikos* and *person-of-peace* evangelism in a friendship triad.

A pastor I was mentoring asked me to give a definition of a triad that he could use with his leaders. I responded that a triad is two to four friends living in a friendship relationship with Christ and with each other and telling others how to be Christ's friend. In this friendship relationship they will:

- Experience the presence of Christ
- Acknowledge that Jesus is Lord
- Prayerfully listen to God for each other
- Apply scripture together to life
- Live in and be led by the Spirit
- Confess personal sins
- Be accountable to and for each other
- Edify and encourage each other
- Live together in friendship body life
- Invite others into the friendship triad
- Multiple into two triads when they become four friends

Friendship Triad Biblical Explanation

Focus on Christ: Christ is the center of a triad. "For where two or three gather in my name, there am I with them" (Matt. 18:20). "God has chosen to make known among the Gentiles the glorious riches of this mystery, which is Christ in you, the hope of glory" (Col. 1:27). "I will come to you" (John 14:16-23). "I want to know Him" (Phil. 3:10-11).

Confess Jesus is Lord: This establishes the reality and extent of Jesus' authority in the lives of those in the triad. Each person in the triad is under submission to the same Master. "Confess with your mouth that Jesus Is Lord" (Rom. 10:9). "Then Jesus said to his disciples, 'Whoever wants to be my disciple must deny themselves and take up their cross and follow me'" (Matt. 16:24). "Thomas said to him, 'My Lord and my God!'" (John 29:24-29). The following are also scriptures about the Lordship of Christ: Matt. 16:16; Luke 12:9; John 1:49, 6:69, 11:27; Phil. 2:11; 1 John 2:11, 4:15.

Apply the Word: Triads give a place for scripture to be applied personally. Questions may be used so those in a triad will apply the Word to daily life: What does the Word of God say? What sin does God reveal to me? What command does God want me to obey? What promises does God give to me? The Bible is not only studied but is applied to life. Personally applying the Word and agreeing around Scripture begins in the friendship relationship of the triad.

"Anyone who listens to the word but does not do what it says is like someone who looks at his face in a mirror and, after looking at himself, goes away and immediately forgets what he looks like" (James 1:23-24)."Whatever you have learned or received or heard from me, or seen in me---pit it into practice. And the God of peace will be with you (Phil. 4:9). "Go therefore and make disciples of all the nations, baptizing them in the name of the Father and the Son and the Holy Spirit, *teaching them to observe all that I commanded you,* and lo, I am with you always, even to the end of the age" (Matt. 26:19-20). "All Scripture is God-breathed and is useful for teaching,

CHAPTER 9: PROTOTYPE FRIENDSHIP   191

rebuking, correcting and training in righteousness, so that the servant of God may be thoroughly equipped for every good work" (2 Tim. 3:16-17).

Pray: Prayer in the two or three group is a unifying element of the Christian life and the central focus of a triad. Friends in a triad learn to pray in Christ's presence. The triad is the place for first experiencing the full expanse of prayer: Listening prayer, intercessory prayer, confession prayer, and edification prayer. In a friendship triad God takes special note of agreeing prayer in a two or three triad and binds His word together with those prayers.

"If two of you on earth agree about anything you ask for, it will be done for you by my Father in heaven" (Matt. 18:19). "In the same way, the Spirit helps us in our weakness. We do not know what we ought to pray for, but the Spirit himself intercedes for us through wordless groans. And he who searches our hearts knows the mind of the Spirit, because the Spirit intercedes for God's people in accordance with the will of God (Rom. 8:26-27). "This is the confidence we have in approaching God: that if we ask anything according to his will, he hears us. And if we know that he hears us—whatever we ask—we know that we have what we asked of him" (1 John 5:14-15). A community cell builds upon the prayer experience of the two or three and will often bring fuller understanding and new revelation.

Confess sins: A friendship triad provides a natural and safe venue to share personal details of problems and sins to a friend in confidence. Confession in a two or three unit substantially reduces the danger of prayer or edification "gossip" that spreads unnecessary personal details. This allows confession in the community cell to deal with spiritual issues without personal and sensational details. "Confess your sins to each other and pray for each other" (James 5:16). "If we confess our sins, he is faithful and just to forgive us our sins and to cleanse us from all unrighteousness" (1 John 1:7-9).

Edify one another: Edification is "the act of one who promotes another's growth in Christian wisdom, piety, holiness, happiness."[117] Edification prayer begins in the triad as members speak into each other's lives. Because needs are shared in detail in the two or three unit, Christ can quickly deal with the root issues in the community cell. In the two or three unit, Christ speaks words of discernment, knowledge, and encouragement through a friend. In a community setting, Christ speaks practical words of prophecy through others in the cell. "Let us therefore make every effort to do what leads to peace and to mutual edification" (Rom.14:19). See Rom. 15:2; Eph. 4:12; 29-30; 1 Thess. 5:11.

Be accountable: Live out the "one another's" (1 John 4:7-21). The friendship relationship in a triad is expressed in the one another's: being accountable for one another, confessing to one another, praying for one another, and edifying and encouraging one another. "And let us consider how we may spur one another on toward love and good deeds" (Heb.10:24).

The two or three unit is the first place to deal with personal conflicts within the body. The more mature person in the triad should help a new believer follow the Biblical pattern that Jesus gave to deal with conflict with another Christian. It is the first place of accountability as the individuals in the triad walk along side of each other. Accountability in a two or three unit is removed from just the narrow confines of personal responsibility and takes on a broader community context for

---

117. Strong's Concordance N.T. 3619.

accountability. The cell is the final place for solving conflicts that cannot be resolved in the two or three unit.

Follow the Spirit: Live in and be led by the Spirit (Rom. 8:14-17; 26-27). Produce the fruit of the Spirit and the ministry and leadership gifts of the Spirit (Gal. 5:16-26). This relationship with Christ naturally moves into the Christian's relationship with the Holy Spirit. Christians in the friendship triad walk by the Spirit, are led by the Spirit, and obey the Spirit.

Live in community body life: "So in Christ we, though many, form one body, and each member belongs to all the others. Other scriptures that deal with body life are Rom.12:5, Acts 2:42-47, Acts 4:32, and Col. 3:12-17. Body life begins in the friendship relationship in a triad and is covered later in this chapter.

Add friends: I agree with Neil Cole's appraisal of evangelism in triads. "These groups spread like wild fire because the breath of God blows on obedient disciples who find fuel in dry lives longing to burn for the Lord. Because the system is simple enough to pass on with one easy description the flame spreads unhindered. Ordinary Christians are empowered to do the most important work any of us can do."[118] "The first thing Andrew did was to find his brother Simon" (John 1:41). "Some Greeks came to Philip. He went to tell Andrew; Andrew and Philip in turn told Jesus" (John 12:20-22)."And I, when I am lifted up from the earth, will draw all people to myself" John 12:32.

Multiply into two triads: "So the churches were strengthened in the faith and grew daily in numbers" (Acts 16:5). Friendship *evangelism* naturally flows out of a friendship triad. The objective is to bring another person into the triad so the original two become three. The friendship triad is the place of basic

---

118. Cole, *Cultivating a Life for God*, 94.

evangelism: The first contact with friends who are "person of peace," the penetration of an individual Christian's *oikos* (sphere of influence), and the cultivation of those "caught" in the net fishing activities of the cell. The new person invited to be part of a triad can be an unbelieving seeker, a hurting Christian, or a person finding their way back to God. The triad is the natural place to assimilate new believers and to provide extra grace for hurting people who are not ready to function in a community cell.

Process Steps

Greg Ogden summarizes what happens in a "disciple-making" unit of two or three Christ-followers or seekers.

> *Let me make explicit what has been implicit. The model of discipline making I propose is one person inviting two others into a covenantal relationship structured around a Bible-based curriculum. For approximately a year they meet weekly for about an hour and a half per session, which then reproduces into the next generation.*[119]

The chart, *Friendship Triad Process*, shows my interpretation of the friendship triad process. A pastor or the catalytic leader of a new church start must begin at this point and experience (prototype) the life and multiplication of a friendship triad with a group of followers. This process is repeated and is the multiplication and expansion catalyst in Jesus' strategy for today.

Four steps explain the practical application of the two or three core unit in more detail.[120]

---

119. Ogden, 176.
120. Ibid., 162.

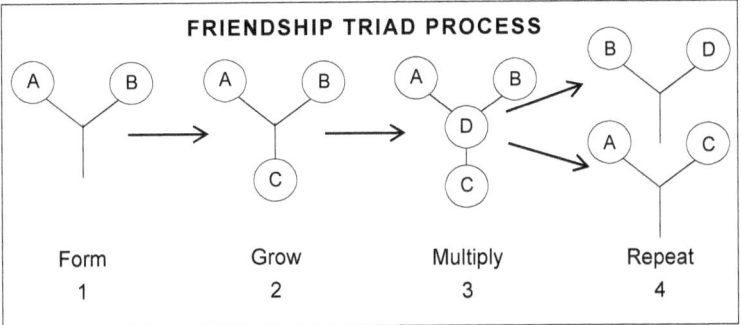

1. *Form* a triad with one other person. In the case of a new church plant or a church that is beginning cells, the pastor/leader chooses another leader to help prototype a friendship triad. At the same time, the wife of the pastor or leader can begin a woman's prototype triad. If small groups or cells already exist in the church but without triads, friendship triads can be formed with two people who are part of the same community cell, men with men and women with women. The two connect in relationships, meet regularly, talk to each other on the phone, text, and send emails. In other words, they use all the normal means of relationship, written and verbal correspondence, social media, and face-to-face activities that family and friends use. They bond in a relationship of friendship around the presence of Christ as Lord, the written Word (the Bible) and living Word (the Holy Spirit) and listening in prayer for each other.

2. *Grow* by adding a friend. The objective is to bring one other person into the friendship triad so that the original two become three. The new person can be a relative, friend, or acquaintance. The friend may be a Christian, a new follower of Christ, a prodigal believer, or a person of peace seeker. The triad continues to do the same thing: Apply scripture to life, pray for one another, confess Jesus Christ is Lord, confess sins, and edify and encourage each other.

3. *Multiply* when a fourth person is added. The second friend can come into the triad in the same way as the first friend: *Oikos* relationships and person of peace seekers. When the fourth person is added, the triad remains together for four to six weeks as a group of four and then multiplies into two basic friendship triads of two. Form the new triads along natural relationships. Look at the process chart again. I am assuming that "A" invited "C" into the triad and that "B" invited "D". Therefore, one new friendship triad is formed out of "A" and "C" and the other triad is formed out of "B" and "D". Relationship is the central principle in friendship. Therefore, the simple rule of a triad is to grow along relationship lines.

4. *Repeat the process.* The two new triads of two persons go back to the second step and repeat the process: grow to four, multiply into two, and repeat the process. The goal is to keep multiplying the two or three unit. Triads are always connected to community cells.

Factors to Remember about a Friendship Triad

The triad is a relationship, *not a meeting.* Even though a triad has a face-to-face time, it is not one more meeting added to a cell meeting and to the worship meeting on Sunday. Relationships are experienced at the deepest, closest, and most intimate level in a friendship triad. Think of a family. A husband and wife form the core of a family unit that may include several children. Parents and children have a close relationship as a community family. However, the relationship between a husband and wife is different from that of the broader family that includes the children. The same qualities of love, care, and accountability operate with the broader family. However, the physical and emotional relationship between a husband and wife is the most intimate within the family. The small size of a friendship triad allows a degree of intimacy and openness that is different from the relationship in a family community cell.

In a two or three triad, *friendship takes precedence over leadership.* Everyone is equally invested in a friendship if it is a true friendship. A friendship relationship may develop among persons who are old and young, rich and poor, employee and employer, and educated and uneducated. However, if one of these factors dominates the relationship then it is no longer a friendship but a mentoring or power relationship. In Thailand, very precise words are used to identify older and younger siblings. In fact the word for "sibling (pêe nóng) is separated into two words that are used as relationship prefixes to designate older and younger (relatives, relations, kinsfolk). A short prefix placed before brother or sister changes it to older brother/sister (pêe) or younger brother/sister (nóng). The prefix system is also used to designate other relationships in business and friendships. As a missionary I was usually addressed as "teacher." If someone used the older brother prefix (pêe Bill) when addressing me then I knew I was no longer seen in the formal role as missionary but had entered into a more familiar relationship like friendship.

The *relationship roles* of father, young man, and child that we see in 1 John 2, form naturally in a friendship triad. These are the roles of a mature spiritual adult, a young spiritual adult who knows the Father and knows how to deal with Satan, and a spiritual child who only know they have a spiritual Father. The roles may need to be introduced in the beginning of the prototype. However, after a cycle or two, the relationships of spiritual adult, young spiritual adult, and spiritual child develops naturally. The original two members of a triad will disciple a person they bring into the triad. When the triad forms two new units, it is natural for the relationships to continue in cell community life.

A spiritual "adult" will give stability and guidance in a new triad with a spiritual "young person" or spiritual "child."

John's teaching on the three relationships of father, young person, and child can best operate in a friendship type relationship rather than a leadership system (John 2). Seek this same dynamic in your triad relationships. Leadership takes place within a friendship triad but it is more like the leading of an older brother or sister. The roles develop naturally in a friendship triad. The most basic kind of one-on-one accountability and equipping take place in the two or three unit. The spiritually older friend walks with a new or immature believer through the early days of Christian living. Every person learns to lead at the initial level of Christian living. The two or three unit is not about processing Biblical facts and knowledge but about experiencing God. The community cell equips in advanced areas of on-the-job training and cognitive lessons.

A triad is *gender specific*: men with men and women with women. For years I have sensed the need within the church for a group that is gender specific. The Promise Keepers phenomenon of men taking the responsibility to be good husbands and fathers confirmed my conviction that Christian men need a way to be in each other's lives. The Promise Keepers movement was made up of men who met in stadiums, but was driven out of accountability relationships in small groups.

Let me state what I have observed and what is obvious: Men and women relate differently. Both communicate but use different vehicles. The nature of men is to relate around tasks while the nature of most women is to relate around conversation. I have observed this in community cells for years. Women most often dominate the conversations of a cell meeting and men sit and listen. The one exception is a male leader who has the task of leading the cell. I believe this is the reason groups in the church usually have more women than men. The triad gives a place for gender specific relationships where women speak into the lives of women and men are in the lives and faces of men. Then men and women triads join together in community cell life.

A friendship triad is a *sub group of a community cell*. It is either forming a new community cell or multiplying within an existing community cell. The community cell leader oversees the triads, makes sure they are: functioning, multiplying when they grow to four members, and caring for new believers.

Some models combine the cell and triad in one meeting time. A portion of the community cell meeting time is reserved for triads to meet. The persons in a triad that meets during a cell meeting may change each week. This eliminates another "meeting" and gives the community cell leader a way to coordinate the triads. It also gives a way that visitors can experience a friendship triad. However, it limits some of the most important aspects of a friendship triad. (1) The friendship triad is a relationship and not an activity or meeting. Having the triad during cell meeting makes it an activity. (2) It limits the continuity of relationships. The people in a triad during the cell meeting depend on who shows up. Whereas, this gives a place for cell visitors, it does not support the intent of the friendship triad of an ongoing intimate friendship. (3) Doing triads during the cell meeting discourages relationships during the week because "we have already done this during the cell meeting." (4) Scheduling triads during the cell meeting reduces the quality of personal relationship between Christians and seekers because it is limited to one time during the cell meeting. (5) Cell triads limit the number and depth of contacts between Christians and seekers. Those in the triads that meet within the cell meeting often only have one contact with Christians whereas a friendship triad is a continuing relationship.

Christians experience *body life* in three relationship groups. The first experience is friendship body life that Christians experience in a friendship triad. Then, life as His body is experienced in a cell community where Christians experience nurturing friendship. Once Christians experience friendship body life together in triads and nurturing body life in a community cell, they experience supervising body life in a cluster of seventy. These three body life experiences affirm to Christians today that they are experiencing what happened in the New Testament.

Ray Stedman devoted his classic book, *Body Life*, to exploring in the book of Ephesians the New Testament meaning of life as the body of Christ. "What is terribly missing is the experience of 'body life'; that warm fellowship of Christian with Christian which the New Testament calls *koinonia*, and which was an essential part of early Christianity. The New Testament lays heavy emphasis upon the need for Christians to know each other, closely and intimately enough to bear one another's burdens, confess faults one to another, rebuke, exhort, and admonish one another, minister to one another with the word and through song and prayer."[121]

Stedman's church experienced body life in a powerful Sunday evening service that began in 1970. The only avenue for experiencing body life within the traditional structure was within some kind of large group venue. He describes this "Body Life service" in the last chapter of his book.[122] Body life is much more than a service. Since the experience of Stedman and his church, God has begun to restore body life in the New Testament small groups of triads and community cells where it was originally experienced.

The Chart *Body Life Triad Checklist* shows the different elements of body life that begin in a triad and continue in community cell life. A triad and cell can be evaluated from the same checklist

---

121. Stedman, 113.
122. Ibid., 145-160.

CHAPTER 9: PROTOTYPE FRIENDSHIP

because they are part of the same community unit. Triads make up cells and therefore when a triad works properly the cell works properly.

The experience of body life begins in the triad and is expressed in the other basic groups of the church. For instance, body life in the triad is friendship body life; body life in the cell is community body life; and body life in

BODY LIFE TRIAD CHECKLIST
- Acknowledge Christ's Presence (Matthew 18:20)
- Confess Jesus is Lord (Romans 10:9)
- Live together in Body Life (Ephesians 4:16)
- Apply Scripture to life (James 1:21)
- Confess sins (1 John 1:7-9; James 5:16)
- Listen to God in Prayer (John 10:27)
- Edify and encourage love and good deeds. (Romans 14:19; Heb. 10:24)
- Be accountable to each other (Ephesians 5:21)
- Live together in friendship body life (Ephesians 4:16)
- Multiply: Invite a Friend (2 Cor. 5:17-20)

the cluster of seventy is mission body life as Christians focus on expanding the church. This same body life rippling effect that begins in the triad to the cell and to the cluster of seventy takes place in the other elements (disciplines or experiences) of abiding in the presence of Christ, acknowledging the Lordship of Christ, applying Scripture to life, listening in prayer for each other, confessing personal sins, being accountable to and for each other, following and obeying the Spirit, edifying and encouraging each other, welcoming friends into Christ's circle, and multiplying.

The triad creates an atmosphere of openness that is essential for learning in community life. "When small groups of people (as few as two or three) become deeply committed and open they create a microcosm of a learning organization. This microcosm not only teaches them the skills they need but become a model for others."[123] Practical love is the foundation for openness and is first practiced in a group of two or three. In the two or three, Christians practice agape. Agape does not grow out of emotions but out of intentions. Agape is a "commitment to serve one another, and willingness to be vulnerable in the context of that

---
123. Senge, 285.

service. The best definition of the love that underlies openness is the full and unconditional construct to another's 'completion,' to (see) another being all she or he can and wants to be."[124]

Greg Ogden believes that "if the goal is to grow self-initiating, reproducing, fully devoted followers of Christ, then this means we need contexts in which the metamorphosis into Christlikeness can become a lifelong quest."[125] Triads are the first step for the "metamorphosis into Christlikeness" for every Christian.

COMPARISON OF A TRIAD AND CELL

Friendship triads and community cells share many of the same characteristics. This is understandable because the two or three unit is a sub group of the community cell and the community cell works through the two or three units. Paul's explanation of Body Life in Ephesians 4:16 is lived out in the triad and cell. This means that the triad and cell: (1) Depend on the Head: Every part is living according to directives from Him. (2) Have unity in diversity: Every part is important and needed. (3) Are interdependent on one another: Every part is mutually contributing to the other parts.

A contrast of triads and cells reveals only subtle differences. However, it is important to understand those differences in order to have realistic expectations for each group. All the dynamics of cell life will most naturally occur first in a friendship triad. The community cell continues and completes what is started in the two or three disciple unit. The Friendship Triad is the place for basic Christian living: experiencing Christ in the midst, discipleship, fellowship, accountability, edification, application of the Word, and evangelism.

---
124. Ibid.
125. Ogden, 152.

Chapter 9: Prototype Friendship

The chart below is a side-by-side summary of teachings in this book about triads and cells. It places the dynamic elements of triads and cells together in one place. Remember: these distinctions are nuanced and are only different in degree, not in substance because the triad is the embryo of the cell.

FRIENDSHIP TRIAD		COMMUNITY CELL
Experience Christ in the Midst	BODY LIFE	Live in His presence, power & purpose.
Spiritual Friendship	RELATIONSHIP	Spiritual Community
Personally Apply Scripture	SCRIPTURE	Apply Scripture within the Body
Contact & Cultivate the Person of Peace	WITNESS	Assimilate *Oikos* into Community
Experience 2 or 3 Prayer	PRAYER	Apply 2 or 3 Prayer in Community
Discover Words Of Agreement	AGREEMENT	Interpret and Apply Words of Agreement
Accountable to One Person	ACCOUNTABLE	Accountable within a Community Group
Personal Edification	EDIFICATION	Community Edification
Discerning Words of Knowledge	PROPHECY	Community Practical Prophecy
Personal Praise	PRAISE	Community Praise
Personal Confession about Details	CONFESSION	Confession Leads to Edification
First Step in Solving Conflict	CONFLICT	Final Step in Solving Conflict
Basic Discipleship	EQUIPPING	Community Equipping
Develop Committed Followers of Christ	LEADERSHIP	Develop Cell Leaders
Separated into Men and Women Units	GENDER	May be Mixed Group with Men and Women

Chapter 10

PROTOTYPE COMMUNITY

"The fact was I had the vision... I think everyone has... what we lack is the method."
• Jack Kerouac, American novelist and poet

The life and structure of Jesus' *ecclesia* is centered in a group of five to twelve Christians who meet regularly in homes or other appropriate venues. A volunteer leader facilitates the group and leads the community members in mutually caring for each other and building each other up (edifying). It carries the mitochondria DNA of the church that met together in the houses of the early Christians.[126]

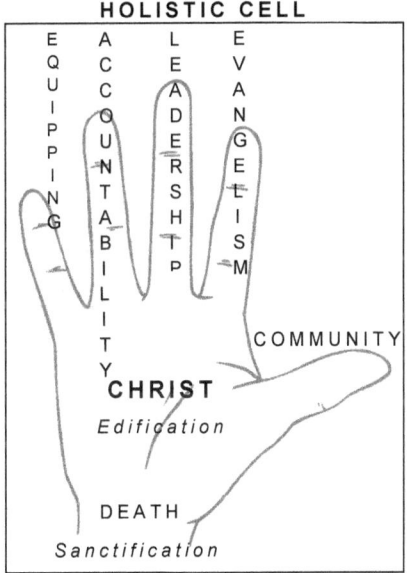

---

126. William A. Beckham, "Community Dimension," in *The Second Reformation: Stage 2* (Moreno Valley, CA: CCS Publishing, 2014), 251.

A holistic community cell is made up of several sub set groups of friendship triads (two or three) that are introduced in the previous chapter. The number of triads in a community cell depends upon the growth stage of the triad. Is it a new triad with two persons, a mature triad of three, or has it grown to the multiplying size of four? A community cell should begin with five to seven persons and multiply as a mature cell when it has twelve to fifteen adults (around four triads). A cell is itself a sub set of a mid-level supervising group of seventy.

The basic elements and experiences of the church take place in a community cell: community, accountability, equipping, leadership, evangelism, edification, and sanctification. Within the community cell, Christians live together in holistic community, develop leaders, penetrate *oikos* relationships, nurture and edify on the individual, cell, and church levels, equip the saints for the work of ministry, evangelize, abide in Christ, are accountable to each other, cultivate contacts through group activities, and live out the one another's.

The diagram of the hand is an illustration of how the different elements of spiritual life fit together. The entire hand represents a community cell that is the spiritual Body of Christ on earth. The opposable thumb allows the five digits of the human hand to function in a unique way. Each finger operates independently but also interdependently with the thumb and each other.[127]

Community: A Place to Live as Spiritual Family

The thumb represents community where all the elements and experiences of cell life are integrated. In the same way our

---

127. Scott Boren, Bill Beckham, Joel Comiskey, Ralph Neighbour, and Randall Neighbour, *Cell Group Church Values: Navigation* Guide (Houston: TX: Cell Church Resources, 2003), 185f. This is a more in depth look at cell community.

fingers come together when we close our hand, Christians gather in community for fellowship, for edification (building up) of the body, for body life of mutual love, care and nurture, for physical and spiritual safety, for transparent and honest communication, and for understanding the truths of God's Word. Cell community is made up of Christians who are "members one of another." They experience Trinitarian community lived out in real time with real people, together in the presence of Christ, the power of the Holy Spirit, and the purpose of the Father. Just as all the fingers operate in relationship to the thumb, every element in the cell operates in relationship to community.

New Testament cell community integrates all the other elements of the Christian life and allows them to operate in the proper way at the proper time. Equipping (discipleship), accountability, leadership, and evangelism fit together as a whole when activated in community. However, none of these four elements will independently unite the others. For instance, a focus on equipping often neglects evangelism. The element of accountability may become legalistic and restrictive if focused upon itself. Integrating the work of the church around leaders often focuses on the particular gifts of the leader and neglects the other important elements. Evangelism as the integrating element often neglects the other four. In addition, the special relationship activities with God of worship, prayer, and the Word cannot independently coordinate all of the other elements. New Testament cell community integrates all the elements and experiences of the church and allows them to operate in the proper way at the proper time.

Remember: Community in cell life is happening among people who are also living in a friendship relationship in a triad of two or three other followers where they are experiencing intimate friendship with each other and with the Father.

Equipping

The power-centers of the hand are the base of the thumb and the side of the little finger. These power centers allow the hand to work in tandem and tightly grip objects. The strength of the church is living in community together (the thumb side) and nurturing the spiritual babies to maturity (the little finger side). A holistic cell is a place for nurturing God's babies. God cares for His spiritual babies within His spiritual family: the community cell. The "babies" may be new believers, the spiritually immature, the emotionally weak members of the body, or Christians going through times of hurt and crisis in their lives.

The "babies" are cared for and equipped by more mature young Christians and fathers in the friendship triads of two or three, the natural subgroups of community cells. Several scriptures make reference to equipping. In Ephesians, Paul explains that gifted leaders are provided to the church to "equip the Saints" (4:12). The writer of Hebrews assures Christians that God's purpose is to "equip you with everything good" (13:21). Paul's intention was that Timothy would be "thoroughly equipped" and to do the same for others (2 Tim. 3:17).

The inability of the church to care for new believers was one of the great tragedies of the 20th century organizational church and the neglect continues today. Large numbers of new Christians have been birthed over the last decades but have been lost to meaningful ministry within a porous large group system. Churches that lack a community cell structure must try to care for the spiritual babies in a sterile institutional setting in a warehouse environment.

Christ provides for the care of His spiritual babies in spiritual families in a small group family setting. Cell leaders are spiritual parents to new believers. Other members of the cell are older brothers and sisters who help guide the steps of the new babies. Activities associated with the little finger are a personal step-by-step disciple experience for new believers, mentoring, and special group events through which new believers are nurtured. New believers are nurtured in a gender specific friendship triad with one or two other Christ followers.

Equipping is a broad category that includes helping Christians walk in sanctification, to be personally edified, and to grow in maturity so that they can help and encourage others.

ACCOUNTABILITY

The Romans believed a "vein of love" ran directly from the heart to the fourth finger of the left hand. This is one of the reasons rings are placed on the fourth finger, or "ring finger" of the left hand. In fact, all the fingers on the hand have a similar vein structure. But, it is a beautiful story that gives a special significance to this finger as the covenant ring finger.

In cell life, the ring finger represents accountability. The same commitments associated with Christian marriage are lived out in cell community. Accountability begins, as does the other elements, in the two or three friendship unit and is completed in the holistic community cell.

The New Testament concept of accountability is revealed in the "one another" passages: "And be kind to one another, tender-hearted, forgiving each other" (Eph. 4:32); "and be subject to one another in the fear of Christ" (Eph. 5:21); "bearing with one another, and forgiving each other..." (Col. 3:13; Rom. 14:19); and join in "mutual edification" (1 Peter 2:5, 9).

One of the names Jesus uses for the promised Spirit illustrates the meaning of accountability. The Spirit is Advocate: "the one Who comes alongside" (John 14:16). This is a beautiful picture of the work of the Spirit and the spirit of accountability. The Holy Spirit loves to come along side of Christians to comfort, guide, teach, support, intercede, and protect. Accountability is the vein of love and life that flows from the Father through the Holy Spirit and from the Spirit through a Christian to another Christian. Accountability is the special *paraclete* ministry of the Holy Spirit to and through every Christian.

The work of the Spirit is multiplied in a cell as He enlists each member to share in His work of "coming alongside" the other members in the cell. The Holy Spirit through me "comes alongside" you and supports and encourages you. Then, the Holy Spirit through you "comes alongside" me, and supports and encourages me. This beautiful ministry changes the hard and harsh pictures many have of accountability.

The Disciples understood what Jesus was talking about when He said the Holy Spirit would "come alongside" of them. In their relationship with Jesus, the Disciples experienced spiritual accountability in its intended meaning. He had come alongside them as He walked with them, encouraged them, supported them, and was their advocate and friend. Jesus promised that the Holy Spirit would continue this relationship.

Members of community cells are accountable to each other in two or three friendship triads and in cell meetings. Leaders are accountable to each other in authority and submission relationships within the cluster of seventy. Accountability within the context of friendship is closer to how Jesus mentored than the context of leadership or discipleship that the modern day church uses.

LEADERSHIP

A holistic cell is a place where simple, spiritual, servant, and sacrificial leadership is exercised and developed. The large finger is significant because it is the most prominent finger, representing the strong and mature people who are fathers and mothers. God as Abba Father (Rom. 8:1t5) is the best picture of spiritual leadership. The heart of God is to parent. Christ calls and prepares leaders to care for the spiritual babies and to lead His flock. God's Trinitarian nature best explains the concept of cell leadership. Christians experience the fatherhood of God, the brotherhood of Christ, and the mothering nurture of the Holy Spirit, and leaders continue these relationships.

Fatherhood implies reproduction. The object of the family cell is to reproduce itself. This reproduction must take place first at the point of leadership. Only then can the cell reproduce numerically. Every cell has a leader and is developing at least one other to be a leader. Potential cell leaders are emerging out of the triads. In addition to leadership in the cell, this finger also represents training of new leaders, coordinating meetings for leaders, and the Jethro structure (3, 12, 70, 120) through which leaders coordinate the work of the ministry.

In 1 John 2:12-14, John explains the nature of this community/family leadership system as the dynamic interaction of spiritual "children, young men and fathers." Fathers (and mothers) are mature Christians. Young men (and women) are growing Christians. Children are new or immature believers. Parents mentor the youth and the youth help mentor the children. Jesus demonstrated the warm, loving relationship of the Father in His relationship to His followers and to the children in the crowds. Mature members in a community cell live out the love and life of Father God. God the Father parents His spiritual children in the spiritual family of the cell.

Leaders are developed in the group system through on-the-job training. Interns naturally emerge out of personal discipleship, life in a triad of two or three, experiences in a cell, special training and deploying events, and experience as an intern.

How are interns for a cell found? Look in the triads and the community cells. Future cell leaders take responsibilities in the triads and that is where the training of a future cell leader begins. Then use the FAT principle. Who is **F**aithful? Who is **A**vailable? Who is **T**eachable? Who is most faithful in the triads of two or three? Who is teachable? Who ministers to others? Who is a peacemaker? Who is part of the solution rather than part or the problem? Life in triads and cell community prepares new believers and reveals potential leaders.

Developing an intern to lead a cell is the most important training in a church. This on-the-job training begins in a friendship two or three triad. If a church can train a good cell leader intern it will have a good cell leader. If it has a good cell leader it will be able to identify and train good supervisors. If it has a good supervising leader over 30 to 70 persons (3 to 6 cells), God will call out some to lead streamlined support congregations of hundred's. Jesus trained His leaders within this structure without a set of materials except the Torah. His on-the-job training was based in relationships, experiences, and demonstration. Ralph Neighbour factored in relationships, experiences, and demonstration in his taxonomy of training and materials.

The basic unit of the squad in the military illustrates the uniqueness of these types of leaders. Stephen Ambrose saw the squad (cell) as the most important unit in the military. In his book *Citizen Soldiers* Ambrose explains the uniqueness of the squad.

> *In assessing the motivation of the GIs, there is agreement that patriotism or any other form of idealism had little if anything to do with it. The GIs fought because they had to. What held them together was not country and flag, but unit cohesion ... Organization for a common and concrete goal in peacetime organizations does not evoke anything like the degree of comradeship commonly known in war. At its height this sense of comradeship is an ecstasy. Men are true comrades only when each (member of the squad) is ready to give up his life for the others without reflection and without thought of personal loss.*"[128]

We see this level of community and commitment to one another in the New Testament movement. As in the military, it was the groups (squads of 10 - 12 adults) in the New Testament that produced this kind of commitment to a common task and to each other.

All other leaders exist in order to support the community cell leader because the community cell is the place for producing leaders for clusters and congregations.

EVANGELISM

The index finger is good for pointing, directing, and picking things up. This finger represents evangelism because the cell points the cell members toward the lost and works together to "pick up" those who are separated from God. Through its cell activities and life in triads, a community cell naturally contacts and connects with the lost in three ways: (1) It draws persons of

---
128. Stephen E Ambrose, *Citizen Soldiers* (New York: Touchstone, 1997), 473.

peace who are seekers to Christ in friendship triads; (2) It cultivates those in relationship with members through their *oikos* sphere of influence; and (3) It attracts the interested in groupnet fishing activities.

Because "God loved the world" (John 3:16), Jesus told His followers "You will be my witnesses" (Acts 1:8). God's love and witness are joined together in community life. The cell experiences body life evangelism when Christ is lifted up in the cell. He draws the unlearned and unconverted to Himself so that they experience Him in such a powerful way that they fall on their face and proclaim: "Surely God is in this place" (1 Cor. 14:24-25).

Jesus is the center of the cell and His desire to go and "seek and to save the lost" is fulfilled through the cell and triads. It is Christ's eternal purpose to also draw all men to Him. Jesus promised, "If I am lifted up, I will draw all men unto myself (John 12: 3). Because Christ is the center of the cell, His desire is to draw the lost to Himself through friendship triads into community cells. Cell community evangelism begins when Christ is lifted up in the cell. The pointer beckons the Lost to Christ by drawing all men.

Friendship evangelism is varied and creative and is a central focus in the two or three triad and the community cell. Within the friendship triads everyone practices a lifestyle of reaching out to and reconciling the lost to Christ. Evangelism is both a personal and community responsibility. In friendship triads, cell members identify the person of peace and reach out to friends and relatives who are part of their *oikos* sphere of influence. Christ followers in community become "fishers of men" and use community "net" fishing instead of individual "pole" fishing as the only evangelism method.

Christians should be prepared to share their own brief (3 minutes at the most) personal testimony of the work of God in salvation and sanctification in their life. Paul's testimony in Acts 22 and 26 is a good pattern: (1) My life before I became a Christian; (2) How Christ first spoke to me; (3) How I made my decision to follow Him; and (4) My life now.

Christians are also prepared to give a clear witness that focuses on bringing a lost person to a point of decision. In his materials, Ralph Neighbour uses John 3:16 as the outline of an interactive witness. Christians in community exercise prayer evangelism by identifying and regularly praying for their *oikos* sphere of relationships. They also learn to identify and penetrate the "person of peace" in two or three triads that are sub units of the community cell. Community cells also practice net fishing by throwing out activities in which they meet seekers.

Friendship evangelism, through the two or three unit, is the place for learning and implementing organic evangelism.

CHRIST IN THE MIDST

The palm represents Christ in the midst of the cell and triad. Several scriptures help us understand Christ's presence in a general way and in specific situations. Paul teaches that Christ is in His Body in all situations. This is the hope of the Christian. "Christ in you, the hope of glory" (Col. 1:27).

Christ promised to be with a Christian in specific situations. "Where two or three gather in my Name, there I am in the midst" (Matt. 18:20). In John 14, Jesus elaborates on how He will relate to His followers after He returns to the Father. Jesus is preparing a place for them in heaven so His followers can be with Him. In addition, He is preparing a place on earth so He can be with them.

Jesus clearly promises to be both "in" and "with" the Christian. The Spirit "lives with you and will be in you" (14:17b). "I (Jesus) will not leave you as orphans; I will come to you" (John 14:18). "If anyone loves me, he will obey my teaching. My Father will love him, and we will come to him and make our home with him" (John 14:23). Jesus' promise in Revelation even puts the promise in the setting of a home. "Here I am! I stand at the door and knock. If anyone hears my voice and opens the door, I will come in and eat with him, and he with me" (Rev. 3:20).

This scripture is depicted in paintings that show Christ standing at a door and knocking. The door is a symbol of Christ knocking at the heart of a person. However, the scene is also a picture at the door of a community cell that is meeting inside a home.

Christ in the midst is a promise to the individual Christian and to a triad of two or three followers. In fact, the promise is given within the context of a group of two or three. However, the promise of His presence is also given to a community cell of twelve because it is made up of several two or three disciple units. This is the most important aspect of a cell: Christ is present when the cell comes together in His name. Christians in a cell don't just talk about Christ, sing about Him, or pray for needs in His name. Christ is the honored guest in the cell. Acknowledging Christ in the cell meeting and cell activities remind us of the power of His manifest presence.

Cell community has at least two advantages over ministry-based specialized small groups such as Bible study groups, fellowship groups, and ministry groups to teens, singles, couples, etc. Christ's presence in the life of each individual gives a common point of reference. The Christ "in me" is the same Christ "in you." That is a powerful connection for coming together as community. However, our connection together is more than just

Christ being in each person individually. Christ, through the Holy Spirit, also inhabits the group as the indwelling, incarnate, resurrected, and manifest Christ. The "with" experience is the powerful experience between Christians and Christ. Christ is "with us" in His community Body, not just in us as individuals.

At a certain point our individual experiences become one in Christ and something supernatural happens. We become spiritual community, the spiritual Body of Christ. In that kind of community all the "fullness of the Godhead bodily" is expressed in a powerful way. This releases the presence, power and purpose of Christ in and through His church. In the New Testament this is called spiritual fellowship and community. Christ's promise of His indwelling and manifest presence is given to both the individual and the community.

The heart of Christ is to abide with His followers and for His followers to abide in Him. Therefore, the cell lives out the very life of Christ as He abides in the cell and as the cell abides in Him (the palm). Christ begins the work of the edification of His body in a friendship triad and competes edification in cell community. These two groups are the place where God deals with the wellness of the church.

COMMUNITY CELL: EXPERIENCING DEATH & RESURRECTION

In the hand illustration, the wrist represents death. In Christ's wrists we see the scars caused by the nails that physically held Him to the cross. The primary place for affirming this principle of death and resurrection is in cell community.

Salvation is possible because of the death of Christ: He died that I may live. For me to receive His life, I must die. This is the meaning of baptism as the symbol of death, burial, and resurrection. Sanctification is by way of death. I must take up my cross daily and follow Christ in order to live the Christian life. The cross is an instrument of death (John 12:24). The cross is also an instrument of power and resurrection: "The cross is the power of God" (1 Cor. 1:18, 24); "triumphing over them by the cross" (Col. 2:13-15).

Each Christian enters into authentic community by way of death. "Unless a kernel of wheat falls into the ground and dies, it remains only a single seed. But if it dies, it produces many seeds" (John 12:24). It remains only a single seed or it abides alone. Alone is the opposite of community. The alone life is overcome in only one way: I must die to my self-sufficiency or personal isolation so that I can be resurrected into His commu-nity. There is no true Christian community without death. God uses us in ministry to the extent that we are willing to die to our own vision for our life.

Jesus demonstrated the meaning of death at Gethsemane: "Not my will but Thy will be done" (Luke 22:42)! Paul shows us the theology of Christ's death in Philippians 2:5-11. Christ emptied Himself (kenosis), turned loose of what was rightfully His, gave up, released, became a servant, humbled Himself, became obedient, obedient to death, even death on a cross.

In Philippians 3:10, Paul again explains the dynamic of death in his relationship to Christ. "I want to know Him, and the power of His resurrection, and the fellowship of sharing in his sufferings, becoming like Him in His death." A Christian must embrace the fellowship of Christ's suffering and be conformed to His death.

It is at the point of "being conformed to His death" that Satan attacks a Christian and a cell. Authentic love appears as the cell experiences death to personal agendas. Each person in a cell must die to personal agendas ... even good ones, if the group is to experience true New Testament community. The agenda may be Bible study, discipleship, evangelism, worship, prayer, edification, or the gifts. All of these are worthy goals but no one of these, or a combination of them, can be the agenda of a holistic community cell.

The person who is gifted in the Bible must die to that gift. The same is true of evangelism, the gifts, discipleship, worship, and even prayer. Christ must be the agenda of His community. True edification only takes place from Christ's presence and my death. I must die to edifying through my knowledge, past experiences and natural abilities. As I die, Christ is able to empower me and to edify through me.

Sanctification flows from Christ through the Holy Spirit to the needs of the cell. Sanctification begins in the Friendship Triads as personal needs are discovered during confession and application of Scripture. The triad is the beginning point of sanctifying and edification and cell community is the completion point.

USE YOUR HAND TO REMEMBER THE ELEMENTS IN CELL LIFE

Look at your hand and name the five dynamic elements and two experiences in a community cell. Begin with the thumb of community, then the small finger of equipping, the ring finger of accountability, the large finger of leadership, the pointer of evangelism, the palm of Christ in the midst where the Body is edified, and finally the wrist where we see the scar of death that leads to a resurrected and sanctified life. This is a simple picture of how Christ, through the Spirit, expresses His life through the most basic unit of His Body ... the cell. These are not tasks the members of the cell must do in their own experience, knowledge, and strength. Christ, through the Holy Spirit, ministers out of His heart in a community cell.

- The heart of Christ is to care for the babies. Therefore, through the cell Christ lives out His heart for caring for the new believers (small finger).
- The nature of Christ is to come alongside and to care for His followers. He does this in the cell as more mature members care for new believers and as the other members support each other in friendship triads (ring finger).
- God reveals Himself as a Father who loves and leads. Leaders are assigned to every cell and leaders are identified and raised up because this is the very heart of God (large finger).
- God so loved the world that He died in order to draw all men to Himself. The cell is an extension of the love and ministry of Christ to reach out to the lost and hurting and to draw them to Himself in His Body (index finger).
- The heart desire of Christ is to form His followers into His spiritual Body on earth (palm). Therefore, through the work of the Holy Spirit, Christ is present in every holistic cell community that gathers in His name. Christians experience prayer, revelation, practical prophecy that results in edification. This experience verifies the presence, power, and purpose of Christ to the group and to any who do not understand the reality of Christ. "Surely God is with us!"
- At the center of the heart of Christ is the cross. Death was God's way to bring about resurrection life. In holistic cell community, every Christian, and the cell as a community unit, learns the power of entering into personal death in order to experience the resurrection life of Christ (scar) in daily walking in sanctification.

With your hand diagram, you can share a picture of cell life wherever you go. Every time you look at your hand, you can remember

Chapter 10: Prototype Community

the dynamic life and ministry of Christ taking place in your cell community. Your cell is the place where you meet Christ, enter into His life, become part of his presence, power and purpose, and are used as an instrument of His life on earth.[129] You can also use the hand illustration to evaluate a community cell.

CHRIST DOES IT!

Recently I was part of a commissioning service for twenty-two cell leaders. The Lord gave me the following word for them. "You are not the leader of your group!" "You cannot make your group work!" Then I explained: "Christ is the leader of your community group and you are His assistant." "You cannot do Christ's work! Only He can do His spiritual work." "The cell does not belong to you. It belongs to Christ and is His Body."

I went on to explain that the responsibility of the community group leader is to take the group to Christ, into His presence, to allow His power to move within the group, and to fulfill His purpose of community edification and friendship evangelism through the group.

These two statements, "Jesus is the leader of your cell" and "only Jesus can make your cell work" solve two leadership problems. It solves the overconfidence of some leaders who, in pride, believe they can make a community cell work by techniques, experience, and the force of personality. It also solves the equally dangerous

---

[129]. Detailed suggestions for understanding the mechanics of a cell church can be found in *The Second Reformation* and Ralph Neighbour's excellent books and materials. Also, Joel Comiskey teaches the nuts and bolts of small groups from many different angles in his books. However, in this chapter I intentionally focused on the dynamics of community cell life necessary to establish an expansion strategy.

problem of fear: a lack of confidence in being a cell leader. If the leader is responsible for providing the wisdom and power for a cell to function, a normal leader will approach the cell with fear.

Consequently, cell leadership becomes a burden of responsibility and a yoke of performance. This is why we must place our cell into Christ's hands. He encourages us: "Come to Me, all who are weary and burdened, and I will give you rest. Take My yoke upon you and learn from Me, for I am gentle and humble in heart, and you will find rest for your souls" (Matt. 11:28-29).

It helps me when I lead a cell to "see" Christ in the cell and to say to Him: "This is your cell. I place it in your hands."

EVALUATE A GROUP WITH SEVEN CELL ELEMENTS	
CHRIST	Christ is the center of prayer, worship, the Word, and edification in the group.
COMMUNITY	Members love, edify and enjoy fellowship and life with each other.
EQUIPPING	Members are intentionally and systematically nurtured for ministry.
ACCOUNTABILITY	Members are mutually accountable and live out the "one another's."
LEADERSHIP	The group has a core of servant leaders and is developing new leaders.
EVANGELISM	Growth is through the Triads and reaching the oikos of the person of peace.
DEATH	Members in the group have died to personal and group agendas.

Chapter 11

PROTOTYPE SUPERVISION

"Mission is finally God's way of being God---faithful to an eternal design, bound to suffering, turning contingencies into opportunities, granting forgiveness and healing, and pouring out the Spirit. As a community of witnesses sent to the ends of the earth, this is what being church is all about."

• Paul Varo Martinson

The first large group expression of the church in the Gospels is the mid-level supervision cluster of seventy.[130] Jesus' meetings with His seventy followers preceded the upper room meeting during Pentecost. (Jesus' meetings with the large crowds in open air venues and at the Temple are evangelism events, not a designated group of the church.)

An expansion prototype begins with a catalytic leader who holds in his/her heart the seed vision of an expansion church. The leader sets that vision into motion, defines and refines it, and works out the details while developing a mid-level supervising cluster. This leader is the pastor in the case of an existing church (no matter the size of the church) or a catalytic leader in the case of a new start. The prototype is completed with the first cluster because once one cluster is functioning the prototype is complete. Simply reproduce it.

---

130. William A. Beckham, "The Tactical Dimension of Seventy," in *The Second Reformation: Stage 2* (Moreno Valley, CA: CCS Publishing, 2014), 266.

A congregation is not the focus of an expansion prototype because the congregation is the by-product of two or three working clusters. In fact, pastors and catalytic leaders must intentionally ignore the picture of the existing traditional large group paradigm while developing the cluster prototype. Only in this way can leaders escape the excess baggage that accompanies the traditional congregation: buildings, programs, Sunday service, and professional leaders.

My observation and experience tells me maintenance growth takes place on Sunday in large group ministries and programs while expansion multiplication takes pace during the week in relationship groups of three, twelve, and seventy. Therefore, the secret of an expansion church is to supervise expansion through the mid-level group of seventy. If a church (large or small) faithfully lives in friendship units of two or three, community groups of twelve, and supervising clusters of seventy, the church can continue to grow internally and expand externally.

1. Set the Mission into Motion

More than any other group the cluster of seventy is directly connected to Jesus' mission. Mission was foremost in His mind when Jesus called seventy of His followers together, trained them, deployed them, and debriefed them (Luke 10). His mission could not be completed by a religion practiced in a temple or synagogue (or church building for that matter) because it was a mission to the world. In the first century God's kingdom took a spatial and geographical dimension. "Rather than sinking roots in Jerusalem and waiting for the world to flood in, Jesus' followers are to move out from Jerusalem, through Judea and Samaria and ultimately 'to the ends of the earth' (1:8). The flow is centrifugal instead of centripetal; the apostles are just beginning their journey, not ending it."[131]

---
131. F. Scott Spencer, *Journeying through Acts: A Literary-cultural Reading* (Peabody, MA: Hendrickson Publishers, 2004), 36.

God's worldwide mission requires mission leadership and a mission structure. Therefore, Jesus appointed the seventy to be the supervising leadership group for the expansion mission of the church. Otherwise, why is the appointing of the seventy and the detailed instructions in Luke 10 included in the New Testament immediately after the setting aside of the twelve? Jesus not only gave a mission but gave a simple mission structure for implementing the mission. Jesus' expansion strategy allows a church of any size to continue to be part of His mission. It does this by organizing around the small units of three and twelve that are supervised in the mid-level cluster of seventy.

The mission God gave to Abraham and his descendants was to bless all nations (Gen. 18:18) and to declare His glory among the nations (Ps. 96:3). This mission spans all generations, extends to every geographical location "to the ends of the earth", and includes "every nation, tribe and people" (Rev. 7:9). In Matthew 24:14 Jesus confirmed the mission with a message and simple method. "And this gospel of the kingdom will be preached in the whole world as a testimony to all nations, and then the end will come." The mission is to preach to "the whole world" and "to all nations." The message is the "gospel of the kingdom." The method is "to preach the gospel ... as a testimony."[132]

The mission is open-ended with a worldwide scope stretching across centuries, thousands of miles, several worldwide political empires, many cultures, and all of the inhabitable continents. The very nature of the mission means that it cannot be completed in one generation, in one geographical area, or in one culture. The cluster of seventy is the centerpiece of Jesus' mission strategy for every generation.

---

132. George Eldon Ladd, *The Gospel of the Kingdom* (Grand Rapids, MI: Wm. B. Eerdmans, 1959), 130.

> *God's story in the New Testament has the "rhythm of mission through all of time. Witness passes on to witnesses, and passes on yet again in witnesses. Jesus' absence became the occasion to draw the Christian community into full participation in God's mission.*[133] *Mission is finally God's way of being God---faithful to an eternal design, bound to suffering, turning contingencies into opportunities, granting forgiveness and healing, and pouring out the Spirit. As a community of witnesses sent to the ends of the earth, this is what being church is all about.*[134]

The cluster (70) is the expansion unit that supervises and oversees the triads and cells that are the spearhead of the mission. Jesus' group of seventy is perfectly designed to supervise the triads and cells without hindering the unique expansion characteristics of Jesus' model. A number of these characteristics are included in other chapters. However, it will be helpful to gather the characteristics that operate within a cluster in one list.

1. *Mobility: A seventy cluster is mobile.*
2. *Organism: It operates naturally and organically.*
3. *Indigenous: The relational group system can be adapted to any culture. Since it is relational it is not "foreign."*
4. *Mobilization: It marshals and mobilizes its total membership. Everyone is deployed in the battle.*
5. *Maximum contacts: It maximizes personal contact with persons of peace and the oikos of family and friends.*
6. *Deployment: It is a "go structure" and not a "come structure."*

---

133. Paul Varo Martinson, "The Ending Is Prelude: Discontinuities Lead to Continuities," in *Mission in Acts: Ancient Narratives in Contemporary Context*, ed. Robert I. Gallagher and Paul Hertig (Maryknoll, NY: Orbis Books, 2004), 320.
134. Ibid., 322.

7. *On-the-job:* Simply by doing it, leaders emerge out of on-the-job experience.
8. *Simplicity:* It has few working parts and the parts it has work simply.
9. *Unencumbered:* It reduces hindering obstacles such as buildings, programs, and professional leaders.
10. *Health:* It promotes "wellness" for new, immature, and hurting believers through edification.
11. *Contagious:* it spreads like an epidemic through friendship triads.
12. *Self-supervision:* It is able to supervise itself through leaders developed within the system.
13. *Dynamic:* It releases the synergism of an interrelated group system of 3/12/70.
14. *Balance:* It prepares to go and returns to debrief.

2. BUILD A LEADERSHIP SYSTEM FOR SUPERVISING EXPANSION

The cluster of seventy is Jesus' interpersonal group (3/12/70) leadership system through which the expansion mission can be organized and supervised. The seventy simplifies, clarifies, maximizes, and multiplies leadership. The traditional church leadership system is complex, organizational instead of relational, and is designed for internal growth instead of external expansion. In addition, it narrows the leadership pool by requiring professionals with degrees and ordination. It asks the wrong question about leadership: who can lead (women?) rather than how can everyone lead someone?

Jesus modeled this leadership strategy with His disciples. Robert Coleman believes "the time which Jesus invested in these few disciples was so much more by comparison to that given to others that it can only be regarded as a deliberate strategy."[135] The life and the systems

---
135. Coleman, 43.

of the church emerge out of the leadership strategy we see in Jesus' three-year ministry. The cluster leader supervises the community cell leader and encourages expansion through the friendship triads.

In his classic book, *The Master Plan of Evangelism*, Robert Coleman challenges pastors to focus ministry on a few men. "One must decide where he wants his ministry to count … in the momentary applause of popular recognition or in the reproduction of his life in a few chosen men who will carry on his work after he has gone."[136]

The chart, *Jesus' Eight Guiding Principles of Leadership*, lists Coleman's eight principles along with a descriptive statement and a key scripture for each leadership principle that guided Jesus in His leadership strategy.[137] Jesus modeled these principles in His expansion group system of 3/12/70. These guiding principles of leadership are not learned or implemented from the pulpit in a building but are connected to the mission and expansion of the church out in the world.

> **JESUS' EIGHT GUIDING PRINCIPLES OF LEADERSHIP**
>
> **SELECTION:** Men were His method.
> *"He chose from them twelve" (Luke 6:13).*
>
> **ASSOCIATION:** He stayed with them.
> *"Lo, I am with you always" (Matt. 28:20).*
>
> **CONCECRATION:** He required obedience.
> *"Take my yoke upon you" (Matt. 11:29).*
>
> **IMPARTATION:** He gave Himself away.
> *"Receive ye the Holy Spirit" (John 20:22).*
>
> **DEMONSTRATION:** He showed them how to live.
> *"I have given you an example (John 13:15).*
>
> **DELEGATION:** He assigned them work.
> *"I will make you fishers of men (Matt. 4:19).*
>
> **SUPERVISION:** He kept check on them.
> *"Do ye not yet perceive? (Mark 8:17).*
>
> **REPRODUCTION:** He expected them to reproduce.
> *"Go and bring forth fruit" (John 15:16).*
>
> Robert Coleman

One cannot think of the mid-level seventy as a meeting. It is a mission task team that gathers to plan, train, deploy, debrief. When trying to get your mind around a seventy cluster, think

---

136. Ibid., 37.
137. Ibid., 7.

CHAPTER 11: PROTOTYPE SUPERVISION   229

of a retreat setting instead of Sunday worship and teaching in a building. In fact, a cluster is more like what happens with a Seal Team than what we experience in a worship service. A cluster is able to supervise and coordinate, to be mobile, and to focus on evangelism and discipleship expansion. In addition, the seventy does not require a building or program organization.

The pastor/catalytic leader oversees the startup and models the role of a cluster supervisor. He puts into place the activities and relationships necessary for a functioning cluster, supervises three to six cell leaders who oversee the disciple triads, and meets periodically with all cells in order to cast the vision, plan, train, deploy, debrief, encourage, give perspective, and supervise growth.

An initial cluster begins with two or three cells and grows to five to seven cells. The cluster leader mentors leaders within the experiences built into the system. This is the reason Paul was able to leave little struggling groups he had mentored, confident that they could carry on the work of the church in their geographic locality. They had the simple system of groups and he taught them to rely on the Holy Spirit. The Spirit became their mentor, teaching them to abide in the presence, power, and purpose of Christ. Mentoring has the quality of friendship that is lived out in the friendship triads.

3. DEVELOP AN EXPANSION STRUCTURE

The question is, "Can the modern church live out the principles, purposes, and qualities of

TRADITIONAL ATTRACTION MODEL			
MINISTRIES & ACTIVITIES IN A BUILDING			
PREACHING	TEACHING	HELPING	EVENTS
SMALL GROUPS			
Fellowship Group	Bible Study Group	Discipleship Group	Evangelism Group

(G R O W T H on both sides)

the New Testament Church without using the design of the New Testament Church?" I say "No!" The traditional model is built upon ministries and meetings and is designed to attract people to a centralized place and service. We keep changing the attraction factor to appeal to the audience. The attraction may be preaching, teaching, music, events, or ceremonies. The attraction model will grow but will not expand. (Look at the chart, Traditional Attraction Model.) Even if a traditional church uses small groups, they are specialized ministry groups that are attached to the ministry and meetings system as one more program attraction for the centralized church.

Without the simple New Testament design of the church, the principles, purposes, and qualities observed in the New Testament and written about in thousands of books, will never be effectively experienced. Applying good church growth principles, purposes, and qualities to the same traditional design will result in basically the same results. Based on ministries and meetings, the traditional model, will continue to grow. However, it will not expand as a New Testament people movement, even with the addition of small groups. Jesus used a relationship model, not an attraction model!

To fulfill Jesus' expansion mission, leaders must use His first century relationship paradigm of church, and that means using His groups of 3/12/70. (Look at the chart, Expansion Cluster of Seventy.) Through these groups functioning as the organic Body of Christ, God can fulfill His mission of producing a pandemic people movement like we see in the New Testament.

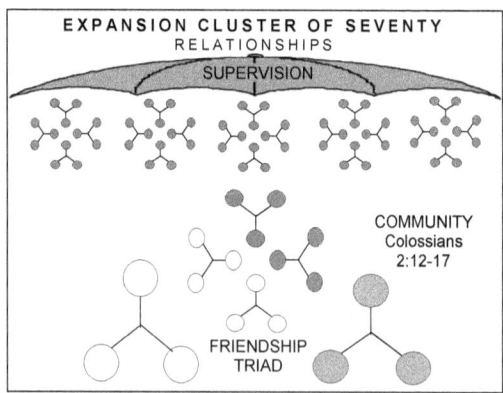

Jesus' expansion cluster is a flexible, low-maintenance, and high-growth model that allows the church to operate with community flexibility and freedom. However, it gives enough structure for training and ministry to take place. Expansion is possible because the cluster and its parts (triads and cells) are more engaged in contacting the lost than in worship and teaching. It is a building-less and program-less model. Think about the dynamics of a retreat.

The seventy gives house churches a functional and organic large group through which they can organize and supervise expansion. In addition, the seventy doesn't necessarily do away with the teaching, preaching, and program large group but gives another option that can focus on expansion. The rule of thumb is never start high maintenance public worship until a strong foundation of cells and clusters is already living out the expansion vision and values of the New Testament church.

4. BALANCE THE LARGE & SMALL GROUPS

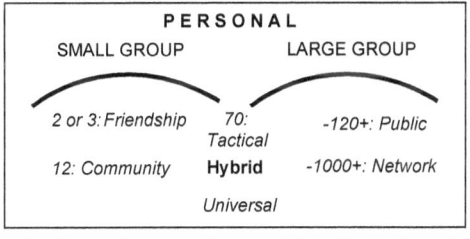

The mid-level supervising cluster of seventy is a hybrid of the small group and large group. Hybrid vigor is a scientific phenomenon that takes place in the animal and plant kingdoms. It is defined as "increased vigor or other superior qualities arising from the cross breeding of genetically different plants or animals." Its scientific name is *heterosis*.

My favorite example of hybrid vigor is the North American bison (buffalo) and bovine (cattle) cross that produces the "cattalo" (male bison and bovine female) or "beefalo" (domesticated bovine bull crossed with a female bison or a female cattalo). The hybrid-cross produces leaner meat and is superior in adapting to climate change and diseases. However, the cattalo hybrids still had the rather unmanageable attitude of the buffalo.

The cluster of seventy offers the benefit of hybrid vigor because the best qualities of the small (mobility, simplicity, organism) and the best qualities of the large (supervision, coordination, tactics) are merged. It is a bridge between the small group community dimension of twelve and the large group-coordinating dimension of the one hundred and twenty (plus or minus). It is key to church growth and expansion and offers an alternative to the traditional large group that has dominated the church for seventeen hundred years.

The hybrid nature of the seventy makes it ideal to supervise the expansion mission. It is a platoon-type supervising unit. (It can be a beginning cluster of 30 (3 cells) or a mature cluster of 70 (5 cells). The cluster of seventy is able to meet underground or out in public. Its size approaches that of a small congregation but it operates without a building, centralized programs, or time-consuming organization. The supervising group is one of the most important and neglected dimensions of the church today.

Worship takes place with the individual as well as in all groups, including the friendship triad of two or three, the community cell of twelve, and the cluster of seventy. However, these expansion groups of the church do not expend time, energy, and treasure on high maintenance worship with professional musicians, bands, and singers. That is reserved for a public worship and preaching service. Worship and praise in the cluster expansion venues should be personal and spontaneous. Think about worship around a campfire, at a retreat, or in family worship. God will provide some who are gifted in praise, music, and instruments but the temptation to perform in choirs, bands, and worship teams should be reserved for large group public services.

5. TEST NECESSARY MATERIALS

The pastor/cluster supervisor is responsible for providing necessary materials and experiences during the development of the prototype cluster. Jesus and Paul's on-the-job training was experience-driven rather than material-driven. Materials and experiences must be tied together but the materials should supplement the experiences and not the other way around. This means the materials will be simple and functional. By the end of the prototype, the following experiences and materials should be in place.

1. Bible Reading Plan for Friendship Triads (Developed by the pastor or church planter)
    a. The focus of the Bible reading is application of the Word to life.
    b. Three questions to ask about each passage of Scripture:
        i. What does the scripture say in the context of this passage?
        ii. What does these verses personally say to me?
        iii. How will I apply these truths to my life?
    You can develop your own questions for your triads. I believe questions should be limited to three or four. The three I suggest cover the key elements of these types of questions. Neil Cole lists sample questions that several churches are currently using.[138]
2. Discussion Questions for a Community Cell
    a. The pastor's message can be used or some other theme.

---

138. Cole, *Cultivating a Life for God*, 125-131.

b. The questions should be mostly "why" and "how" questions that get to root needs and to edification. "What" (what happened) and "who" (who did what to whom) questions lead to long stories that consume time and cover up the root needs.
c. An initial set of questions should be developed from theological themes that imprint the vision and values of the community system. This startup package could be repeated each year in order to reinforce the theology, vision, and values of the community and relationship system. The dynamic spiritual themes are most important, such as:
   i. Christ's presence (Matt. 18:20)
   ii. Mary's Heart & Martha's Hands (Luke 10:38-42)
   iii. Christ's power (1 Cor. 14:25)
   iv. Expansion multiplication (Matt 28:18-20; John 1:41, 12:20-22: Andrew)
   v. Friendship (2 Cor. 5:17-21)
   vi. Listening prayer (Matt. 18:19)
   vii. Applying Scripture (instead of studying Scripture) (James 1:22)
   viii. Edification (1 Cor. 14:12)
   ix. Confession/transparency (Rom. 10:9; James 5:16)
   x. Jesus' community pattern of 3/12/70 (Luke 9 &10).
3. New Believer personal equipping materials
   a. These materials should be simple.
   b. The Cell Leader should oversee the equipping of new believers in the community cell. Equipping should not be the focus of the Friendship Triad because this can change its focus from evangelism and expansion. Look at Ralph Neighbour's discipleship materials.
4. The Order and Agenda of the Community Cell Meeting

a. Some use the 4 W's: Welcome, Worship, Word, and Witness/works.[139]
   b. All cell meetings should have three experiences:
      i. Presence: welcome Christ, worship, word (discussion)
      ii. Power: edify through listening prayer and practical prophecy ... speaking a word from God to a need. (1 Cor. 14:24-25)
      iii. Purpose
         a) Encourage the Friendship Triads.
         b) Follow up on the *oikos* of new people (persons of peace) in the Friendship Triads.
         c) Disciple new believers and immature Christians.
         d) Follow up on those discovered in cell net fishing events.
5. Leader Training Materials and Activities
   a. This is on-the-job training. Leaders are developed within the group system. A leader is successful in a smaller leadership role before moving to another role. For instance, a cell leader is first a successful participant in a Friendship Triad and a cluster leader of seventy is first a successful leader of a community cell.
      i. A cell leader intern will emerge out of a Friendship Triad.
      ii. A cluster supervisor will emerge from the leaders of community cells.
   b. Simple materials and activities (retreat) can be used to prepare cell leaders.
   c. Simple materials and activities (retreat) can be used to prepare supervisors.

---

139. Ralph W. Neighbour, Jr., *The Shepherd's Guidebook* (Houston, TX: Touch Publications, 1994), 169-177.

6. Provide a Strategy Process

The chart below, *Triad, Cell, and Cluster Prototype*, is a picture of the prototyping process that a pastor/supervisor must implement. It shows the basic five-point process of developing a prototype cluster. The cluster works because the friendship triads and the community cells work. In the chart, notice the triad chains, the community cells, and the supervising cluster. We will return to this chart and its process in the next section on strategy.

The first pattern triad and pattern community cell are the building blocks of the prototype cluster. In fact, when the friendship triads and community cells are working properly the cluster of seventy fulfills its purpose naturally. The cluster prototype is a leadership prototype that supervises expansion through the triad and cell. The cluster of seventy is the basic prototype and is a large group alternative to the traditional large group with a building and programs.

Overlay the five-point expansion process on top of the triad, cell, and cluster chart. Begin with a friendship triad and see what happens. There is a natural force in Jesus' interpersonal system that moves it from friendship triads, to community cells, and into a supervising cluster.

BASIC FIVE-POINT PROCESS
1. Begin prototype triads: a men's chain and a women's chain.
2. Form the first prototype cell out of triads (two full triads of four persons or three growing triads of three each).
3. Multiply the prototype cell by expanding the friendship triads and following up on "persons of peace" and *oikos* family & friends.
4. Form the first supervising prototype cluster out of two cells
5. Grow to a full cluster of six cells and then multiply into two

Chapter 11: Prototype Supervision

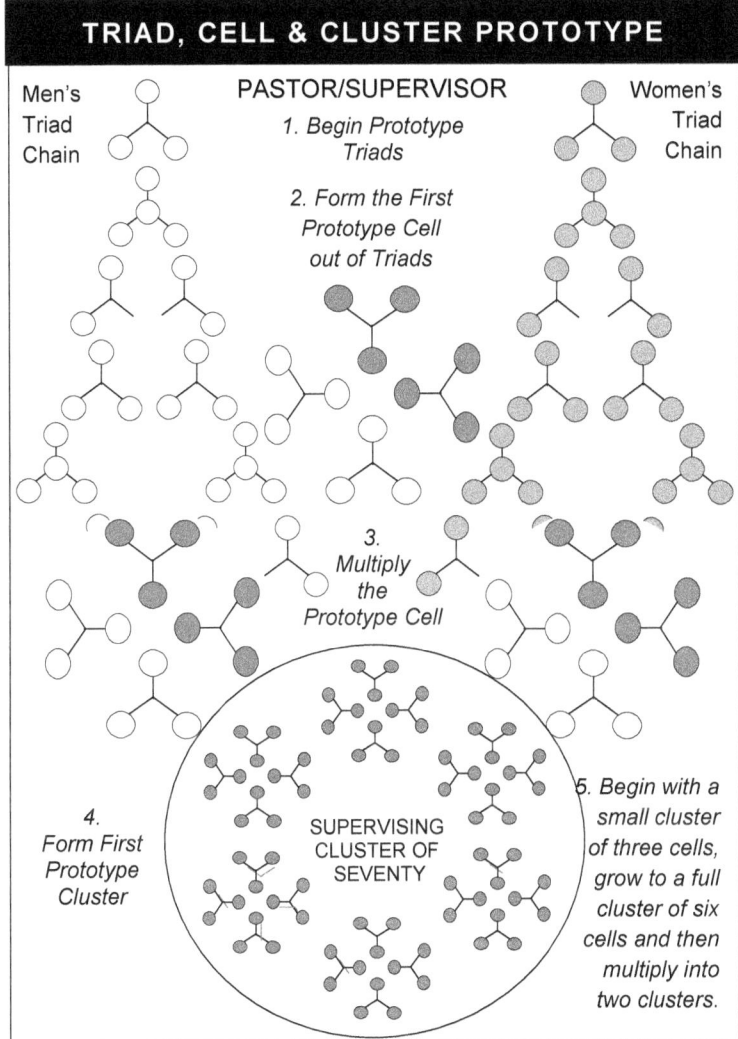

Pastor Influence

Pastors and church leaders fear loosing control of a small group movement. As long as the focus is Bible study, we can manage the theology and the response. But when we release our people to the Living Word, the Holy Spirit, things can begin to happen, especially with immature Christians. It is not easy for pastors/leaders to trust ordinary Christians when they are released to listen to the Spirit and participate in edification through practical prophecy.

This is one reason Martin Luther did not follow through with his intention to let the Reformation flow through ministry in the homes. He was afraid he would lose the movement to the "enthusiasts" who were the groups outside the structure of the Catholic Church. In fact, the "enthusiasts" used the small group structure that Luther was setting into place. These were the Baptists and Mennonite groups, and probably some groups operating with the gifts. In the end, Luther removed the small group ministry activities from his movement because of the fear of loosing control.

However, Jesus' three groups of 3/12/70 provide the opportunity for a pastor to influence members and leaders more than in the organizational system of the traditional church. The pastor has several spheres of influence where the vision God gives to him can be passed on to the church.

1. Sermons
2. Pastoral ministry
3. Assigning the scripture that will be read and applied in triads.
4. Developing the question to be applied in cells.
5. Input into the lives of all supervisors and cell leaders.

6. Choosing the materials and activities that will be used to disciple new believers.
7. Developing materials and activities for three training retreats that focus on experiencing the dynamic life of triads, cells, and the seventy.
   a. Friendship Retreat (triads: evangelism)
   b. Community Retreat (cell life: edification)
   c. Supervision Retreat (seventy: supervision/expansion)

Section III

Paradigm perspectives

Chapter 12: A Trip to the First Century

Chapter 13: The Danger of Paradigm Paralysis

Chapter 14: Jesus' Strategy Behind the Great Commission

Chapter 15: Movements Are Built on Governing Principles

Chapter 16: Jesus' Strategy Overview

Chapter 12

A TRIP TO THE FIRST CENTURY

"An organization derives power from the association of individuals, but a body derives its power from the sharing of life."
• Ray Stedman

Let me take you on a journey to the first century! You are transported back to Jerusalem and participate in the final events of Jesus' life. You witness His death and resurrection; are part of the group Jesus teaches for 40 days after His resurrection (Acts 1:3); are one of the 500 who witness the ascension of Jesus (1 Cor. 15:1-6) and hear Him say: "But you will receive power when the Holy Spirit comes on you; and you will be my witnesses in Jerusalem, and in all Judea and Samaria, and to the ends of the earth" (Acts 1:8). You are in the Upper Room and experience the return of Christ in the promised Spirit. You are one of the 5000 that hear Peter's sermon at Pentecost (Acts 2: 14-39). For two months you meet privately in the homes of Christians in Jerusalem and publically gather together with all the believers (Acts 2: 46).

After two months you leave Jerusalem and return home to Antioch. You are getting off your camel in front of your home. What do you do? Can you reproduce the church and fulfill the Great Commission that you heard about and experienced in Jerusalem?

There is another element in this scenario: All memory of the traditional church has been erased from your mind. You are starting with a clean slate concerning the church; you carry no historical baggage, good or bad. All you know about church is what you have experienced with Jesus and the people of the Way over a period of several months.

You have two models in your religious repertoire that you can use to begin Jesus' movement. One: You can begin a centralized temple complex with a ceremonial system led by professionals like Judaism. Or, two: You can operate with Jesus' organic system through the relationship units that He used: 3/12/70. Which option will reproduce the expansion movement we see in the first three centuries of the church?

Logic suggests you will do what Jesus taught you during your forty-day training session, and what the leaders shared during the following weeks. You learned and experienced His organic, relational, and mobile strategy. Jesus knew it would be natural for those who had experienced it to share it; and through relationship that it would expand.

Now back at home, you meet with family and friends in groups of two or three, have community together in your home and the homes of new believers, and supervise and organize the units like Jesus did with His cluster of seventy. You meet publically in various venues and introduce this new Way to the general populace. Friendship groups of two or three and community cells begin to spring up all over Antioch. You hear from travelers that the same thing is happening throughout the Mediterranean world. As you begin to get resistance against the public gatherings, the movement shifts and focuses more on the smaller and more personal venues. Jesus' pandemic people movement has begun.

Transported to the Fourth Century

Our problem is that our time-travel clock miscalculated and our transporter stopped three centuries off the plan. The search for church was hijacked in Rome in the fourth century and Jesus' model has been seriously compromised by the grandeur of Constantine's centralized organization of the church.[140]

Two parallel paradigms (a framework of concepts) are at work in church history. Look at the contrast in the chart, *Two Church Paradigms*. Constantine's paradigm of the church is characterized by a public meeting, preaching, programs, a large group, professional leaders, education, walls and buildings, ceremonies, organization, noun leaders (ranked by positions and titles), a come structure, and produces only internal growth. Jesus' paradigm of the church is characterized by private gatherings,

TWO CHURCH PARADIGMS	
JESUS	CONSTANTINE
1st Century	4th Century
Private Gathering	Public Meeting
Witness	Preach
Task	Programs
3/12/70	One Large Group
Lay Persons	Professionals
Relationships	Education
Without Walls	Walls/Buildings
Ordinary Leader	Extraordinary Leader
Community	Ceremonies
Organism	Organization
Verb Leaders	Noun Leaders
Go	Come
Expansion	Growth
Mobile	Static
Political Persecution	Political Patronage
Forward Base	Headquarters
Prepare Ministers	Provide Ministries
Movements	Revivals

---

140. William A. Beckham, *The Second Reformation: Stage 2* (Moreno Valley, CA: CCS Publishing, 2014), 45-78. I explain the relationship of Constantine's church and today's traditional model in chapter 3, "Before and After Constantine" and chapter 4, "Constantine in the Modern World."

witness, task, groups of 3/12/70, lay persons, relationships, no walls, community, organism, verb leaders (doing), and a go structure, that produces external expansion.

These paradigms are vastly different because "an organization derives power from the association of individuals, but a body derives its power from the sharing of life."[141] Which option is best for carrying out Jesus' Great Commission? Constantine's model distorts the organic nature of the church, redefines the Great Commission to education, and reverses the direction of the church from going (expansion) to coming (growth).

Today we must duplicate Jesus' design that He used during His ministry and that the early Christians used in the first century expansion of the church. This means we aim for the right century and maximize Jesus' first-century model and minimize Constantine's fourth-century model. Transplanting Constantine's brick and mortar model reproduces more centralized organizational institutions instead of birthing Jesus' Body DNA that produces organic expansion.

The paradigm of church I am suggesting has not suddenly surfaced after seventeen hundred years. A strong case can be made that God has continued to work through a parallel large-group/small-group stream that flowed throughout history alongside the traditional model established by Constantine.[142] Jesus' paradigm operated in history underneath Constantine's paradigm. It was never lost, just overshadowed by the more visible and organizationally powerful public structure of Constantine.

---

141. Stedman, 26.
142. William A. Beckham, "The Church with Two Wings," in *Church without Walls: A Global Examination of Cell Church*, Michael Green editor (UK: Paternoster Press, 2002), 33.

Most pastors and church leaders would agree that the Church is the focus of Jesus' Kingdom mission. Our problem is the definition and nature of that Church. Are we talking about Constantine's centralized organization from the fourth century or Jesus' organic expansion model of the first century?

JESUS' CHURCH PARADIGM WORKS

The scenario of returning to the first century forces us to look at the essentials of the church from the New Testament paradigm. This doesn't mean everything that was added to the church in history is wrong. But we need to assess our tendencies to focus on and invest in buildings, seminaries, denominations, mass media, and most church programs such as Sunday School, to just mention a few. This isn't about the props (they didn't have pianos) or inventions of history (they didn't have electricity or computers). This is about function. How has the church operated in its spiritual and organic nature to produce effective witness and expansion in every period of history?

Jesus designed the church to function in every cultural environment, in every period of history, in every social condition, and with every people group (*ethnos*). The scenario suggested above of returning to the first century forces us to contrast the church in its organic and relational body to the church as an organization in a building with professional leaders.

Why did Jesus' paradigm work? What did the New Testament Christians have that Christians of every age have (but that we may not be using)? They had and we have:

- *Christ's presence. Christ promised the Trinitarian presence in His discourses in John.*

- *Christ's prayer: Listening and intercession, from the heart and through the Spirit.*
- *Christ's power: Resurrection, revelation, and witness (Acts 1:8).*
- *Christ's purpose: Make disciples in Jerusalem, Judea, Samaria, and the world.*
- *Christ's principles: The teachings are preserved in the New Testament Canon.*
- *Christ's provisions: Salvation, sanctification, spiritual gifts, and edification.*
- *Christ's church pattern (form, structure, model): Jesus' relationship units of 3/12/70.*

The followers of Jesus "would receive power so that, between the Spirit's coming and the Son's coming again, they were to be his witnesses in every-widening circles. In fact, the whole interim period between Pentecost and the Parousia (however long or short) is to be filled with the world-wide mission of the church in the power of the Spirit."[143]

It is a mistake to assume that any paradigm will do. To determine the validity of this truth, apply reverse strategy. Take Constantine's paradigm and apply it to the first century. Would the church have expanded? Would it even have survived? Now, take the church strategy you are using and apply it to the New Testament. Would the church have expanded or survived? The people expansion paradigm of the Early Church was built upon the presence, prayer, power, purpose, principles, and the provisions of Christ, but the traditional church cannot exist without programs, professional preachers, paid pastors, and a public place (building).

---

143. John Stott, *The Spirit, the Church, and the World* (Downers Grove, IL: InterVarsity Press, 1990), 44.

We must apply Jesus' paradigm to the 21st century. The centralized church paradigm constrains leaders within historical boxes and drains them of the passion and creativity we see in the New Testament when leaders used Jesus' dynamic relationship system. It takes away the freedom and mobility of leaders to be the church around the world through relationship units. The traditional paradigm of church binds pastors and church leaders to an organizational system that makes it very difficult to live as the organic Body of Christ.

British theologian Michael Green recognizes that "when churches have been set in a maintenance mode for so long, it is hard for them to do an about turn and concentrate on mission." However, he believes "many of our churches now realize the weight of tradition that has been holding them down, and are willing at last to start making changes. There are lots of people in these churches who long for a fresh wind of the Holy Spirit to blow away dead leaves, strip them back to New Testament essentials, and to show them afresh the top priorities that Christians need to maintain. There is a hunger for renewal in the air."[144]

NEW THINKING

God is beginning to reveal His first century expansion paradigm to leaders in the 21st century. Visionary pastors are finding success as they unlearn the organizational paradigm. We know this because of the dissatisfaction expressed about the organizational church, even by successful pastors. Maybe you are one of these pastors who love and serve the church but know something is missing.

---

144. Michael Green, *Thirty Years that Changed the World: The Book of Acts for Today* (Grand Rapids, MI: Wm. B. Eerdmans, 2004), 9.

Jim Putman, pastor of Real Life Ministries, a church in Post Falls, Idaho, gave an enlightening interview with Outreach Magazine in 2013. (In 2011, his church was ranked number 52 on the list of the 100 largest churches in the United States.) The interview was about his new book, *Disciple Shift*, in which he suggests several shifts the church must undergo. His primary shift is to a discipleship paradigm.

Putman was asked why he believes the current model of the church isn't working and why the church needs to shift to "a disciple-driven church and plant churches with that DNA."

> *Because it's not Jesus' methodology! We've been handed a box historically, and we're just trying to live within that box, rather than ask if it was the right box to begin with. But the box doesn't make disciples. So we have to look for what's different about the way we're doing things and how Christ did things. A lot of these young guys planting churches know the old model doesn't work but they think, if I were in charge, then it would. And they're taking these new big words and the new fads, and it sounds good. At the beginning, it's kind of like Vegas. As you drive in, you see all the great-looking buildings and flashy lights. It's so inviting. But when you really go down that road, so to speak, you find only glitz, and you're left with empty pockets. It starts out well but doesn't end well ... So for me, it's about looking at the biblical design and model of the church we see in Acts. Live out that model, and you will see it actually works for all people in all cultures for all time.*[145]

---

145. Jim Putman, "A Better Way to Make Disciples," Outreach Magazine, September 5, 2013; http://www.outreachmagazine.com/features/4838-jim-putman-needed-shifts-in-making-disciples.html?

In the same interview, Putman was also asked: "What about the way we're doing things isn't the way Jesus intended the church to be?"

> When Jesus told His disciples, "Go and make disciples," He didn't mean for them to do it any way they wanted. He had just made disciples, and He said, "What I've done with you, now you go do the same." And they did that! And it worked! Because Jesus' ways met the needs of real people! In Acts 2, you see that the people lived in relationship, and in that relationship, they're devoted to the apostles' teaching, to breaking bread and fellowship, to caring for the hurting, even being willing to sell what they have and give it away. Jesus taught them to do all of these things ... Many leaders want to rally their people to a great cause, but they often don't teach their people to do this in real relationship. So they burn out quickly. My point is that we focus on one aspect of the design for the church and then the pendulum swings all the way over, and now we're missing something else! God's church is organic, attractional and missional, and organized. All of this is tied together in relationship because love is to be what we are known for. It's not only one of those things; it's all of them.[146]

In his definitive book, *Evangelism in the Early Church*, Michael Green states that the modern cell church model offers hope:

> For providing one of the best ways of being church in a world where religion is a leisure option, and the gospel needs to be presented in a way that attract people's attention and meets their needs. And in an age when they have no desire to belong to an institution, but are deeply committed to a small circle of friends, the cell has a great deal to offer. It is my conviction that in the next 50 years the West will discover cells as a

---
146. Ibid.

powerful tool for evangelism, nurture and leadership training. This, under God, may well mean a renewal of the Christian faith in the West. That is my prayer.[147]

IDENTIFYING THE PROBLEM

We must identify the church's problem and the solution. Leaders today recognize the church is not doing the basic task Jesus assigned: Go and make disciples. That is the problem. Some pastors and church leaders have correctly concluded, along with Jim Putman, that the centralized and organizational paradigm of the church cannot solve the problem of the church "because it's not Jesus' methodology" and "the box doesn't make disciples. So we have to look for what's different about the way we're doing things and how Christ did things."[148]

I agree that discipleship is a central function of the church, but it is an objective, not a strategy. Therefore, there is one more step beyond identifying the problem (in this case the inability to make disciples) and identifying what won't work (the traditional model). We must identify the solution. Making disciples is not the solution but the goal. Jesus' solution is His relationship and small group architecture of 3/12/70 that is His spiritual Body on earth. That is the way He organized and supervised His church, the way the Early Church expanded, and His strategy for the church today.

The church has become a complex organization through years of history. Therefore, pastors and church leaders must unlearn seventeen hundred years of wrong strategy and methodology. The challenge for traditional churches is to "practice the latter without leaving the former undone" (Luke 11:43). You may

---

147. Michael Green, *Church without Walls* (UK: Paternoster Press, 200), xii-xiii.
148. Ibid., Jim Putman, "A Better Way to Make Disciples."

do the "latter", Constantine's traditional centralized church, but don't leave the "former" undone, Jesus' first century decentralized and organic model.

It has taken God six decades to restore small groups back into the church: from 1950, when the church in China was forced into house churches because of persecution, until today. Now the church must do three things: (1) Add a mid-sized large group expansion system of seventy to the small group system, (2) make Christ the focus of existing small groups, and (3) establish friendship triads of two or three as the front line of expansion evangelism.

Pastors of all modern church models (traditional, creative, cell, and house church) can and must build an expansion prototype that will allow them to participate in God's pandemic people movement in the 21st century. The simple strategy solution of returning to Jesus' organic relationship system of 3/12/70 that I propose in this book will help restore the methodology for fulfilling Jesus' Great Commission to "go and make disciples."

Chapter 13

THE DANGER OF PARADIGM PARALYSIS

"The maxim 'Nothing but perfection' may be spelled 'Paralysis.'"
• Winston Churchill

Many pastors are disillusioned and disappointed with the old church model and readily admit it has significant problems and certainly is not 100% effective. However, even though the traditional church paradigm may not always work, it is all that traditional pastors and leaders know. Escaping old paradigms is extremely difficult because human nature demands that a new paradigm be perfect before a leader will abandon old safe paradigms. "The devil we know is better than the devil we don't know."

The expectation of a perfect new model causes paralysis of analysis where leaders over-think their church situation and the proposed change. Winston Churchill identified perfectionism as a key component in the paralysis of thinking. "The maxim 'Nothing but perfection' may be spelled 'Paralysis.'" Fear is the other major factor in the paralysis of analysis. We are petrified of getting caught outside of our safe paradigm box, exposed and vulnerable.

Peggy Noonan, former speechwriter for President Reagan, went through a time in her life when she experienced what is called in the corporate world "the paralysis of analysis" and what she calls "over-thinking." Noonan explains that "over-thinking is a TNT drama that occurs on a stage, inside your head, where you are the director, producer, actor, actress, supporting cast, key grip, sound manager, and executive assistant to the executive assistant of the casting director."

The drama playing inside the heads of 21st century pastors is the traditional church. It plays mind-games with us and paralyzes our ability to think outside that drama. A 19th Century poem explains the paralysis of analysis.

> *The centipede was happy quite,*
> *Until the Toad in fun said,*
> *'Pray, which leg goes after which?'*
> *Which worked her mind to such a pitch,*
> *She lay distracted in a ditch,*
> *Considering how to run.*

Noonan explains that the way out of this paralyzing mental state is to choose to get out of the past and move into the "here and now." "It doesn't cost you anything to end your relationship with the drama inside your head. You can decide to focus on things in the present that are deserving of your time and attention whenever you choose. The here and now is calling... will you answer?"[149]

I believe Noonan left out one step that is necessary to escape "over-thinking" or the "paralysis of analysis." In normal life some kind of "aha" moment (expression of discovery or realization) shocks us out of our suspended state so we are able to choose to live in the "here and now." Christians call that "aha" experience "revelation," "illumination," or "inspiration."

---

149. Peggy Noonan, "10 Ways over-Thinking Destroys Your Happiness," Huffpost, Healthy Living, The BLOG: Posted 08/26/2013,5:12EDT.

The Work of the Holy Spirit

I am not using the terms "revelation," "illumination," and "inspiration" in a narrow theological sense as they are used to refer to Scripture. The Bible is a special revelation from God that He illuminated to chosen men who were inspired by God to write the revelation down as they received it.

I am using these words in a practical (but extremely important) sense of how God continues to speak into the lives of Christians through the Holy Spirit. This continuing revelation of the Holy Spirit will not contradict Scripture or add anything new. However, without this active revelation through the Holy Spirit, we are religious people confined to ancient words in the Bible. The Bible is the Living Word precisely because of the work of the Holy Spirit as the Agent and Administrator of continuing revelation. This was the focus of Paul's Trinitarian prayer in Ephesians 1:17-23.

> *I keep asking that the God of our Lord Jesus Christ, the glorious Father, may give you the Spirit of wisdom and revelation, so that you may know him better. I pray also that the eyes of your heart may be enlightened in order that you may know the hope to which he has called you, the riches of his glorious inheritance in the saints, and his incomparably great power for us who believe. That power is like the working of his mighty strength, which he exerted in Christ when he raised him from the dead and seated him at his right hand in the heavenly realms, far above all rule and authority, power and dominion, and every title that can be given, not only in the present age but also in the one to come. And God placed all things under his feet and appointed him to be head over everything for the church, which is his body, the fullness of him who fills everything in every way.*

I personally experience what Paul prayed for every Christian in Ephesians 1. I receive "the Spirit of wisdom and revelation to know Him better." The "eyes of my heart" are "enlightened" so I know "the hope to which he called me" and "the riches of his glorious inheritance in the saints." I see and experience his "incomparably" great resurrection power and His heavenly dominion that is wrapped up in Christ who is "head over everything for the church, which is his body." In my personal experience, this is not a one-time moment, but an on-going and deepening revelation. I believe this is the common experience of all of us who have chosen to love and pursue God and to give ourselves to the work of His Kingdom and church.

So we recognize that Paul's prayer is God's promise to every Christian. God the Father through the Holy Spirit will continue to reveal the meaning of the church to Christians, will continue to give illumination about what the revelation means, and will continue to inspire us as the Body of Christ on earth, even as our Head, Christ, sits on His throne in Heaven. The Christian participates in revelation through Scripture, prayer, and the Spirit.

> *The Scripture is no bearer of religious mana. Its holiness and power is not something which rubs off mechanically, but is imparted only through the ministry of the Holy Spirit. This instrumental character of Scripture is suggested by Ephesians 6:17 and Hebrews 4:12, both of which liken the word of God to a sword. The Ephesians passage, in particular, portrays Scripture as the instrument (sword) of the Holy Spirit. The power of the word of God is manifested only as the Holy Spirit pleases to manifest it under certain conditions ... The primary spiritual condition for the manifestation of the word of God is prayer. The apostles gave themselves to the word of God and prayer (Acts 6:4). The good gifts of God in creation are sanctified by the word of God and prayer (1 Tim. 4:5). The*

> *word of God will find an open door only as the saints pray (Col. 4:3) and the word of God will speed on and triumph only as this is the prayer of the Church (2 Thess. 3:1).*[150]

The Holy Spirit teaches us the words and ways of revelation primarily through prayer (Rom. 8:26). As we pray and listen, the Holy Spirit gives us revelation and wisdom about His nature and the nature of His church on earth, and in heaven. The church and individual Christians are edified within community as the Holy Spirit speaks words of revelation (practical prophecy) through prayer to a specific need through a human instrument of His choice. The specific word of edification, through practical prophecy, never contradicts the spirit and meaning of Scripture.

Personal and community revelation, illumination, and inspiration didn't stop with the closure of the Canon. Through prayer and the Word, the elements of revelation, illumination, and inspiration continue in the work of the Holy Spirit to individual Christians and to the Church. This continuing revelation is required for the church to be the spiritual and organic Body of Christ.

The Spirit continues to make God's revelation known to the Christian and the Church. "The Spirit is the agent of the extension and continuation of revelation" and is "promised as the Paraclete who is to abide for ever (John 14:16); thus ensuring that revelation shall be continued in perpetuity."[151] Paul explains the continuing revelation work of the Holy Spirit in 1 Corinthians 2:6-16:

> *We do, however, speak a message of wisdom among the mature, but not the wisdom of this age or of the rulers of this age, who are coming to nothing. No, we speak of God's secret wisdom,*

---

150. Bernard Ramm, 121.
151. Alan Richardson, s.v. "Revelation," *A Theological Word Book of the Bible* (New York: The Macmillan Company, 1960), 199.

> *a wisdom that has been hidden and that God destined for our glory before time began. None of the rulers of this age understood it, for if they had, they would not have crucified the Lord of glory. However, as it is written: "No eye has seen, no ear has heard, no mind has conceived what God has prepared for those who love him" – but God has revealed it to us by his Spirit.*
>
> *The Spirit searches all things, even the deep things of God. For who among men knows the thoughts of a man except the man's spirit within him? In the same way no one knows the thoughts of God except the Spirit of God. We have not received the spirit of the world but the Spirit who is from God, that we may understand what God has freely given us. This is what we speak, not in words taught us by human wisdom but in words taught by the Spirit, expressing spiritual truths in spiritual words. The man without the Spirit does not accept the things that come from the Spirit of God, for they are foolishness to him, and he cannot understand them, because they are spiritually discerned. The spiritual man makes judgments about all things, but he himself is not subject to any man's judgment: "For who has known the mind of the Lord that he may instruct him?" But we have the mind of Christ.*

Paul is clearly describing the Christian's experience of continuing revelation: "We have ... the Spirit who is from God, that we may *understand* what God has freely given us. This is what we speak, not in words taught us by human wisdom but in words *taught by the Spirit*, expressing spiritual truths in spiritual words" because "we have the mind of Christ."

This is not the same as the revelation of Scripture but it is revelation illumination to the spiritual Body of Christ. In combination with scriptural revelation, body revelation illumination makes the Bible the living Word of God and Christians become the spiritual Body of Christ.

REVELATION REQUIRED

Constantine's organizational paradigm of the church is so prominent and powerful that pastors and church leaders are often caught in a state of "over-thinking" and "paralysis of analysis" when trying to think outside the box. Only a special word of revelation, inspiration, and illumination from God through the Holy Spirit will cause a pastor to replace Constantine's paradigm, even with Jesus' original paradigm. Consequently, what God wants and needs to do in the 21st century will not come from the head through learning but only from the "Spirit and Wisdom" of revelation.

The purpose of this book and the one that preceded it (*The Second Reformation: Stage 2*) is to share the information and concepts that God has used to reveal Christ's paradigm of the church to me and many other pastors. This radical paradigm shift requires revelation about the institutions that have boxed God's people into ceremonies, buildings, and hierarchical systems. The revelation is really about God who expressed Himself in the person of Christ when "the Word became flesh," continues to express Himself through the person of the Holy Spirit who is given to every Christian to teach him/her all things, and preserves His revelation for Mankind in the Bible.

Revelation is an "autobiography of God, i.e., it is the story which God narrates about himself. It is that knowledge about God which is from God. In the broadest sense revelation is the sum total of the ways in which God makes himself known ... Special revelation is God's word in a concrete form to a specific person or group ... General revelation is God's witness to himself for all men."[152]

I am not talking about blinding flashes, burning bushes, and thundering voices of revelation. I am talking about revelation as the "still small voice." This kind of revelation wisdom is God speaking personally to each Christian through prayer about His purposes and plans for life and for His Church.

> *The LORD said, "Go out and stand on the mountain in the presence of the LORD, for the LORD is about to pass by." Then a great and powerful wind tore the mountains apart and shattered the rocks before the LORD, but the LORD was not in the wind. After the wind there was an earthquake, but the LORD was not in the earthquake. After the earthquake came a fire, but the LORD was not in the fire. And after the fire came a gentle whisper. When Elijah heard it, he pulled his cloak over his face and went out and stood at the mouth of the cave. Then a voice said to him, "What are you doing here, Elijah?" (1 Kings 19:11-13).*

God speaks to every Christian willing to "stand with Elijah on the mountain in the presence of the LORD," to "watch" with Habakkuk "on the ramparts," and to "listen to what God will say" (Hab. 2:1-3). Early in His ministry, Peter confessed that Jesus was the Messiah. Jesus explained that God the Father had revealed this to Peter and that this revelation confession was about Christ and the Church: "Blessed are you, Simon son of Jonah, for this was not revealed to you by man, but by my Father in heaven. And I tell you that you are Peter, and on this rock I will build my church, and the gates of Hades will not overcome it" (Matt. 16:17-18). Living out Jesus' Great Commission

---

152. Ramm, 17.

Chapter 13: The Danger of Paradigm Paralysis

and simple strategy requires total focus on Christ and revelation from God.

Peter continued this revelation theme in the first sermon to the Church at Pentecost (Joel 2:28-32; Acts 2:17-21). He "stood up with the Eleven, raised his voice and addressed the crowd:"

> *Fellow Jews and all of you who live in Jerusalem, let me explain this to you; listen carefully to what I say. These men are not drunk, as you suppose. It's only nine in the morning! No, this is what was spoken by the prophet Joel: "In the last days, God says, I will pour out my Spirit on all people. Your sons and daughters will prophesy, your young men will see visions, your old men will dream dreams. Even on my servants, both men and women, I will pour out my Spirit in those days, and they will prophesy. I will show wonders in the heaven above and signs on the earth below, blood and fire and billows of smoke. The sun will be turned to darkness and the moon to blood before the coming of the great and glorious day of the Lord. And everyone who calls on the name of the Lord will be saved."*

Notice Peter carefully explains that these people are not drunk but are experiencing the revelation of the Spirit that is being "poured" out upon them as prophesied by Joel. The revelation of the Spirit is more important than the manifestations.

Saul of Tarsus (Paul) was paralyzed in his box of Judaism. He had religion but not revelation. As brilliant as he was, knowledge could not get him outside of the box of religious law. He heard one of the greatest sermons ever preached from Stephen and yet it had no impact on him. Evidently a ringleader, he held the coats of those who stoned Stephen to death. Still ravenous in his religious zeal, Saul was "breathing out murderous threats against the Lord's disciples" (Acts 9:2). He was on a mission to

Damascus to continue the assault on Christians when his life was changed by revelation. Jesus, the One crucified and the One Stephen preached about and died for, spoke to Paul. In that moment of revelation, Paul was forever changed. What knowledge, learning, and religion could not do, revelation did.

This is a day that cries out for revelation. Pastors and church leaders, we will not change from the traditional paradigm without revelation of Jesus' paradigm. This is more than revelation about the structure of the church. This is about the form of the Church, about the Church as Christ's Body. There is a substantial difference between analysis and revelation. The church will not escape paradigm paralysis by more analysis. Only revelation from God about the church can restore it as the organic Body of Christ.

"THOSE DAYS"

The prophet Joel prophesied about "those days" when God's Spirit would be poured out upon His people in a real and practical way. "Those days" are not restricted to the time of the Apostles, or to the first three centuries. "Those days" are God's continuing Holy History.

We are living in "those days" because Christ assured us that "the kingdom of God has come near" (Mark 1:15b). To borrow a phrase from Paul about life after death: If we must live as God's church without revelation outside of those days "we are of all men most to be pitied."

Today is the *kairos* (the supreme moment of opportunity and fulfillment) in contrast to *chronos* (time measured in duration with clocks). Jesus said: "The time (*kairos*) has come" (Mark 1:15a).

Revelation has a *kairos*, "appointed time", and though it requires patience to receive, it will "certainly come and will not delay" (Hab. 2:1-3). Surely God has something to say today to those of us who are pastors and church leaders in this critical period of history.

Listen with Elijah to the "gentle whisper." Watch with Habakkuk "on the ramparts" and wait for the revelation vision. Go beyond "flesh and blood" and receive God's revelation of Christ and the Church. Embrace Joel's "days" of revelation when "sons and daughters will prophecy," "young men will see visions," and "old men will dream dreams."

Until the revelation personally comes, you and I will not change from Constantine's organizational program paradigm of the church to Jesus' organic relationship paradigm. Because of the power of the old paradigm and our familiarity with it, we tend to over-think the situation and the solution when confronted with another paradigm, even Jesus' paradigm. We reason: "Surely the solution is more complicated, larger, and more impressive than friendship triads, community cells, and supervising units of seventy!"

Pastor, listen to God about the paradigm of the Church that Jesus modeled. This is the spiritual process we see in the Bible: God breaks through entrenched and hardened human thought with a word of revelation. You and I are not going to change paradigms unless and until we receive God's revelation. That revelation is often not experienced in the spectacular and sensational events but in His "gentle whisper."

Trapped "In-between" History

The church has accepted a sad and restricted view of church history: The church is living "in-between" in a perpetually suspended state of history in an organizational paradigm. At times the church is so detached from Jesus' mission that it seems to be living in an alternate universe to what we see in the New Testament. "In-between" is not a very rewarding or productive place to be and is certainly not where God intends the church to be.

The traditional church is caught in a crack in history between the New Testament church as the Body of Christ and church as the glorified Bride of Christ promised in Heaven. Paul explains the intent of Christ to prepare the church on earth for its heavenly nature. "To make her holy, cleansing her by the washing with water through the word, and to present her to himself as a radiant church, without stain or wrinkle or any other blemish, but holy and blameless" (Eph. 5:26-27).

The cleansing of the church is obviously taking place on earth in order for Christ to present the glorified church to himself in Heaven. On earth the church is in process: It has glory (radiance) that is not full and it is being cleansed of stains and wrinkles and other blemishes so it will be blameless. The church does not enjoy the full heavenly glory but is being made glorious through sanctification here on earth.

The church is not suspended in time between the presence and power of the church as Christ's Body on earth and the glory of the church in Heaven. The church is participating in the Body of Christ in history in His presence and power that we see in the Early Church and is being formed into the glorious church that will be totally realized in Heaven.

This is why Jesus promised: "I tell you the truth, anyone who has faith in me will do what I have been doing. He will do even greater things than these, because I am going to the Father" (John 14:12). Through the grace of God and the power of the resurrected Christ, the nature of the church as Christ's Body in the first century and the nature of the church as Christ's heavenly Bride is part of the nature of the church in history ... including our history.

THE CHURCH OF LAODICEA

The Church "in-between" God's holy history is the Church of Laodicea described in Revelation 3:15-22:

> *To the angel of the church in Laodicea write: These are the words of the Amen, the faithful and true witness, the ruler of God's creation. I know your deeds, that you are neither cold nor hot. I wish you were either one or the other! So, because you are lukewarm – neither hot nor cold – I am about to spit you out of my mouth. You say, 'I am rich; I have acquired wealth and do not need a thing.' But you do not realize that you are wretched, pitiful, poor, blind and naked. I counsel you to buy from me gold refined in the fire, so you can become rich; and white clothes to wear, so you can cover your shameful nakedness; and salve to put on your eyes, so you can see. Those whom I love I rebuke and discipline. So be earnest, and repent. Here I am! I stand at the door and knock. If anyone hears my voice and opens the door, I will come in and eat with him, and he with me. To him who overcomes, I will give the right to sit with me on my throne, just as I overcame and sat down with my Father on his throne. He who has an ear, let him hear what the Spirit says to the churches.*

The danger is the false self-image. The church at Laodicea

thought it was rich, wealthy, and self-sufficient. From its perspective it didn't "need a thing." This church was tepid and lukewarm. It had devolved into a religion of convenience, comfort, and compromise. Nothing good was said about this rich-poor church. It floated along in the neutral zone of history.

Jesus gives the solution for the church that is suspended between two worlds and is neither hot nor cold: "Buy from me gold refined in the fire." Pastors and church leaders, lets admit it: We are buying programs and strategies from everyone who will sell one. In fact, what I am "selling" you in this book is just one more man-made program or strategy that you can buy . . . unless God reveals that the concepts are His. What I am saying has no lasting meaning unless He "refines" it, reveals it to you, and you "buy" it.

The church in the 21st century has a Laodicea spirit that is tied to its Laodicea structure. It is hanging on in neutrality, neither hot nor cold, trying to survive between the power of the Early Church as the Body of Christ and the glory of the Church as the Bride of Christ in Heaven. It is trapped in an organizational body that is in-between the spiritual Body of Christ on earth and the glorified church as the Bride of Christ in Heaven.

We must be careful that we don't spend our spiritual wealth for an organizational system and religious programs. Don't believe the false advertising that brings you to the end of your ministry with buyer's remorse. Buy from Christ! His product is the only one "refined in the fire" that will accomplish His Kingdom purpose in every moment of history.

Chapter 14

JESUS' GREAT COMMISSION STRATEGY

"A central methodology is to plan the outpost of the kingdom of God, which are principally Christian Churches, in every nation or ethnos."
• C. Peter Wagner

On May 13th, 1940 in his first speech to the House of Commons after becoming Prime Minister, Winston Churchill set the tone for the dark days ahead during World War II.

> *I have nothing to offer but blood, toil, tears and sweat. We have before us an ordeal of the most grievous kind. We have before us many, many long months of struggle and suffering. You ask: What is our policy? I will say it is to wage war by sea, land and air, with all our might, with all the strength that God can give us, to wage war against a monstrous tyranny never surpassed in the dark and lamentable catalogue of human crime. That is our policy. You ask: What is our aim? I can answer in one word: victory.*

Churchill inspired England and the Free World for the journey ahead with His statement of intent, resolve, "policy," "aim," and challenge. However, he gives very little strategy, methodology, and context for the process. Four long years later Gen. Dwight D. Eisenhower, Commander of the Allied Forces, issued the following general order to encourage Allied soldiers taking part in the risky D-day invasion of Europe on June 6, 1944. Final victory came one year later.

> *Soldiers, Sailors and airmen of the Allied Expeditionary Force!*
>
> *You are about to embark upon the Great Crusade, toward which we have striven these many months. The eyes of the world are upon you. The hopes and prayers of liberty-loving people everywhere march with you in company with our brave Allies and brothers-in-arms on other Fronts. You will bring about the destruction of the German war machine, the elimination of Nazi tyranny over the oppressed peoples of Europe, and security for ourselves in a free world.*
>
> *Your task will not be an easy one. Your enemy is well trained, well equipped and battle-hardened. He will fight savagely. But this is the year 1944! Much has happened since the Nazi triumphs of 1940-41. The United Nations have inflicted upon the Germans great defeats, in open battle, man-to-man. Our air offensive has seriously reduced their strength in the air and their capacity to wage war on the ground. Our Home Fronts have give us an overwhelming superiority in weapons and munitions of war, and placed at our disposal great reserves of trained fighting men. The tide has turned! The free men of the world are marching together to Victory! I have full confidence in your courage, devotion to duty and skill in battle. We will accept nothing less than full Victory!*
>
> *Take comfort. Good Luck! And let us all beseech the blessing of Almighty God upon this great and noble undertaking.*

Eisenhower gave no more strategy in his general orders than Churchill gave in his earlier statement! These two historical statements, issued four years apart, help us understand that a mission statement is not the same as a strategy plan. Mission and vision statements, no matter how inspiring, are not enough to win wars. That requires a strategy with methods, tools, logistics, and tactics.

JESUS' GREAT COMMISSION

The Great Commission is a vision statement in which Jesus tells us what to do but not how to do it. It is a rallying cry for His movement; a call to finish what He started. Peter Wagner correctly believes the goal of the church as stated in the Great Commission "is to plant the outpost of the kingdom of God, which are principally Christian Churches, in every nation or ethnos."[153] The question left unanswered in the Great Commission is how to do that in the way He did it.

The Great Commission is recorded in five versions: Matthew 28:18-20; Mark 16:15-16; Luke 24:44-49; John 20:19-23, and Acts 1:6-8. In order to establish a biblical foundation for the strategy of the church, we will concentrate on the most familiar version in Matthew 28:18-20.

> *Then Jesus came to them and said, "All authority in heaven and on earth has been given to me. Therefore go and make disciples of all nations, baptizing them in the name of the Father and of the Son and of the Holy Spirit, and teaching them to obey everything I have commanded you. And surely I am with you always, to the very end of the age.*

Pastors and church leaders, we must rethink and reinterpret Jesus' Great Commission. As a general order, the Great Commission is a powerful statement about Jesus' mission for the church.

---
153. C. Peter Wagner, *The Book of Acts* (Ventura, CA: Regal, 1994), 53.

However, it is not an all-inclusive strategy statement. Therefore, the Commission can be frustrating because it cannot be completed with the components in the statement itself. It anticipates some of the elements of Jesus' strategy: The mission, making disciples, the witness, the call to the nations, the heart of the church of baptizing and teaching in the name of the Father, Son, and Spirit, and the power of the Spirit. However, key elements are left out of the Great Commission: Prayer is not mentioned, nor is worship, the Bible, leaders, edification, body life, accountability, and community. In addition, Jesus doesn't include the tools, workforce, leaders, tactics, or methods that He demonstrated during His 3 ½ year ministry.

The Great Commission has been referred to as the "great omission" because the traditional church doesn't do the commission. I don't believe this is a valid criticism because a great deal of energy and manpower of the traditional church has been given to missions in an attempt to fulfill the Great Commission.

Huge parachurch ministries and denominational resources and departments are devoted to the Great Commission. In addition, we have churches that operate under the banner of "Great Commission Churches" with Acts 2:42 as their defining mission. "They then that received his word were baptized: and there were added *unto them* in that day about three thousand souls. And they continued steadfastly in the apostles' teaching and fellowship, in the breaking of bread and the prayers." The responsibility for completing the Great Commission is a rallying cry for others: "And the gospel must first be preached to all nations (Mark 13:10)."

Praise God for the emphasis on faithfully living out the Great Commission, even when all the money and effort doesn't produce New Testament expansion. The point I am making is that

Chapter 14: Jesus' Great Commission Strategy

effort and money have not been lacking in fulfilling the Great Commission, but Jesus' strategy has been missing.

Jesus' Mindset

To implement the commission, it helps to go back to Jesus' mindset when He gave it. We should think of Jesus' mission statement in the context of a SEAL team and not a group of religious leaders or businessmen. Jesus is not sending His followers out to begin spiritual businesses, to run religious orders, or to maintain centralized organizations in special buildings. Jesus is sending His followers out on a military mission that will bring in the Kingdom. I can see them with their full spiritual battle gear on as they receive the mission objective. This is a mission of asymmetrical (guerilla) warfare. They will be mobile and able to live off the land and penetrate society. Jesus has already put them through boot camp and advanced training. They know how to do it. Paul captures the spirit of Jesus' commission in Ephesians 6: 10-18:

> *Put on the full armor of God so that you can take your stand against the devil's schemes. For our struggle is not against flesh and blood, but against the rulers, against the authorities, against the powers of this dark world and against the spiritual forces of evil in the heavenly realms. Therefore put on the full armor of God, so that when the day of evil comes, you may be able to stand your ground, and after you have done everything, to stand. Stand firm then, with the belt of truth buckled around your waist, with the breastplate of righteousness in place, and with your feet fitted with the readiness that comes from the gospel of peace. In addition to all this, take up the shield of faith, with which you can extinguish all the flaming arrows of the evil one. Take the helmet of salvation and the sword of the Spirit, which is the word of God. And pray in the*

> *Spirit on all occasions with all kinds of prayers and requests. With this in mind, be alert and always keep on praying for all the saints.*

In the Great Commission, Jesus gives a general description of His vision and lays the conceptual foundation for His strategy. "Going" gives us direction. "Make disciples" gives us the central focus. "Baptizing" brings the church community into the equation. "In the name of the Father, Son, and Spirit" gives the spiritual relationship. "Teaching them to observe all things Jesus commanded" gives a curriculum. "I am with you always, to the end of the age" shows relationship to Him during the process.

The strategies of the church too often focus on one or two of the elements in the Great Commission. However, no individual element or combination of them has successfully replicated the powerful expansion that was evidenced when the Early Church first implemented Jesus' strategy. There is not one of these elements in the Great Commission that tells how to do what is commissioned. Even if all the elements in the commission are put together they do not equal a strategy. All we have are some of the ingredients without the recipe!

An unclear strategy leads to the church "preserving itself well, content to maintain a rear-guard action, content to protect the status quo." However, "that's not what God has called the church to do. God wants the church to do more than merely hold its own. We're in a battle against the powers and principalities of this world. Aggressive action is needed."[154]

---

154. Jim Putman & Bobby Harrington, *Disciple Shift* (Grand Rapids: MI: Zondervan, 2013) 23.

JESUS IS THE CENTER OF HIS COMMISSION AND STRATEGY

The church as an organization cannot do Jesus' commission. Notice, Jesus placed Himself at the center of His commission. He is the content and the context of His strategy. The commission objective is all about Him: His authority; His nature as Father, Son, and Spirit; and His presence. Jesus begins the commission with His authority and Lordship, "All authority has been given to me," and gives His purpose to the work (make disciples of Christ). The commission proceeds with His nature of Trinity (baptize in the name/nature of the Father, Son, and Spirit). It ends in the *shekinah*: the promise of the never-ending presence of Christ. "I AM with you."

The concept of "all" is used four times in the commission and is a key focus in His strategy: "All authority," "all nations," "everything (all) Jesus commanded," and "always" (for all time). The commission has one primary verb: make disciples. In addition, "go" is a strong participle that carries the force of a command. So, Jesus is saying: "Go and make disciples, baptizing and teaching them to observe."

The followers of Christ saw the Great Commission as an opportunity to show their gratitude to Christ more than as a command to fulfill. "Mission, they saw, was grounded in the very nature of God who gave; it must be no less evident in those who claimed to have relation with such a God."[155]

Before formally giving the commission, Jesus had already trained His followers to do the commission. For more than three years, Jesus had been living out this great commission of the Father. Jesus used the unit of two or three. His inner circle was

---

155. Michael Green, *Evangelism in the Early Church* (Grand Rapids, MI: Eerdmans, 1970), 240.

three and He sent the disciples out two by two. Jesus utilized the group of twelve with His leadership group and then the Early Church continued this general number in the homes of Christians. Jesus trained, deployed, and debriefed the seventy in His mission task. God built His Trinitarian nature of presence, power, and purpose into His organic units of 3/12/70 so that God the Father, Son, and Spirit can lead the troops to complete the commission in every generation.

JESUS' SIMPLE STRATEGY

The Great Commission is not an isolated statement. It was given from the context of His great expansion model that would go and make disciples to all nations through His simple small group relationship strategy of 3/12/70. Jesus' Great Commission and His simple strategy go together. What kind of commander would Jesus be, if He came to the end of His ministry and gave a commission to His followers without also providing the strategy tools and training for doing it? Something went before the command---the model of how to do the command. The Great Commission had a context because Jesus had already trained the ones who heard the Great Commission.

In the Great Commission, Jesus gives the mission objective. However, before that the disciples went through Jesus' boot camp and several campaigns over a period of 3 ½ years. He had already trained them how to do the mission in His simple strategy of relationships and groups. We must use the Great Commission as a mission statement about Jesus' expansion strategy that produces a people pandemic.

The fact that Jesus modeled a simple implementing strategy does not diminish the importance of the Great Commission. To the contrary, it restores the Great Commission to the place Jesus gave it as a clarion call to implement the relationship strategy He had already set into motion, to use the tools He had already given, and to organize into mobile and inexpensive groups of 3/12/70. The only way the church can fulfill the Great Commission is to use His strategy and His tools that are part of the relationship units He demonstrated. His authority of Lordship, His Trinitarian nature, and His presence are lived out and experienced in His relationship units of 3/12/70.

The Great Commission is the last recorded personal instruction of Jesus to His followers. In order to expand, the church must not only be challenged by Jesus' Great Commission but must implement Jesus' simple strategy that produces a people movement. Jesus' 3/12/70 group units provide a strategy context where each element in His commission can be experienced.

SIX STRATEGY INTERPRETATIONS

In addition to Jesus' relationship strategy of 3/12/70, at least five other strategies have developed in history in an attempt to carry out Jesus' Great Commission. All can be explained as part of the Great Commission, but none is completed by itself. Elaborate strategies have been developed around one of the following Great Commission models: Authority/power, going/missions, disciples/discipleship, baptizing/church, and teaching/education.

(1) Some leaders focus on the authority and public power demonstrations of Jesus. This leads to a strategy of public power evangelism, preaching, and healing in crusades. Jesus prepared the crowds through His preaching and healing and Peter and the Apostles gathered the Early Church through this public power approach. However, in the first century the government began to shut down the public power demonstrations and the expansion

of the church took place as a people movement that spread through relationships rather than public power encounters.

(2) The word "go" has inspired the church to have a presence of some kind in the world. The church, denominations, and parachurch ministries have been sending ministering missionaries into the nations for centuries. Ministry presence demonstrates the love, care, and compassion of Christ and Christians. However, "going" is Jesus' direction, not His strategy. It just puts people in the place where His strategy can be activated.

(3) "Make disciples" is the central verb of the Great Commission. Therefore, discipleship has been the strategy of choice of many pastors and mission leaders. The promise is: If one Christian disciples another and that person disciples another, exponential multiplication takes place and we can win the world in a few years. However, what happened in the Early Church is more than a discipleship movement. The everyone-win-one ministries would have already fulfilled the Great Commission, if discipleship were Jesus' strategy. The assumption about exponential multiplication is true. However, Jesus' exponential multiplication used relationship groups to organize and supervise the one-on-one discipleship contacts as the organic Body of Christ.

(4) The Great Commission includes "baptizing" and that is the sign of entrance into the church. Planting public churches fulfills the institutional part of the commission to baptize. However, the issue is the kind of church that is being planted: Christ's organic church or Constantine's organizational church.

(5) "Teaching them to observe" has been a popular interpretation of the Great Commission. For years the church has tried to carry out the Great Commission through education in schools and in the traditional church.

(6) Then there is Jesus' expansion strategy that moves through the world through Jesus' simple strategy of relationships lived out in the group units of 3/12/70. In fact, Jesus' small group system activates every element in the Great Commission.

The church has tried to implement the Great Commission by focusing on one of the elements that Jesus includes in the Great Commission statement. Using the first five elements, the church can maintain, grow in place, and produce isolated pockets of expansion from time to time. However, no one of these elements, or a combination of them, will produce the expansion we see in the Early Church without Jesus' simple group expansion system of 3/12/70

THE GREAT OMISSION ABOUT THE GREAT COMMISSION

The centralized church model we are currently using is not designed to fulfill the Great Commission, no matter the good intentions and diligent effort. These churches send sincere people as missionaries and use the names "missional" or "Great Commission Church." However, a centralized church reproduces the same centralized design whatever it calls itself and wherever it goes. The Church is not doing the Great Commission until it is doing what Jesus taught the Disciples to do: To be His body in relationship units of 3/12/70 in Jerusalem, Judea, Samaria, and the end of the earth.

The great omission is trying to carry out Christ's Great Commission without His simple strategy system of relationships and community groups. It is absurd to believe this commission was a stand-alone command without context. Jesus' commission was not waiting around for Constantine's model to be developed in the fourth century so it could be successfully implemented. Jesus intended the great commission to be carried out with His great community church: His spiritual Body on earth. Some methods, tools, and strategies are better than others for fulfilling the expansion mission. Jesus' strategy is the best way to accomplish His strategy of expansion. The strategy of many traditional churches is to maintain and that is what they do. Other churches have a strategy of growth and develop methodologies to grow. Jesus' strategy was expansion.

The traditional church with its buildings, professional religious hierarchy, and programs is not Jesus' Great Commission model for expansion. Jesus not only gave a commission and promise but He also provided a great commission context/design of expansion. This was not a commission that could be fulfilled with an organization, or would be completed with lone ranger Christians scattering all over the earth. Jesus' commission is given to the community of faith: the Church, the Body of Christ.

Chapter 15

MOVEMENTS ARE BUILT ON GOVERNING PRINCIPLES

"I strongly believe the Cell Church Movement is God leading the church back to the place it never should have left."
• Robert Lay

Over a period of fifteen years, Touch Cell Church Network in Brazil developed into an important movement of hundreds of churches representing all the major denominations in the country. The Network gives us a preview of what God can do through movements that are fueled by Jesus' relationship paradigm of the church.

In 1978, Robert Lay, a Mennonite Brethren "connector"[156] and innovator, moved his young family from Curitiba, Brazil to California to study Christian education and to complete a Masters degree in music. While a member of a local Baptist church, he participated in a twelve-week training on "friendship evangelism" that Ralph W. Neighbour, Jr. facilitated on video. After returning to Brazil in 1982, Lay began implementing the concepts from the video in a Portuguese-speaking couples class in his home German-speaking Mennonite Brethren Church.

In 1985, Lay traveled to Singapore to study a Cell Church model designed by Neighbour.[157] After returning home, he began trans-

---
156. Gladwell, 38.
157. Neighbour, *Where Do We Go From Here?*, 359-377.

lating the training materials and implementing the model in the couples-class that he was leading. Eventually the class became a separate Portuguese-speaking church.

Shortly after his trip to Singapore, I met Robert Lay at a conference in Harrisburg, Virginia. It was at that conference that Dion Robert (pastor of Eglise Protestante Baptist Oeuvres et Mission in Abidjan, Ivory Coast) made a simple statement that Robert and I have repeated many times over the past decades: "Vision plus vision equals division."

The last day of the conference, Robert and I ate a sack lunch together high up in the bleachers of the church gymnasium and dreamed about how God could begin a cell church movement in Brazil.

Robert returned to Brazil and began a ministry that has taught cell church concepts and components, mentored leaders who are transitioning their churches, and provided necessary resources for a movement. A decade and a half later, the Cell Church Network in Brazil consists of hundreds of churches and thousands of Christians in regions from the Amazon to Argentina and from the Atlantic to the Andes.[158] All major denominations are represented in this stream of the growing Cell Church Movement in Brazil that is part of a yet broader church movement. The Cell Church Network is now expanding into local communities (Jerusalem), surrounding regions (Judea), mission areas of Brazil (Samaria), and is positioned to go to other countries (the world) (Acts 1:8).

---

158. According to estimates from Cell Church Ministries, approximately fourteen thousand pastors have completed a special training called Acts (Advanced Cell Training), and five thousand churches, thirty-five thousand cells, five-hundred fifty thousand Christians, and seventy denominations or groups are part of the Network.

CHAPTER 15: MOVEMENTS ARE BUILT ON GOVERNING PRINCIPLES

In this chapter, I am coming full circle back to Brazil where God gave me many of the ideas for two books: *The Second Reformation: Stage 2* and this book, *70: Jesus' Expansion Strategy*.

GOVERNING PRINCIPLES

Underneath movements are statements, stated or unstated, that define the basic truths that drive the movement. These statements fit Peter Senge's concept of "governing ideas"[159] that succinctly express the vision, mission, values, and even system structures of an organization. Governing ideas "paint pictures of the future"[160] and are the "essences" or the "state of being"[161] that, taken as a unit, answer the question, "What do we believe in?"[162] Governing ideas "simplify the complex world into a single organizing idea, a basic principle or concept that unifies and guides everything."[163]

We see governing principles in the Bible and in Church History. Peter at the home of Cornelius made a governing principle statement that "God is no respecter of persons" (Acts 10:34-35). This basic maxim was confirmed at the Jerusalem Council about the Gentiles (Acts 15). Paul cites the principle in Romans 2:11, Galatians 3:28, and Ephesians 6:9. James uses the principle several times in James 2. This governing principle gave the Early Church the theological rationale and cultural and religious absolution so that it could evangelize the uncircumcised Gentiles.

Beginning in the 12th century the Waldensians, the earliest "protestant" denomination, was guided by the motto "Into

---

159. Senge, 219-220.
160. Ibid., 223.
161. Ibid., 374.
162. Ibid., 224.
163. Collins, 90-92.

darkness light!" During that same period of history, the Moravians, an early proponent of a more New Testament paradigm of the church, used the motto "Our Lamb has conquered, let us follow Him!"

The governing principle of the Reformation was "the just shall live by faith." The central governing principles for Baptist were salvation by grace through faith, the priesthood of the believer, and the authority of Scripture alone for faith and practice. Presbyterians followed the theological principles that God is totally sovereign, Man is totally sinful, and grace is totally sufficient. John Wesley founded Methodism on the governing principle of "be holy as God is holy." Wesley also had a governing principle about having a method of living the Christian life, thus the name Methodism.

The mantra of the Pentecostal movement at the beginning of the 20th century was the governing principle of the Holy Spirit's continuing presence and power through the gifts and healing. The Catholic Church followed a governing principle about authority: The Catholic Church is the universal church with God's authority on earth and the Pope has the keys to the kingdom.

GOVERNING PRINCIPLES IN THE MOVEMENT IN BRAZIL

Four statements developed over the period of a decade (2000 – 2010) and now define the Cell Church Movement in Brazil. These statements spontaneously emerged in the movement without promotion and were broadly accepted by those in the Network. The statements began to appear on T-shirts, were displayed on conference banners and incorporated into indigenous songs, were included in strategy planning, and were used to explain the vision and values of the movement.

Looking back it is obvious God used these principles to crystalize vision, clarify concepts, and mobilize leaders in the Cell Church movement in Brazil. It became obvious to the pastors that if the statements were applied in their churches they would maximize growth and minimize maintenance.

The first two statements emerged during the early years and express the basic vision and values of the Network: "Every house a church" and "every member a minister." The third and fourth statements give ministry direction to the Network: "Every Church a training center" and "every Church a sending base." The Network has come to accept these four statements as God's governing principles. Two additional statements have been introduced in recent years: "Every church multiplying movements" and "every church transforming society." However, the first four defined the movement in its beginning. They unify the Network and provide a frame of reference for making both macro (big picture) and micro (detail) plans and decisions.

The Biblically based governing principles in Brazil, especially the first four, have freed these churches from some of the most powerful chains of traditionalism and institutionalism. "Every house a church" breaks the edifice barrier that ties the church to expensive buildings and forces the church into an organizational paradigm. "Every member a minister" breaks the professional clergy model of hired holy men, a professional leadership class performing duties for consumer members. "Every church a training center" breaks the barrier of institutional training for a few special leaders rather than on-the-job training for multiple-leadership needs. "Every church a sending base" releases the church from dependence on outside agencies to fulfill the Great Commission to go to Jerusalem, Judea, Samaria, and the world.

During a recent conference in Brazil, I sensed the need for another governing principle: Every Christian a missionary. This statement makes every Christian part of the contagious factor of the Gospel that contributed to the expansion of the Church in the early centuries. Using a basic friendship triad, the Church is no longer just sending missionaries but every Christian is being a missionary. This is what happened in the New Testament Church: Every Christian was infected with a spiritual dose of the Gospel and infected those around them. The Early Church spread along the lines of a classic epidemic. The friendship group of two or three is the contagious factor in the church. The community cell of twelve is where Gospel contagion is maintained at the maximum degree for the maximum amount of time through contact with Christ, body life with Christians, and the edification of each Christian and of the Church. The infectious epidemic is supervised in the expansion group of seventy.

The peril of the Church is to underestimate the strength of the institutional barriers that have been attached to the traditional model for seventeen hundred years. It is difficult for a church with the DNA of a traditional denomination to go back into the movement womb and be born again. However, many pastors of denominational churches in the Cell Church Network in Brazil believe their church has experienced such a new birth. God used the governing principles as the midwife of that birth.

The Church is an Expansion Movement

Multiple indicators in the Bible confirm God's intention to continue the Christian movement that swept across the first century world. These indicators give a scriptural rationale for God working through spiritual movements in every period of history,

CHAPTER 15: MOVEMENTS ARE BUILT ON GOVERNING PRINCIPLES

in every part of the world, and in diverse social, cultural, and economic situations. The Cell Church Network in Brazil is an example of such a movement.

Commentators consistently *use the word "continue" to describe what happened in Acts*. F. F. Bruce, imminent New Testament scholar and church historian, ties the history of the movement in Acts to Christians today.

> *Acts is the continuation of the story of Jesus. That is to say, Jesus, who began to act and teach on earth in the years immediately preceding A.D. 30, has continued to act and teach since that year by His Spirit in His servants; and the history of Christianity ought to be the history of what He has been doing and teaching in this way down to our own times – a continuous Acts of the Apostles.*[164]

Michael Green does the same thing in his classic book on evangelism in the church:

> *Luke wrote his Gospel to show what Jesus began to do and to teach when he was on earth. He wrote his Acts to show what Jesus continued to do and to teach after his resurrection, through the agency of the Holy Spirit in a handful of dedicated people whose message became irresistible. God is still engaged in this dynamic enterprise. He has not given up on us.*[165]

The conclusion of the Book of Acts suggests that what was recorded in the first twenty-eight chapters would continue as a movement in succeeding generations. Luke placed a period after

---

164. F. F. Bruce, *The Spreading Flame* (Grand Rapids, MI: Wm. B. Eerdmans, 1958), 161.
165. Michael Green, *Thirty Years that Changed the World: The Book of Acts for Today* (Grand Rapids, MI: Wm. B. Eerdmans, 2004), 10.

Acts 28:31 to close out his history of the early Church but the inconclusive ending of the book makes it feel like a comma. Acts encourages us to believe and pray "that Acts 29 is possible: that the fresh wind of God's Holy Spirit that launched the infant church is still available, still active, still ready to work in and through us if only we are willing."[166]

The book of Acts "challenges readers to consider how they themselves will continue the story of the gospel's progress."[167] The continuing connection between the church in Acts and the church in history "inevitably intersects with our personal narratives. Horizons meet and inform."[168] "The sense that the story is not finished summons readers to supply the ending themselves."[169] "The ending is prelude."[170]

The *work of the Holy Spirit* is an indicator that God intended the New Testament movement to continue in history. In the New Testament, the Holy Spirit knows no boundaries of time, culture, demographics, or geography. In His conversation with Nicodemus, Jesus used the picture of the blowing wind to explain the powerful work of the Spirit in a person's life. (John 3:8). Luke recorded the same wind phenomenon at Pentecost. "A sound like the blowing of a violent wind filled the whole place" (Acts 2:2). Then the wind turned to something like "tongues of fire that separated and came to rest upon each of them" (Acts

---

166. Ibid., 10.
167. David G. Peterson, *The Acts of the Apostles*, The Pillar New Testament Commentary, ed. D. A. Carson, (Grand Rapids, MI: Wm. B. Eerdman Publishing Co, 2009), 724.
168. Paul Varo Martinson, "The Ending Is Prelude: Discontinuities Lead to Continuities" in *Mission in Acts: Ancient Narratives in Contemporary Context*, ed. Robert I. Gallagher and Paul Hertig (Maryknoll: Orbis Books, 2004), 313.
169. Beverly Roberts Gaventa, *Acts*, Abingdon New Testament Commentaries (Nashville: Abingdon Press, 2003), 370.
170. Martinson, 321.

2:3). The tongues of fire became languages that the Spirit spoke through the disciples to the different language groups in the crowd who came from "every nation under heaven" (Acts 2:4). Peter explained the events to the Christians and to the crowd as a fulfillment of Joel's prophecy of the Spirit being "poured out" (Acts 2:17). His sermon is full of words about prophesying, seeing visions, dreaming dreams along with wonders in heaven, signs on earth, and the "glorious day of the Lord" (Acts 2:20).

All of these vivid pictures suggest something is happening that is powerful, unrestricted, uncontrollable, and ongoing. The prophecy of Joel linked what was happening at Pentecost to what had happened in the Old Testament and to what was about to happen throughout the world. The reader of Acts naturally expects the same Spirit to birth the same kind of movement in every period of history, geographical location, and cultural context.

In addition, the *concept of time* in the New Testament establishes a theological foundation for considering God's work in history as a movement. God's redemptive history through Christ holds the movement together from the Old Testament to the New Testament and beyond.[171] The western system of measuring time begins at a center point in history with the birth of Christ and then proceeds in opposite directions, one forward and the other backward. Oscar Cullmann asserts that this unique method of calculating time and history as "before Christ" (BC) and "after Christ" (AD), corresponds to the Primitive Church's conception of time and history.

The eternal Christ ties together events that take place over thousands of years, in many different cultures, and in vast expanses of geography. Prophecy is a connecting link in this timeline.

---

171. Oscar Cullmann, *Christ and Time* (London: SCM press, 1962), 19.

The fulfillment of prophecy indicates a continuing context in which the prophecy makes sense. For instance, the prophecies about Jesus' birth are announced in the Old Testament and fulfilled in the New Testament. Without some kind of continuing process and context, the original prophecy and the subsequent fulfillment would not be connected, much less understood.

The *historical nature of the Bible* is one of the strongest indicators that it is the story of a movement that was intended to continue. The nature of Biblical history indicates God is just as interested in the world today as the world in the past. "History is not a random flow of events. For God is working out in time a plan which he conceived in a past eternity and will consummate in a future eternity."[172] Religions such as Buddhism, Hinduism, and Confucianism stand or fall on their philosophical ideas. Their history is just incidental background whereas Judaism and Christianity are rooted in history. The very essence of the story of the Bible is that its theology, revelations, and persons are demonstrated in history. "The Word became flesh and dwelt among us" (John 1:14). That is both a statement of theology (the Word) and history (became flesh and dwelt among us). All theology in the New Testament is tied to what happened in the life of Christ in history.

More than four decades ago, Billy Graham challenged the church with a timeless word about Christian history.

> *Every generation is crucial: every generation is strategic. But we are not responsible for the past generation, and we cannot bear full responsibility for the next one. However, we do have our generation! God will hold us responsible at the Judgment Seat of Christ*

---

172. John R. W. Stott, *You Can Tell the World*, ed. James E. Berney (Downers Grove, IL: InterVarsity Press, 1979), 8.

for how well we fulfilled our responsibilities and took advantage of our opportunities.[173]

Theologians Robert Gallagher and Paul Hertig captured the relationship of the church today to past and future history.

Christians in this century are not second-class believers trying to live out a first century church theology through a historical wine-skin of the fourth century. God placed no expiration date on His presence, power, or purpose in history. While the unique events that include the incarnation, the death of Christ, his resurrection, his ascension, and the pouring out of the promised Spirit at Pen-tecost took place in the first century, they are not unique in terms of the implications and applications of those events in history. God has the same purpose in every period of history. "Through the Spirit, you and I are invited to become part of the on going saga---the history of the church. The church discovers its identity in history when it enters into the narrative where Acts abruptly concludes.[174]

MOVEMENTS

Movements are scary, and at times, messy and confusing. We can't make them happen with organization, machinery, and human effort. However, at the same time, we must have some kind of organization, machinery, and human effort to support the life of a movement. All movements have some combination of the elements of mission, men, methods, materials, models, mentoring, and time. Some would include "money" on this list. However, its very nature and definition means a movement does

---

173. Billy Graham, *Why the Berlin Conference?* (Address, World Congress on Evangelism, Berlin, West Germany, October 1966).
174. Robert I. Gallagher and Paul Hertig, eds, *Mission in Acts: Ancient Narratives in Contemporary Context* (Maryknoll, NY: Orbis Books, 2004), 2-3.

not depend on money or extraordinary leaders. Spiritual movements are organic, not organizational. They spread naturally through relationships, not through the machinery of an organization.

The mission of the movement in Brazil is expressed in its governing principles that are implemented in its effective method of the cell church. It had access to materials and a way to teach the concepts in several modules. Ralph Neighbour's discipleship and leadership materials were available as a startup sample and the Network used and adapted them. A group of respected innovators bought into the vision early. They not only owned the vision but the vision owned them. These leaders had a sense of God's history taking place among them. From this came enough early successful models to establish the ideas as a viable strategy. The leaders of the early models became mentors to the movement.

Mentors are essential for maintaining movements. The question is: How do we mentor and resource a movement? Michael Gerber, author of The E-Myth says "It is literally impossible to produce a consistent result in a business that is created around the need for extraordinary people."[175] This is true of a movement. A movement cannot depend on experts for mentoring. In Brazil, Robert Lay invited outside "experts" to teach in large conferences (Ralph Neighbour, Joel Comiskey, Bill Beckham, Ben Wong, and others). However, Robert and the Brazilian leadership team actually mentored the movement in smaller regional venues and in one-on-one coaching relationships. Every pastor of a successful cell church (one that is a little farther along in the process) became a resident "expert" and mentor.

Watching a movement develop is a thrilling and humbling experience. God sovereignly works in history in His own way, in His

---

175. Gerber, 60-61.

own time, and through the people of His choice. Looking back it is evident that Robert Lay and other leaders in Brazil were God's instruments for developing and maintaining a movement.

Even at the beginning, during my brief time with Robert Lay in the bleachers in Virginia, I sensed that we were dreaming together in a special way. T. E. Lawrence's explanation of his experience in Arabia during World War I expresses what God is doing in Brazil.

> *All men dream: but not equally. Those who dream by night in the dusty recesses of their minds wake in the day to find that it was vanity: but the dreamers of the day are dangerous men, for they may act their dream with open eyes, to make it possible.*[176]

Robert Lay and the leaders in Brazil are God's "dangerous men" in relation to the kingdoms of this world because they are "dreamers of the day" "with open eyes" who "act their dream" out, and make possible the dream that God gave.

A "Dangerous" Event

Every time I participate in the final session of a National Cell Church Conference in Brazil, I sense something special happening. Conferences close with the Lord's Supper. The large crowd includes pastors and people from the full spectrum of denominations. This is a "dangerous" event!

I can still see the event in my mind: The crowd gathers in small groups of eight to ten persons all across the large conference room. A leader from each group goes to the front of the auditorium and picks up the elements of bread and wine for their

---

176. T. E. Lawrence, *Seven Pillars of Wisdom* (Blacksburg, VA: Wilder Publications, 2011) 7.

group. Leaders of the movement tell the simple meaning of the bread and wine and each group shares together in the supper of the Lord.

When preparing for the Lord's Supper in a recent conference in a large Presbyterians church, the pastor commented: "This is not a Presbyterian table but Christ's table."

Throughout history these denominations fought over theological concepts and practices, including the Lord's Supper. Now they share in the Body of Christ together. I know this is a miraculous event because of the unity of the Body expressed. This is the difference between fighting theology and unifying theology. Unifying theology is in the person of Christ and His spiritual Body on earth as Paul expressed in Ephesians 4:1-6:

> *As a prisoner for the Lord, then, I urge you to live a life worthy of the calling you have received. Be completely humble and gentle; be patient, bearing with one another in love. Make every effort to keep the unity of the Spirit through the bond of peace. There is one body and one Spirit – just as you were called to one hope when you were called – one Lord, one faith, one baptism; one God and Father of all, who is over all and through all and in all.*

Unifying theology that is centered in Christ and His mission puts fighting theology in its proper place. In the Network in Brazil, Presbyterian churches are still Presbyterian, Baptist churches are still Baptist, Pentecostal churches are still Pentecostal, and Methodist churches are still Methodist. However, pastors from different denominations often partner together and preach and teach in each other's churches. They are united in a common Christ and a common mission. No one looks for an opportunity to make a theological point. Christ is the point!

Chapter 15: Movements Are Built on Governing Principles

Unity may be the single most powerful testimony that God is restoring the Church to its original nature and order. Robert Lay, the Director of the Cell Church Network in Brazil, sums up what God is doing in the church today.

> *Of course, the Holy Scriptures reveal God's eternal and unchangeable plan and will for all times. Biblical values and principles are eternal, because they come directly from God, and are rooted in His very nature. When we depart from these principles, God will show us the way back in living them out again in our time. I strongly believe the Cell Church Movement is God leading the church back to the place it never should have left.*

Chapter 16

JESUS' STRATEGY OVERVIEW

*"Everything in strategy is very simple,
but that does not mean that everything is very easy."*
  • Military theorist, Carl von Clausewitz

The chart, *Visualizing Jesus' Strategy*, gives an overview of Jesus' strategy process. It shows four strategic elements flowing through Jesus' ministry: preparation, prototype, harvest, and assimilation. The chart can be used in many different church situations: new starts, existing cell churches that have plateaued in growth, churches with small groups, house churches, and traditional denominational churches.

VISUALIZING JESUS' STRATEGY

HARVEST	PREPARATION	PROTOTYPE
NET FISHING & JOHN'S DISCIPLES	STARTUP CIRCLE	CORE — 3
	COMMITMENT BUS	CELL — 12
OIKOS (Family & Friends)		CLUSTER — 70
	ASSIMILATION →	120
PERSON OF PEACE	LEADER TRIANGLE	CONGREGATION

The different elements of Jesus' strategy process are like the elements of music. The building blocks of a song are: melody, harmony and rhythm. These are present in songs of every genre. Comparing the elements of music to a person: melody is "face," harmony is "flesh," and rhythm is "bones." As in music, Jesus' strategy elements are fluid, interactive, and flexible. They flow along together, interact, adapt to each other, blend together, and ultimately produce a unique song.

Strategy "Blurring"

Military theorist Carl von Clausewitz stated an important truth about strategy: "Everything in strategy is very simple, but that does not mean that everything is very easy.[177]

Categorizing Jesus' process into four elements addresses a major frustration in developing strategy. Without separate elements, the attempt to develop a strategy *blurs* into one mass of activities. Leaders find it difficult to determine what comes next and how the different parts relate. Without distinct categories, it is almost impossible to implement an effective working strategy because the stages are compromised. Preparation, prototype, harvest, and assimilation merge into one blob and all look the same with no distinctive steps in the process.

Jesus' four strategy elements help leaders understand the relationship of the elements to each other, their order, and their strategic implications. This gives a way to arrange the simultaneous and sequential processes at work in a church implementing Jesus' expansion model. The four elements move toward the same objective of creating one reproducible prototype cluster of five to seven cells. Once a functioning cluster is developed, it

---

177. Carl von Clausewitz, *On War*, trans. Michael Howard and Peter Paret (Princeton, NJ, 1976), 128.

Chapter 16: Jesus' Strategy Overview

has enough people, organization, leaders, and resources to multiply another tactical cluster of five to seven cells (70) and then, if desired, to form a streamlined support congregation (70 – 150) after the third cluster is developed.

Operational strategy is the planning and the execution that leads to the fulfillment of goals set in an overall strategy. Tactics is deployment of personnel to execute the strategy. Logistics focuses on making sure personnel are where they are meant to be and that they have all the support (normally supplies, but can include other things) that are required. Jim Collins describes a successful strategy as a "build up followed by a breakthrough broken into three broad stages: disciplined people, disciplined thoughts, and disciplined actions."[178] Each element in Jesus' strategy process can be defined with an initial question.

Preparation

The first question is how will leaders effectively prepare to become an expansion church? God made careful *preparation* to build His first church by preparing a nation and the necessary political and social climate. John the Baptist prepared the way and Jesus prepared a group of followers.

Abraham Lincoln was asked: "How would you chop down a large tree if you only had six hours?" After carefully thinking, Lincoln replied: "The first five hours I would use to sharpen my axe." This is a principle of life: The longer and better preparation, the shorter and better the implementation.

---

178. Collins, 57.

The first thing Jesus did when He began His ministry was to draw together a circle of followers. The people in this group were characterized by one thing: They were willing to follow Him. His leaders and committed followers, who would become His prototype, came from this pool of people in His circle of ministry. The circle was adjusted throughout the process: sometimes larger and sometimes smaller.

Some of those in Jesus' circle removed themselves and some were excluded (Matt 10, John 6:60ff). The Rich Young Ruler was obviously a desirable candidate for Jesus' circle. However, he could not be part of the circle because he was unwilling to forsake the things of his life in order to follow Jesus. Ralph Neighbour's decision process that I explain in chapter 4 is helpful in determining where each person is in commitment to the vision: unaware, aware, willingness to receive, controlled attention, commitment, and characterization.

The pastor of an existing church or a new start who wants to begin an expansion model both starts the same way: gathering some "warm bodies." In your mind, draw a circle and begin to evaluate who would join you in that circle. The only difference between an existing church and a new start is that members in an existing church may be added to the circle while in a new start people must be found. Members of an existing church are not necessarily more ready to be part of a new way of doing church. In fact, church members come into the startup circle with traditional values and therefore must go through value changing experiences before they can be part of something different. In a new start a catalytic leader and team must gather a large enough pool of potential followers to begin the process.

The people gathered in a startup circle may be new believers, John's disciples from an existing church, "persons of peace" contacted through friendship triads, *oikos* family and friends, or people contacted in ministry activities and events. Although it is a temporary structure, the startup circle is an extremely important strategy concept for both an existing church and a new start.

While forming a startup circle, the pastor of an existing church or the catalytic leader of a new start must be aware of two groups: the committed, submissive, and productive and the immature, uncommitted, and dysfunctional. This is necessary because 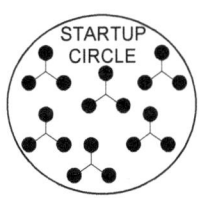 a healthy prototype cannot be formed from the uncommitted, unhealthy, unprepared, unconverted, and dysfunctional; and from leaders in the traditional system who are not submissive. Jesus understood this and we must trust his understanding of the human heart and of the prototype process.

During the preparation phase, the leadership team that is forming agrees on vision and values, establishes a culture, develops a strategy, and chooses necessary discipleship and leader training tools and protocols. (Look at the Preparation column that is in the center of the full chart on the previous page).

Friendship Triads during the Preparation Process

Pastors and catalytic leaders must gather an initial group of followers in a Startup Circle and help them experience a triad of two or three and then to become part of a community cell of twelve. In this process, the leader builds a committed team (commitment bus), forms a leadership team (triangle), and develops a prototype.

Every person in the startup circle should be part of a friendship triad of two or three in order to experience the presence of

Christ, the power of confession and edification, and the purpose of friendship and *oikos* evangelism. The Apostle John's teaching about the three levels of discipleship in 1 John 2 operates naturally during the beginning of the preparation process.

Not everyone in the startup circle will be at the same place of maturity and commitment. The catalytic leader/leaders will prayerfully identify those in the startup circle in the three categories of spiritual maturity: mature parents, growing young people, and spiritual children. It is not necessary to designate these roles but allow them to emerge in the dynamic life of the friendship triads. Friends do not designate a leader but they allow roles of influence to operate in the friendship. The catalytic leader/leaders will observe the triads and identify the potential spiritual parents who can model the Christian life for the spiritual young people. The young people will walk along with the spiritual children. Spiritual young people can be distinguished from spiritual children because they are part of the solution rather than part of the problem.

The friendship triad reveals the heart of early followers: is there a submissive or rebellious spirit? If an older Christian with a lot of church experience will not be part of, or cannot function in humility in, a disciple triad of two or three persons, that person is not a spiritual parent and should not be part of the next step of the pattern cell. On the other hand, a new Christian may become a spiritual young person or even a parent very quickly within the nurturing dynamic of a friendship triad. Keep the startup circle until the first small cluster is complete (3 cells).

All leaders, including the pastor or catalytic leader, should experience life in a friendship triad in a startup circle. The startup circle is the vision and commitment bus. At the proper time, leaders will be chosen to model a pattern cell: three to model a leadership friendship triad, and another nine will later be chosen to help model a holistic cell community. Those in the initial Startup Circle who are not part of the pattern cell remain in a disciple triad of two or three in the startup circle. The triads in the startup circle should follow the protocol of a normal triad as explained in chapter 9, both before and after the completion of the pattern cell.

Not everyone during the preparation period will move at the same speed. Some will not be ready to be part of early prototype cells. The prototype must be protected from dysfunctional people, rebellious followers, and agenda driven leaders.

PROTOTYPE

The prototype question is how will leaders form healthy cell communities into a reproducible prototype of five to seven functioning cells that operates as a supervising cluster?

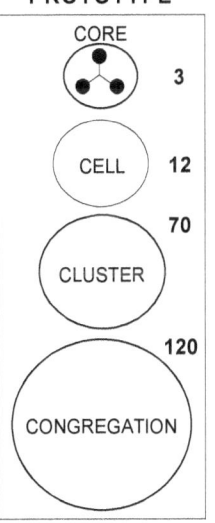

Jesus developed a working *prototype* with His inner circle of Peter, James and John, twelve close disciples, and seventy committed followers. It is logical to conclude that after the ascension, Jesus' cluster of seventy was the nucleus of the one hundred twenty in the upper room.

"Prototypes are essential to discovering and solving the key problems that stand between an idea and its full and successful implementation. Significant innovation cannot be achieved by talking about new ideas, you must build and test prototypes."[179]

---
179. Senge, 271.

A prototype answers the questions and satisfies the needs of different types of leaders: the entrepreneur, the manager, and the technician. For an entrepreneur, a prototype "is the medium through which his vision takes form in the real world." For a manager, a prototype "provides the order, the predictability, the system so important to his life." In a prototype, a technician "is free to do the things he loves to do ---technical work."[180] A prototype is a working model.

In reality, a leadership team must develop three primary prototypes, not just one: a friendship triad of two or three, a community cell of twelve, and a supervision cluster of seventy. (See Chapters 9, 10, 11.) These are the three basic experiences of the church, of Christians, and of leaders: basic Christian friendship, basic Christian community and basic Christian supervision. These three prototypes are developed in order, smallest to largest. Each group is a subset of the next larger group, resulting in a telescoping effect. The friendship triad (3) telescopes into the community cell (12), and the community cells telescope into the tactical cluster (70). The basic elements, systems, materials, and momentum necessary to operate as a cluster of seventy are completed during the prototype.

The congregation (120) of two or more clusters of seventy supports the supervision seventy with logistics and provides a forward base for expansion. However, the prototype focus for expansion is the cluster of seventy, not the congregation of 120. This is necessary because of the historical baggage that accompanies the congregation that includes a building, traditional programs, and professional leaders. A teaching and preaching traditional congregation is high-maintenance, high-cost, low-growth, and immobile. The preaching, teaching, and program congregation is the single greatest impediment to the expansion of the church in the 21st century.

---
180. Gerber, 57.

Chapter 16: Jesus' Strategy Overview

Focusing on the cluster of seventy, as Jesus did, allows leaders to decouple from the buildings, programs, and professional leaders that are attached to a brick and mortar traditional church. The tactical supervision cluster Jesus used is a high-growth, mobile, leader friendly, low-maintenance, and low-cost large group model. The seventy releases an organic vigor and vitality because it is set free from buildings, programs, and professional leaders that stifle growth.

Sophocles (400 B.C.) understood the importance of a prototype: "One must learn by doing the thing, for though you think you know it, you have no certainty until you try."

Harvest

The harvest question is how will the catalytic team attract and gather a pool of committed believers necessary to build each stage of the prototype? How does a team contact unaware lost persons, identify and cultivate seekers, and gather immature believers so that each new Christian becomes a productive part of the church? The harvest element gives a way to gather the numbers of people necessary to form the initial team, to organize the prototype core, and to establish the supervision cluster.

Jesus' ministry provides a helpful picture of organic evangelism in the Early Church. He modeled harvest by planting three kinds of evangelism seeds. (1) Jesus gave specific instructions about identifying and cultivating the "person of peace" and sent his followers out to find them. A "person of peace" is a seeker who is open to a relationship and to hearing about the gospel. (2) Jesus also practiced *oikos* household evangelism by reaching out to relatives, friends, and natural contacts that occur during the normal relationships of life. (3) In addition, Jesus' followers used net fishing (broad witness).

Early in His ministry, Jesus called His first followers and revealed the evangelistic focus and purpose of His ministry (Matthew 4:16-22). "And walking by the Sea of Galilee, He saw two brothers, Simon who was called Peter, and Andrew his brother, casting a net into the sea; for they were fishermen. And He said to them, 'Follow Me, and I will make you fishers of men.'" Net fishing was the picture that came into the minds of the Disciples when Jesus said, "I will make you fishers of men?" The Disciples were commercial fishermen and fished together in a boat with nets as a community. They were not involved in casual recreational fishing but had a strategy for catching the most fish possible.

In 1854-1855, Soren Kierkegaard, the Danish Christian philosopher, published a book with the purpose of shocking the church of his day out of its institutional withdrawal from witness to the world. It is interesting that Kierkegaard used Jesus' "fishers of men" analogy as a charge of neglect against the church.[181]

Jesus' objective during His 3 1/2 years of ministry was to gather and train enough leaders to build a prototype. We see different approaches to harvest during the early and later stages of Jesus' ministry. "First fruits" harvest for Jesus was John's disciples. These are people already prepared by someone else. In first fruit harvest, quality is of paramount importance.

The Spirit ushered in multiplication harvest after the church reached critical mass. Multiplication harvest is always dependent upon the first fruits harvest because the methods, model and work force necessary for multiplication harvest are developed out of the "first fruits" leaders and productive Christians. These initial followers must experience organic growth within the disciple unit of two or three and the community cell of

---

181. Soren Kierkegaard, *Attack upon Christianity* (Princeton, NJ: Princeton University Press, 1944), 203.

twelve. In an existing church, the first fruits for modeling an expansion prototype will be committed members in the church or Christians prepared by others. When working properly the friendship triad will be the primary unit of growth, multiplication, and expansion.

ASSIMILATION

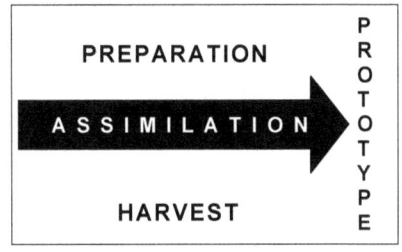

The assimilation question (look at the arrow) is how will the team nurture the immature while forming mature believers into a prototype without compromising the prototype? Assimilation moves out from the harvest, across preparation, to the prototyping process. Jesus successfully assimilated followers of many different levels of spiritual maturity, ethnic background, social conditions, geography, and age. Assimilation is the process by which new believers are brought into and nurtured in the family. "The Lord added daily, those who were saved."

Church leaders today face the same dilemma Jesus faced. What do you do with the crowds of followers while trying to develop a leadership team and a reproducible prototype? (These "crowds" may be large or small but they are the people who are listening but not yet fully engaged in the vision.)

Jesus would not compromise His leaders or His model. Therefore, He practiced controlled assimilation during the beginning of His ministry. He did not bring the uncommitted, unhealthy, or unconverted crowd directly into His prototype! Jesus ministered to the crowds in low maintenance teaching that could address the specific needs of immature believers. This is why He continued His public ministry down to the very end. His public ministry was necessary to prepare the crowd of followers who had believed, but were not yet ready to be part of His leadership core.

During the prototype stage, the catalytic leader supervises assimilation of insincere seekers and immature believers in triads within a special startup circle. Placing those from the crowd into friendship triads in the startup circle, gives a way to prepare and assimilate new believers and those open and interested. A friendship triad will reveal the true heart of someone from the crowd. If a person cannot function in a simple triad, he/she is not ready to be part of a prototype community cell.

A friendship triad of two or three is the natural assimilation group because its size and nature encourages intimacy, openness, honesty, participation, and practical agape. The fact that a triad is gender specific adds another significant positive factor to their use. The triad is so small it removes the temptation of the immature to perform, entertain, act out, or shut down communication. Assimilation in a triad protects the fragile new leadership prototype cell from unconverted, uncommitted, immature, and dysfunctional people until the essential cell systems are operational. A friendship triad is an embryonic experience that prepares Christians for cell community life.

During the operational stage, the harvest is assimilated directly into triads and cells. Each cell leader helps assimilate the harvest into friendship triads and then from the friendship triads into his/her cell. The cluster supervisor oversees assimilation of the harvest of all the cells into his/her cluster.

EVANGELISM & ASSIMILATION

Evangelism and assimilation are not mutually exclusive. Passionate evangelism must happen from the beginning of the project. At issue is what to do with the fruit of the initial harvest. It is not best for those unfamiliar with community to go directly into the prototype cell. In all likelihood the team is still in the process of putting the system and leaders into place. This is true of a new church start and the transition of a traditional church.

The prototype stage is designed for small amounts of assimilation, not to absorb large numbers of people directly into it. After the prototype is set and the operational stage begins, new believers will normally be part of a friendship triad and then assimilated directly and immediately into cells. During the early stages of the prototype, leaders must be more flexible about the kind of groups the interested and immature will be in.

The way we assimilate new believers is different during the prototype and multiplication stages because the objectives are different for each. The objective during the early prototype stage is to gather and develop a nucleus of leaders until a prototype is strong enough to harvest without compromising its vision and values. The objective after the initial cluster is developed is to mobilize as large a number as possible for the work of ministry. This means that leaders will approach assimilation differently during the two stages of development.

Unless the problem of initial assimilation is solved, interested seekers and new believers will not receive the benefit of a fully working community, and the leadership team will not be able to focus on developing an effective pattern of a friendship triad, community cell, and supervising cluster.

Alternative small group experiences other than a community cell are better venues for assimilating those who respond early in the church planting or transition process. In fact, the triad of two or three is the first and natural assimilation group. The objective is to hold those who respond early in a prototype in triads and in other appropriate activities and groups, and to prepare them to enter into community just as soon as the leadership team has experienced community in it different forms: in a pattern triad, a community cell, and a supervising cluster.

Section IV

Strategic conversations

Chapter 17: A Conversation about Jesus' Integrated Strategy

Chapter 18: A Conversation about Strategy Expansion

Chapter 19: A Conversation about the Large Group

Chapter 20: A Conversation about Two Strategic Points

Chapter 21: A Conversation about Strategy Building Blocks

Chapter 22: A Conversation with Church Planters

Chapter 23: A Conversation with Pastors

Conclusion: The Spirit of Namaan

Chapter 17

A CONVERSATION ABOUT JESUS' INTEGRATED STRATEGY

"From him the whole body, joined and held together by every supporting ligament, grows and builds itself up in love, as each part does its work."
• Paul in Ephesians 4:16

At some point during the past two decades, I realized the community cell (small group) alone does not adequately explain the dynamic expansion movement in the New Testament. Two additional elements began to take shape in my understanding of the church: A smaller group of two or three persons and a mobile mid-sized group of 30-70 persons. Along with the community cell, these groups are part of Jesus' architecture of the New Testament church.

Jesus' integrated strategy of 3/12/70 allows a leader to implement Paul's 2 Timothy 2:2 leadership system: "And the things you have heard me say in the presence of many witnesses entrust to reliable men who will also be qualified to teach others."

Maybe God knew we had to begin the stage-by-stage process with cells before the other two neglected groups could be effectively attached. For whatever reason, God has invested more than 60 years in getting cells/groups back into the modern church (since 1950 in China). Now God is re-introducing the two missing groups that are necessary for experiencing New Testament expansion.

The Cell Church began with the centerpiece of the community cell but lacked the bookend groups of three and seventy as equally important elements. Without the dynamic life of the two or three unit and the vision and supervision of the seventy, the community cell as we have done it is too complex, too vulnerable to dysfunctional members, and too demanding on cell leaders to be God's expansion instrument today. This is the reason church planting by Cell Churches has been no more effective than that of the traditional system. (See Chapter 22 for an explanation of the Cell Church's weakness in church planting.)

For the sake of context, it is important to point out again that the group of three has been used as a helpful discussion and training technique. For instance, this is the technique that several para-church organizations such as the Navigators have used to disciple. The cell church movement has used the two or three as a discussion and prayer group and as a leadership training method. In addition, cell churches have used the cluster of seventy to supervise cells under the umbrella of existing cell churches. However, neither the group of three nor the group of seventy has been given equal importance to the cell group today.

THREE-LEGGED STOOL

The church has been a three-legged stool using only one leg: The group of 12 cell community. The friendship triad of two or three and the cluster group of seventy are especially crucial for the expansion of the church. Without the proper working of the three units, the Cell Church Movement has

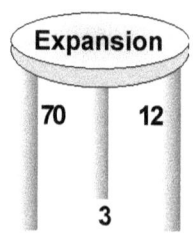

operated only a little better than the growth rate of the traditional church rather than at New Testament expansion speed.

Successful church planting movements naturally use some form of these three expansion units. For instance, Training for Trainers (T4T) has impressive growth that it attributes to a simple strategy centered on a small disciple/training group of four persons. However, I believe all successful movements, including T4T, naturally develop a way to not only multiply disciples and witness but also to nurture Christians in community and to supervise and organize expansion with appropriate leaders.

These three elements of expansion develop naturally in movements because they are the DNA infrastructure upon which Jesus' forms His church.

All three elements (3/12/70) are indispensable to the inherent integrity of an expansion movement. Unfortunately, leaders of successful movements who use one of these elements often do not realize the importance of the other elements in their strategy. In fact, they may not even recognize the presence of one of the elements, even thought it is there, supporting the strategy. This neglect affects a movement: Its length (how long it lasts), width (how far it spreads), and depth (how much of an impact it has).

EXPLANATION OF THE CONTAGIOUS TRIAD

The basic friendship group of two or three is the dynamic contagious element of the church. It is contagious on the inside in making disciples and contagious on the outside in reaching the lost.

Because the two or three unit is a friendship group it is a relationship, not a meeting. It is the embryo of the community cell and the place where Christians first experience the presence, power, and purpose of Christ within a friendship context.

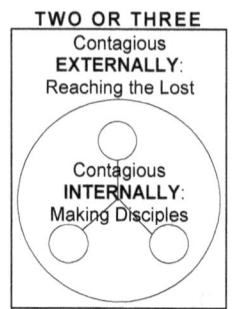

The focus on Christ in the midst makes the friendship triad extremely contagious in making disciples and reaching the lost. John Hayward, a professor of mathematics in Wales, UK, applies the mathematics of epidemics to church growth in an attempt to explain and duplicate the kind of person-to-person epidemic we see in the Early Church.[182] The two or three unit is the contagious epidemic factor in Jesus' relationship expansion system.

EXPLANATION OF THE NURTURING COMMUNITY

The cell group of twelve is the nurturing community element that prepares Christians for Christ's ministry of expansion. It is a nurturing family and is the place for experiencing the presence, power, and purpose of Christ in community. Edification, listening prayer, and body life are the central focuses of the twelve. The community experience is rooted in personal and group relationships but it has a regular weekly meeting.

The community cell has been the primary strategy of the Cell Church Movement since it's beginning. The truth is cell churches have grown internally through community cells but have not produced an expansion movement because the other

---

182. John Hayward, *Mathematical Modeling of Church Growth*, p16; Department of Mathematics; University of Glamorgan; Pontypridd CF 37 1DL, Wales; Technical Report UG-M-95-3 July 1995.

two groups have not been connected to the twelve: The contagious factor of two or three is necessary for developing disciples and reaching the lost and the supervising factor of thirty to seventy persons is required to organize and supervise external church planting expansion.

EXPLANATION OF THE SUPERVISING CLUSTER

The cluster of seventy is the supervising expansion element of the church. Expansion is organized and supervised in the mid-level group of thirty to seventy persons (three to six cells). Groups larger than seventy are encumbered with structure and organization that restricts mobility, focuses on programs more than relationships, and entangles the church in a maintenance rather than expansion system. Jesus' seventy (1) requires no special building (it is the church "without walls"), (2) operates with ordinary leaders rather than professionals, (3) required little or no money, (4) focuses on relationships rather than programs, (5) organizes, supervises, and involves every follower for expansion through the basic units of three and twelve, (6) is mobile enough to make adjustments in geopolitical, geographical, generational, demographic, and economic circumstances, and (7) operates near the frontlines of the battle so that it could give logistical support, expansion training and debriefing, and tactical direction.

To this time, cell churches have used the group of seventy primarily to supervise internal growth under the umbrella of its large group wing and not to organize and supervise church planting. In fact, cell churches have used the traditional method of church planting: Begin a worship service. Consequently, the cell church is not yet a church planting expansion movement and will not be until the contagious quality of the two or three and the supervising quality of the cluster of seventy are properly incorporated into the cell system.

In the 21st century, God is once again applying His integrated expansion formula of 3/12/70.

Eleven Disciplines in Jesus' Integrated System

The chart, *Jesus' Integrated Expansion System of 3/12/70*, shows the homogeneous nature of the three expansion elements of the church.

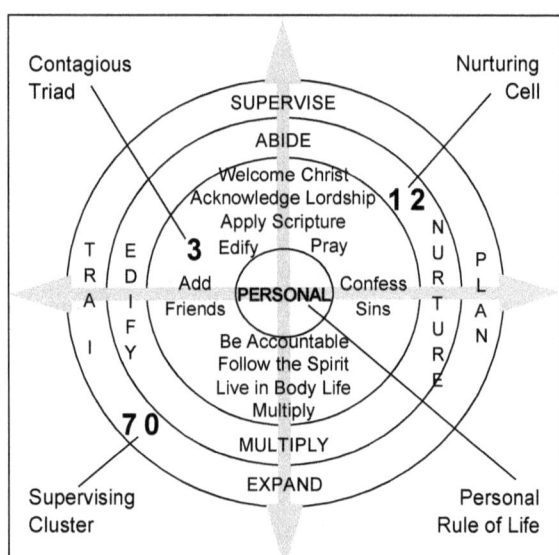

This integrated relationship strategy allows a leader to implement Paul's 2 Timothy 2:2 leadership system:

> *"And the things you have heard me say in the presence of many witnesses entrust to reliable men who will also be qualified to teach others."*

Notice that Jesus' relationship strategy begins from the inside out. At the center of the church are eleven experiences or disciplines. A spiritual discipline is an action or activity that a Christian repeats in order to live the life of Christ. God provides these disciplines to every believer (2 Pet. 1:3-9) but each believer must choose to practice these disciplines. The following disciplines begin as a seed in the two or three friendship triad and are lived out in a community form in the twelve and in a mission form in the seventy. Each Christian personally learns how to practice these disciplines in an intentional experience in a friendship triad.

> 1. *Experiencing Christ's presence: Welcome & Worship Christ (Matt. 18:20)*
> 2. *Acknowledging Christ is Lord (Rom. 10:9)*
> 3. *Listening in prayer for each other (Rom. 8:26-27)*
> 4. *Living in and being led by the Spirit (Rom. 8:14; Gal. 5:25)*
> 5. *Applying Scripture to life (James 1:23)*
> 6. *Confessing sins to each other (James 5:16)*
> 7. *Being accountable to spur each other toward love and good deeds (Heb. 10:24)*
> 8. *Edifying one another (Rom. 14:19; 15:2; Eph. 4:12; 29-30; 1 Thess. 5:11)*
> 9. *Living in friendship body life together (Rom. 12:5)*
> 10. *Adding friends to Christ's friendship circle (Jn. 1:41)*
> 11. *Multiplying the friendship unit (Acts 16:5)*

The disciplines flow through a succession of stages that derive from or act upon the preceding stage. Each discipline functions in an elemental form in the triad of two or three and then in a fuller expression in community. In a cluster of seventy the disciplines are focused toward mission, leadership, and expansion. Each discipline cascades out from the friendship triad, into the nurturing community cell, and finally expresses itself in supervising expansion in the cluster of seventy. In this process the disciplines become a personal way of life that are applied in friendship, community, and the ministry task.

Each discipline is independent with a unique quality that it provides to Christians and to the church. However, the disciplines are interdependent and function with the other disciplines as an integrated body that results in spiritual synergism. Paul describes the integrated synergistic nature of the Church in Ephesians:

> *And in him you too are being built together to become a dwelling in which God lives by his Spirit (Eph. 2: 22).* *"From him the whole body, joined and held together by every supporting ligament, grows and builds itself up in love, as each part does its work (Eph. 4:16).*

The disciplines of the Christian life are introduced and learned in a friendship triad. Then, each Christian must choose to personally live out the disciplines as a "rule of life." In the triad relationship all of the important disciplines of the Christian life are practiced. These disciplines naturally interact and are part of the on-going friendship relationship. They are not checked off as a list of activities to complete.

Four Catalytic Dimensions

In a friendship triad relationship, all of the important disciplines of the Christian life are practiced: Experiencing the presence of Christ, making Christ Lord, praying and listening, applying scripture to life, confessing sins, walking by the Spirit, being accountable to each other, edifying and encouraging each other, living in friendship body life, adding friends to Christ's circle, and multiplying the friendship triad.

Chapter 17: A Conversation about Jesus' Integrated Strategy

These disciplines naturally interact and are not checked off as a list of activities to complete. Friends in a triad share time together, talk on the phone, communicate through social media, and find occasions to be together. This is friendship body life.

In addition to friendship body life, a triad has a regular face-to-face time (weekly?) where the friends focus on four catalytic disciplines: the presence of Christ, confession of Christ as Lord, applying the Word, and prayer. These four catalytic disciplines set the other disciplines into motion. Within the context of these four disciplines, the Holy Spirit applies the other disciplines as He sees their necessity for one of the persons in the triad or for the spiritual development of the friendship relationship of the triad.

THE FLOW OF THE DISCIPLINES IN A TRIAD

Presence	Spirit	Body Life		
Lordship	Accountability		Add	Friends
Word	Confession		Multiply	
Prayer	Edification			

Imagine you are with your triad friends at McDonalds. The experience will be natural and normal: friends sharing time together. However, the experience will be intentional as a spiritual friendship with each other and with Christ. In a conversational way you will welcome Christ, confess that He is Lord, apply scripture you have been meditating on, and listen to God for each other in prayer. These catalytic disciplines of Christ's presence, Lordship, the Word, and prayer give a simple framework for the Spirit to activate the other disciplines at the proper time and in the proper way.

However, in some way all of the disciplines will be lived out in the triad and then expressed in the community of twelve and the cluster of seventy.

Chapter 18

A CONVERSATION ABOUT YOUR STRATEGY

*"However beautiful the strategy,
you should occasionally look at the results."*
• Winston Churchill

Jesus used two types of large groups: public and private. His public large group attracted the crowds. The modern seeker sensitive large group approach follows Jesus' pattern and in theory uses Sunday as a public ministry to seekers. However, seekers and crowds were only the first part of Jesus' strategy. He also brought His "followers" (the seventy) together in a private mid-level large group venue so that He could cast the vision of His mission and prepare them for expansion. He supervised His followers, trained them, deployed them, and debriefed them in His mid-level group of seventy.

Jesus' "private" large group of seventy was directed toward supervision and support of ministries and missions rather than producing services, offering religious ceremonies, educating about Bible knowledge, and providing programs and entertainment that attract the masses. If you are the pastor of a traditional church or a creative church with groups, you can expand your church and plant churches that expand through this private expansion "large" group. The size, denominational affiliation, worship style (liturgical or free), location (urban, rural, suburban), and age of your church are not the determining factors in expansion: The expansion equation of 3/12/70 is.

If you pastor a cell church, you are growing internally with your cell system but you do not expand externally with new church plants. You continue to use the traditional model of a Sunday worship and teaching program with new church plants. This slows expansion. You can participate in expansion church planting by using Jesus' organic mid sized large group system of 3/12/70.

If you are a church planter you can start churches that will expand as a people movement outside of the restrictive design that requires an expensive building, professional leaders, and time-consuming programs.

Let me give several suggestions that can help you develop an expansion arm for your traditional church, creative small group church, mega church, cell church, or new church start.

1. Honestly Evaluate Your Strategy

Winston Churchill understood the danger of using a strategy that looks good but does not produce the original objective. "However beautiful the strategy, you should occasionally look at the results."

Jesus was result-oriented. The God who expanded His Kingdom from Heaven to earth gave us the parable of the shepherd leaving the 99 sheep to find the one. God cares deeply for people and therefore designed His church with an expansion strategy that would touch the maximum number of people.

Chapter 18: A Conversation about your Strategy

However, in spite of impressive growth in some mega churches today (some of the largest of which are cell churches and churches that use small groups), the church in the West is not expanding as a movement.

This is a stark contrast to areas of persecution where Christians are forced into Jesus' small group and relationship strategy and expansion is taking place. New Testament movements in restricted areas of the world remind us of what happened in the early centuries of the life of the church. Expansion increased in the face of persecution and began to decrease when freedom increased.

In a large portion of the world, the church is boxed into Constantine's centralized growth system of buildings, programs, and professional leaders. It has done an impressive job of producing growth by attracting seekers to a friendly large group with professional music, events, and various types of small groups. It creatively utilizes mass media and social media to promote and hold the giant organization together. But we need to be honest; these churches are not expanding as a relationship movement throughout Jerusalem, Judea, Samaria, and the world.

The church has arrived at a dangerous place where the good is the enemy of the best. The good strategy that has produced impressive growth in mega churches will not take you or your church to its expansion best that we see in the New Testament. I believe there is a way to move from a good growth strategy into Jesus' best expansion strategy and that is the purpose of this book.

Now is the time for a brutally honest evaluation of your church paradigm. Pastor of a mega church: Will your church system expand God's Kingdom or grow an earthly church kingdom? Pastor of a cell church: Are you successfully expanding the kingdom with new church plants that carry Jesus' expansion DNA? Pastor of a smaller church, do you realize your vulnerability in depending on Constantine's brick and mortar system? How much more energy and effort can you and your people give using your current system? Church planter: Will you survive or break through the 50-100-barrier when so much of your time and resources are invested in finding a building and setting up programs? Do you long to be part of a genuine New Testament people movement?

2. KNOW THE DIFFERENCE BETWEEN GROWTH AND EXPANSION

Expansion is not about where a new church is planted but about what is planted. Plant a traditional church anywhere in the world and contained growth is the result. A brick and mortar system that is dedicated to preaching and teaching programs will not produce expansion. A mobile organic system that flows through relationships is required.

You as a pastor, church leader, or church planter must understand the difference between internal growth and external expansion. Internal growth is a church growing larger in one locality and/or one facility. Pastors of churches with buildings and come structures naturally focus on growing larger in that one location. If it can't maintain growth in its central system, the house of cards comes tumbling down.

If one of these churches grows numerically, it may establish a mission church in another location. In the mission model, a mother church sends out a number of leaders and members to establish a new daughter mission. However, the model for the new mission is the same brick and mortar design that is devoted to the same type of internal growth.

Some churches grow larger by establishing multiple sites that are connected around an extraordinary preaching pastor, impressive ministries, or a professionally produced Sunday program. This is also internal growth in the sense that the church is growing larger as one entity in several locations. These churches are not growing larger in the sense of expanding. They are just getting fatter. With the popular satellite model, large churches begin a satellite church on a new church campus in another area of a city. The senior pastor of the mother church often preaches at both churches personally or via satellite. New churches also use the popular hive model to transplant a leader and a portion of the original church into a new area. A hive is different from a satellite because it is generally a separate ministry whereas a satellite remains one of the coordinated campuses of the mother church.

Beginning a daughter mission, starting a satellite, or hiving off into a new church is each a good method. However, these methods reproduce the church that birthed them. The daughter mission church is like the mother church. Hive off a good growth church and you get another centralized growth church. If you hive a traditional church, even a growing and creative one, you will get a traditional creative church. Begin a satellite church from a traditional centralized mother church and you reproduce the mother church. If you begin a satellite of a church that is growing, you will get a church that is growing. However, the end result is not expansion.

These models have been primarily used to begin traditional staff-based and program-based designed churches instead of community relationship-based churches. Pastors of small group churches need the New Testament small group cell model that cell churches use. However, this is not enough: cells are only half of the New Testament strategy. Pastors of all churches, including cell churches, also need the New Testament expansion mid level large group of seventy.

If a pastor uses cells as a method of internal growth but ties the cells to Constantine's large group model in church planting he/she will continue to be frustrated in church planting. The New Testament design gives the possibility for a church to grow large in numbers with internal growth and to expand substantially in external new church growth through Jesus' expansion strategy of 3/12/70.

3. Return to Jesus' Church System

At the risk of seeming unspiritual I want to talk about Jesus' church as a system design. We should not be surprised that God created the church as a system. God's creation is full of systems such as the solar system, eco system, and body system.

In fact, Paul describes the church as an integrated body system. "Instead, speaking the truth in love, we will in all things grow up into him who is the Head, that is, Christ. From him the whole body, joined and held together by every supporting ligament, grows and builds itself up in love, as each part does its work" (Eph. 4:15-16). A lone Christian "has lost connection with the Head, from whom the whole body, supported and held together by its ligaments and sinews, grows as God causes it to grow" (Col. 2:19). Paul elaborated on the church system in 1 Corinthians 12. "The body is a unit, though it is made up of many parts; and though all its parts are many, they form one body. So it is with Christ" (1 Cor. 12:12).

Michael Gerber defines a system as "a set of things, actions, ideas, and information that interact with each other, and in so

CHAPTER 18: A CONVERSATION ABOUT YOUR STRATEGY   329

doing alter other systems."[183] An integrated and interconnected framework "whose properties cannot be reduced to those of its parts is called a system."[184] There are several general types of systems: mechanistic (machine), animate (person), social (organization), and ecological (nature). Peter Senge uses a rainstorm to illustrate a system:

> *A cloud masses, the sky darkens, leaves twist upward, and we know that it will rain. We also know that after the storm, the runoff will feed into groundwater miles away, and the sky will grow clear by tomorrow. All these events are distant in time and space, and yet they are all connected within the same pattern. Each has an influence on the rest, an influence that is usually hidden from view. You can only understand the system of a rainstorm by contemplating the whole, not any individual part of the pattern.*[185]

Senge believes we are better at breaking problems into separate elements than connecting elements together as a whole.

> *From a very early age, we are taught to break apart problems, to fragment the world. This apparently makes complex tasks and subjects more manageable, but we pay a hidden, enormous price. We can no longer see the consequences of our actions; we lose our intrinsic sense of connection to a larger whole. When we the try to "see the big picture," we try to reassemble the fragments in our minds, to list and organize all the pieces. But, the task is futile---similar to trying to reassemble the fragments of a broken mirror to see a true reflection. Thus, after a while we give up trying to see the whole*

---

183. Gerber, 141.
184. Ibid., 47.
185. Senge, 6-7.

altogether. We must destroy the illusion that the world is created of separate, unrelated forces.[186]

It is impossible to begin an expansion movement with the traditional church system. Pastors in the modern church, whether a large church, small church, denominational church, independent church, Bible church, Pentecostal church, or cell church, are in the same boat. Constantine's centralized boat may be a luxury liner or a rowboat but it is still subject to the same forces of buoyancy, power, and motion. Some outside force such as wind, a paddle, or an engine is necessary to move a boat. In addition, the ship/boat must have some kind of steering system. Constantine designed the church as a centralized ship/boat.

Suppose Jesus has another design that operates with another set of natural laws? For instance, suppose Jesus' church is designed to fly. No matter how well the principles of navigation on water are applied, Jesus' design of flying will not take place.

The overused definition of insanity does apply here so I am going to use it: "Doing the same thing the same way and expecting different results." If our church system is designed for centralized growth, it is insane to expect expansion. Expansion requires another system and operates with an entirely different set of "laws". Michael Gerber asks a question that shows the relationship between systems and people.

> *How can I create a business whose results are systems-dependent rather than people-dependent? That is not to say that people are unimportant. Quite the contrary. People bring systems to life. People make it possible for things that are designed to work to produce the intended results. Great*

---

186. Ibid., 3.

businesses are not built by extraordinary people but by ordinary people doing extraordinary things.[187]

Without an organic relationship system, a church is dependent on personalities who can run the organizational system of the church. Jesus designed the church as a small group relationship system in order for it to be His organic body. Because the Church is the Body of Christ, each Christian can contribute something special to the body by living in Christ. The next five steps are necessary for the restoration and implementation of Jesus' New Testament church system.

4. Mobilize Ordinary Leaders

Jesus' system is better than His leaders because it was built on the principle of the ordinary. Paul explains in 1 Corinthians 1:26-31 that Jesus' simple system mobilizes ordinary leaders to do extraordinary things.

> *Brothers and sisters, think of what you were when you were called. Not many of you were wise by human standards; not many were influential; not many were of noble birth. But God chose the foolish things of the world to shame the wise; God chose the weak things of the world to shame the strong. God chose the lowly things of this world and the despised things – and the things that are not – to nullify the things that are, so that no one may boast before him.*
>
> *It is because of him that you are in Christ Jesus, who has become for us wisdom from God – that is, our righteousness, holiness and redemption. Therefore, as it is written: "Let the one who boasts boast in the Lord.*

---

187. Gerber, 60.

God uses ordinary leaders in an extraordinary way. This was necessary because there are never enough extraordinary leaders to fuel an expansion movement. Therefore, in order to mobilize Jesus' system through ordinary leaders, Jesus designed His expansion system to work with ordinary leaders. Consequently, Paul observed that not many of Jesus' followers were "wise," "influential," and "noble" but God chose the "lowly things of this world," "the despised things," and the "things that are not" to "confound the wise."

Jesus and Paul understood what business leaders like Michael Gerber have discovered from trial and error.

Great businesses are not built by extraordinary people but by ordinary people doing extraordinary things. But for ordinary people to do extraordinary things a system---a "way of doing things"---is needed to compensate for the disparity between the skills your people have and the skills needed to produce the result.

It is literally impossible to produce a consistent result in a business that is created around the need for extraordinary people. On the other hand, if you intentionally build your business on the skills of ordinary people, you will be forced to ask the difficult questions about how to produce a result without the extraordinary ones. You will be forced to find a system that leverages your ordinary people to the point where they can produce extraordinary results.[188]

Jesus' system in the first century operated with the principles of ordinary people and extraordinary systems that define the best companies today. Jesus' system was better than His leaders and allowed ordinary leaders and people to do extraordinary things.

---

188. Ibid., 60-61.

We must return to His "way of doing things" in order for Him to once again produce His kind of church.

Peter W. Schutz, CEO of several major companies, based his business model on mobilizing ordinary people to achieve extraordinary results. Schutz explains the relationship of ordinary people and "superstars".

> *The only competitive edge of a lasting nature that I have ever enjoyed in these circumstances is to achieve extraordinary results with ordinary people. Why ordinary people and not superstars? It is because most people, including most managers and leaders, are ordinary people. Why not recruit only Superstars? First of all, they are rare. My role as a leader was to back (the rare "superstars") with a supporting organization of ordinary people whose enthusiasm and passion inspired them to outperform their counterparts with the competition.*[189]

Jesus' leadership strategy of mobilizing the ordinary and maximizing relationships worked well. Within a generation, His followers turned the world upside down (Acts 17:6). Whenever and wherever in history ordinary leaders and people used His simple system, expansion took place. The movements we see today are not happening because of extraordinary leaders and our impressive brick and a mortar mega church system, but through Jesus' simple system of groups in homes and with ordinary leaders and people.

One way we can tell if we are using Jesus' system is by who gets the credit. When we are using His system "the one who boasts,

---

189. Peter W. Schutz, The Competitive Edge: Extraordinary Results with Ordinary People in a "Flat World," *Howe School Alliance for Technology Management* Volume 12, Issue 2 (Fall 2008). This article is based on a presentation made at the Howe School Alliance for Technology Management Conference, Hoboken, New Jersey, June 12, 2007.

boasts in Him." It is a warning about our system and our leaders when our system only works with extraordinary leaders and we glorify those leaders. The central characteristic of Jesus' system is the humility of those who do it. "No one may boast before Him." We should be very suspicious and fearful of any system that is complex and requires extraordinary leaders.

5. Go Back to the Basics

Go back to Jesus' basic unit of church life. If you personally cannot or will not live in a friendship triad,

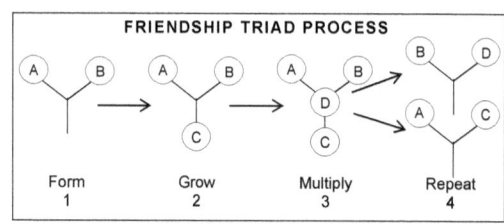

you will not develop an expansion strategy. The triad provides a place to experience the mechanics and dynamics of the church in an embryonic form. So, when developing strategy for the church, always begin with the friendship triad. In a friendship triad Christians experience the promised presence of Christ through the Holy Spirit. This gives life and power to church strategy. Confession of Christ as Lord and confession of sin are part of a friendship triad. Christians apply Scripture to life. Here is where Christians listen to God for each other in prayer and Christ through the Holy Spirit edifies and encourages individual Christians and the Church as a whole. Through friendship triads the first line of evangelism expansion is initiated and the values necessary for expansion are internalized.

Jesus' expansion strategy is self-organizing and naturally grows from the smaller and basic unit to the larger and more complex. Triads of three spontaneously become community cells of twelve and community cells instinctively join together as a cluster team of thirty-seventy (3-6 cells). Self-organizing is one of God's principles of life and creation. When an embryo is being formed, a single cell begins to divide, and when the proper number of cells have multiplied, the cells begin to differentiate and self-organize.

A triad has the DNA information for forming the entire Body of Christ. Begin with the basic triad and it will self-organize into Jesus' community cells and the cells will self-organize into Jesus' supervising cluster. The supervising cluster of seventy is the optimum size and nature for expansion. However self-organization does not happen the other way: The system will not self organize from the more complex to the simple. Clusters do not self-organize into cells and cells do not self organize into triads. The process goes the other way, from the more basic (triad to cell) to the more complex (cluster).

Constantine's organizational church does not self-organize but must be constantly managed and organized. Otherwise, it either flies apart or grinds to a halt. This is why pastors feel like CEOs and why it takes so many paid staff, volunteers, and committees to keep the traditional brick and mortar church running. It is an organization and must be organized. Jesus' system is an organism and self-organizes.

6. Change Values by Providing Experiences

In the preface to this book, I shared the comment of Ralph Neighbour about experiencing and prototyping the dynamic life of a strategy. "We must become evidence of what we want practiced." This truth is key to your success in using Jesus' expansion system in your church. You cannot just teach about a strategy. You must become the strategy and you must provide experiences in order for your people to internalize Jesus' church values.

A leader cannot help others implement a strategy until he/she personally experiences, internalizes, and becomes "evidence of what God wants practiced."

It is dangerous and counterproductive to assume we can change values by transferring religious information and spiritual knowledge. Pastors value preaching and teaching and are trained to inspire and motivate. However, values are not changed or implemented because of information, inspiration, or motivation. Values are internalized and implemented because they are experienced and become part of our inner being ... who we are. "The organizational realm of church ministry can be 'manufactured' --- the organic level can't."[190] The organic level of ministry must be internalized through experience.

A Chinese proverb reminds us of the order of learning: "When you hear something you will forget it. When you see something, you will remember it. But not until you do something, will you understand it."

As you develop a prototype of Jesus' relationship system you will discover it contains the power to change your values and the values of your people from Constantine's organizational system to Jesus' organic relational system. (See Section II in this book for a detailed teaching on prototyping the dynamics of Jesus' expansion system.)

When you and your prototype leaders experience the mechanics and dynamics of a friendship triad and community cell you are living out the basic values that Jesus' disciples experienced during their time with Him. Jesus built His DNA value code into His system. By living in His group system, Christians internalize His values that are expressed in His Great Commission (Matt. 28:18-20) to expand through the earth, His Great Command to

---

190. Schwarz, 98.

love God and one another (Matt. 22:36-40), and His Great Ministry (Luke 4:18-19) to proclaim good news to the poor, freedom for the prisoners, recovery of sight for the blind, to set the oppressed free, and to proclaim the year of the Lord's favor.

In triads and community cells, we experience the following values: Christ's presence and power, total dependence on God, the Lordship of Christ, death to our own methods, ways, and will, humility in realizing we can't make God's church work, prayer listening and speaking, application of the Word, confession and transparency, accountability, sanctification, edification, and evangelism (friendship, oikos, person of peace, and net fishing).

This is why you as a pastor or church planter must experience a triad and a community cell. This has nothing to do with the size or success of your church. In fact, the first value that a pastor or church planter will experience in Jesus' simple system is humility. If you are too busy as a senior pastor to model the basic units of Jesus strategy, then that reveals a need to learn humility in your life and ministry. "Do as I say" has never been an effective strategy. Jesus' 3/12/70 strategy provides a way that every leader can say "Do as I do!"

Jesus built His values into His system. His system will not work without His values and His values will become part of those who experience His system.

7. USE A PARALLEL APPROACH TO STRATEGY

In the past I attempted to develop a comprehensive approach for church strategy: Prototype Jesus' new system while at the same

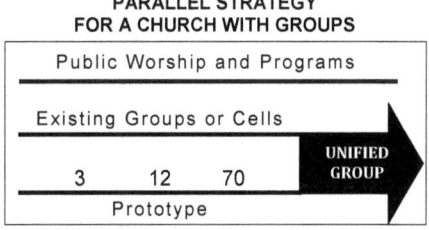

time changing the old public worship and program system and any small group system that was in use. This simultaneous approach to strategy has proved to be complicated and confusing. Changing the old values and methods of the traditional system is a mammoth task that almost always negatively affects a new prototype and slows down the process. It is futile to expect people to change the system and values they know for a system and values yet unknown. In my experience, a small traditional church is just as hard to transition simultaneously as a large traditional church.

In the case of an existing church, I recommend that you visualize your church in three parallel tracks. Leave the public worship and program system alone until you successfully develop a small parallel prototype of Jesus' expansion unit of 3/12/70. (Look at the chart: Parallel Strategy for a Church with Groups.) Don't be distracted by trying to change the existing public system. The same is true of an existing small group system. Tying your initial expansion prototype to the transition of the existing small group system in your church complicates the process and diverts attention away from Jesus' strategy.

First experience Jesus' simple strategy of a friendship triad, a community cell, and a cluster of seventy. Then consider changes to your existing program system after the prototype is completed. Only after you have a cluster of seventy that is growing and expanding through its triads and cells should you consider changes that need to take place in your Sunday public programs. If you have groups you can begin to introduce the 3/12/70 strategy into them when you have prototyped the triad and cell. Until that point, leave your existing groups alone. They are doing what you have told them to do. Only change them after you have a prototype that works.

Again, do not try to change your existing public service and programs while you are developing an expansion prototype. You can operate as a parallel track because you are developing a small prototype that does not require any immediate change to your public worship program or even your current small group system. This releases your prototype from the natural resistance to change of your existing system. This parallel strategic prototype approach allows you and a group of leaders to experience the dynamics, mechanics, and values of what you want your church to do before introducing it and trying to change your current system.

If you are a pastor, the leader of a house church, or a church planter, focus on Jesus' simple strategy. Once you have a working expansion prototype (3/12/70), your way forward is quite evident: Keep multiplying your expansion prototype.

The same idea applies to a new church start: Beginning a public service while developing the first expansion cluster diverts the time, energy, and focus of the new start from relationship expansion to developing and maintaining a come structure public service. If you are a new start, you should develop two or three clusters of seventy before launching any kind of public service.

Trying to move the public service along concurrently with a cluster prototype neutralizes the very reason for a prototype: developing the basics of a new process.

8. Trust God's Organic Strategy to Work

My Dad was a serious quail hunter. He also raised pointer bird dogs and for a period of time had some of the best hunting dogs in the county. Every litter of puppies sold for a high price because of the reputation of his foundation female: Queen, an almost totally white pointer with one liver colored eye.

One day we were hunting with several friends in an area that was being converted from overgrown farmland to grazing land. Trees and bushes had been clear cut and stacked, leaving a perfect habitat for quail. We parked at an abandoned farmhouse. When the dogs were released that crisp November morning, they all began to hunt up a long hill behind the house. We were loading our guns and still had to climb through a fence and walk toward the dogs.

Little Sport was in his first hunting season and it was already evident he was a long-range covey dog. He was beyond all the other dogs at the top of the hill making a sweeping circle. Suddenly, he stopped so quickly it looked like he turned inside out. He froze like a statue in the classic pointer stance: tail straight, one front foot lifted off the ground, and nose pointed toward the covey of quail. At least we hoped it was a covey of quail but you never knew with a young dog.

One of the other hunters said: "Jimmie, Little Sport is down. Will he hold?" He meant: Will he stay on point or commit the cardinal sin of a bird dog and flush the birds before we could get within shooting distance?

My Dad without hesitation replied: "He's bred to." Translated into scientific language my Dad was saying: "It's in his DNA!"

Little Sport did hold and as the other dogs saw his point they honored his point and stopped and pointed toward the covey. Queen honored the point but as if to verify the point of her young son crept carefully forward until she actually smelled the quail. Then she froze in her point. We kicked up a large covey of quail. What a beautiful sight in the early morning light: five or six dogs stretched out up the hill all honoring Little Sport's point.

This is what Little Sport was bred for. He was genetically designed to hunt quail, to point, and to hold point. Little Sport was greatly valued because he did what he was bred to do, and he loved doing it. For the next two hunting seasons a local hunter kept offering my Dad more and more money for Little Sport. Finally the hunter made an offer my Dad couldn't refuse. In the 1960s, $750.00 was an unheard of price to pay for a hunting dog. Little Sport was a treasure of great price like in Jesus' parables in Matthew 13:44-46.

> *The kingdom of heaven is like a treasure hidden in the field, which a man found and hid again; and from joy over it he goes and sells all that he has and buys that field. Again, the kingdom of heaven is like a merchant seeking fine pearls, and upon finding one pearl of great value, he went and sold all that he had and bought it.*

Jesus' church is a treasure of great price because it is Jesus' spiritual Body on earth and is designed to expand into Jerusalem, Judea, Samaria, and the world. God engineered the church for expansion and Jesus designed it with the spiritual DNA of 3/12/70 that self-organizes into a reproducible system of relationships.

Jesus is the pearl of great price because He gave His life for us and for His Body to be able to fulfill His mission on earth. His church is also a pearl of great price. My prayer is that you will find His pearl of great price and buy it!

CHRIST IS THE SYSTEM!

After studying Christ's system for several decades I have come to see that Christ is the system. The church system is His Body that He indwells, empowers through the Holy Spirit, guides through prayer, and heals through edification. His mission is the church's mission (Luke 4:18-19).

> *The Spirit of the Lord is on me, because he has anointed me to proclaim good news to the poor. He has sent me to proclaim freedom for the prisoners and recovery of sight for the blind, to set the oppressed free, to proclaim the year of the Lord's favor.*

His love is the church's love. "This is how we know what love is: Jesus Christ laid down his life for us. And we ought to lay down our lives for our brothers and sisters" (1 John 3:16). His kingdom view of the world is the church's kingdom view: "Jerusalem, Judea, Samaria, and the ends of the world." His peace is the church's peace. "Peace I leave with you; my peace I give you. I do not give to you as the world gives. Do not let your hearts be troubled and do not be afraid" (John 14:27). His unity is the church's unity: "being diligent to preserve the unity of the Spirit in the bond of peace (Eph. 4:3). His suffering and death is the church's suffering and death. "I want to know Christ—yes, to know the power of his resurrection and participation in his sufferings, becoming like him in his death, and so, somehow, attaining to the resurrection from the dead" (Phil. 3:10-11). His victory is the church's victory. Paul describes the church as Christ's system in Ephesians 4:11-16.

> *So Christ himself gave the apostles, the prophets, the evangelists, the pastors and teachers, to equip his people for works of service, so that the body of Christ may be built up until we*

CHAPTER 18: A CONVERSATION ABOUT YOUR STRATEGY

> *all reach unity in the faith and in the knowledge of the Son of God and become mature, attaining to the whole measure of the fullness of Christ. Then we will no longer be infants, tossed back and forth by the waves, and blown here and there by every wind of teaching and by the cunning and craftiness of people in their deceitful scheming. Instead, speaking the truth in love, we will grow to become in every respect the mature body of him who is the head, that is, Christ. From him the whole body, joined and held together by every supporting ligament, grows and builds itself up in love, as each part does its work.*

When we live in and through Christ's system He gives rest, peace, and power. We can spend our time working to enter into Him so that He can do the ministry through us. In Colossians 1:29, Paul identifies the focus of the Christian's labor and striving ... and the source of power. "For this purpose also I labor, striving according to His power, which mightily works within me." (NASB) When Christ is the system I can spend my energy entering into Him so that it is His power that works mightily within me. Organization as a church system demands more and more of my work, labor, and striving, but the church as the organic system of Christ gives life, peace, and power.

By the creative power and will of the Father, the redemptive work of Christ on the Cross, and the indwelling presence and power of the Holy Spirit, the Church is Christ's spiritual Body on earth. Therefore, Christ is the system!

In this book I present the following concepts about Christ's system.

Christ's system is a simple integrated body
Christ's system works with ordinary people
Christ's system is relational in groups of 3/12/70

Christ's system is better than its leaders
Christ's system self-organizes from the inside out
Christ's system develops leaders within its system
Christ's system operates with local resources
Christ's system spreads as a people epidemic

Chapter 19

A CONVERSATION ABOUT THE LARGE GROUP

"The fault here of course lies much deeper than mere architecture. But the building is a witness. It is a signpost telling the world of the church's class consciousness and exclusiveness."
• Howard Snyder

Have I belabored or overstated the danger of the traditional large group for expansion in the 21st century? I don't believe so. Until you and I as pastors, church leaders, and church planters understand the fourth century root of Constantine's large group church, we will not embrace God's first century expansion strategy for the church in the 21st century.

This does not mean the brick and mortar system is bad in all it does, and it is not realistic to expect the current large group expression of the church to be replaced with another method. It is too entrenched and does too many good things. But, Constantine's large group model that we use cannot expand the church. And this is what God wants to do in your church: Expand the church into a New Testament pandemic people movement in your Jerusalem, Judea, Samaria, and the world.

Therefore, before considering strategy I want to look at the large group option one more time. Pastors must settle the issue of the large group because of the overwhelming dominance of the large group in the church today and because what is in the heart and mind of a pastor or church leader will guide vision and strategy.

The church in the New Testament had a public expression when it was possible and it is natural for the church today to do the same. However, the question is what kind of public large group? If we want to expand the 21st century church, we must do two things about the large group of the church: (1) Mold the existing large group expression of the church into a form that will not hinder expansion and (2) find an effective large group that can support, supervise, and organize expansion outside the current brick and mortar centralized model.

Church Safe Zones and Danger Zones

Howard Snyder believes the impact of church buildings on the ministry and mission of the church "lies much deeper than mere architecture."[191] "The building is a witness. It is a signpost telling the world of the church's class consciousness and exclusiveness." Church buildings as edifices are a symptom of the disease of institutionalism that Constantine inserted into the blood stream of Jesus' organic church in the fourth century.

Snyder places a church into safe and danger zones according to how it relates to its church building. He categories the church in these four zones as the Phantom Church, Body Church, Tabernacle Church, and Cathedral Church. I have developed his concepts into the following chart.[192]

This chart is about more than having a building or not having a building. It defines four approaches we can take about the large group expression of the church. The two outside models of

---
191. Snyder, Wineskins, 69-73.
192. Ibid.

CHAPTER 19: A CONVERSATION ABOUT THE LARGE GROUP 347

phantom church and cathedral church are options at the extreme ends of organism and organization. Snyder's phantom church can be compared to an independent house church and his cathedral church is the traditional brick and mortar church. Both are in the danger zone for operating as the New Testament church. The cathedral church has too much organization and the phantom church is too nebulous to supervise organic expansion.

ORGANISM DANGER	SAFE		ORGANIZATION DANGER
PHANTOM CHURCH	BODY CHURCH	TABERNACLE CHURCH	CATHEDRAL CHURCH
Considers a building to be unspiritual & unscriptural. Talks about community, but is highly individualistic. Nebulous existence. No way to supervise or organize expansion. Little form of any kind. Impromptu and informal meetings. No organic interrelatedness. Lacks structure that will promote & conserve growth.	Holds no property and needs none. Its structures are largely organic. Life of the church is in a network of cells. Meets for corporate worship in free or inexpensive venues. Grows as an indigenous people movement. The Body Church is closest to the New Testament design. Operates as a streamlined forward operating base.	A building is important, but secondary. A building is not a "holy place." The purpose of the facility is to extend the Kingdom. A building is a temporary tabernacle or tent. A building is functional & flexible. Groups are essential to church life. The building is designed for ministry. Ministry is flexible, mobile, and focused on expansion.	The building is seen as the church regardless of the size or design. Activities connected to a building and programs. The building shapes the lifestyle and ministry. Many churches fit this: Catholic, Pentecostal, Protestant, Charismatic, and Evangelical. Reinforces the idea to the world that the building is the church. The church requires an extraordinary leader and operates as an organized institution.

Some combination of the two positions in the middle is the best model for expansion: Body Church and Tabernacle Church. They are "safe" and give the church a form while maintaining the spiritual life and organic nature of the church. Only the Body Church and Tabernacle Church will expand the church organically and relationally as a New Testament movement. Snyder's Body Church and Tabernacle Church are the type of large groups I am suggesting in this book: The mid-level cluster of seventy and the streamlined congregation of 120. The biggest problem today is the Cathedral Church with its building and what it represents: stability, study, safety, structure, and worship service.

The Cathedral Church dominates the 21st century church world and is the great obstacle to expansion because it requires a public meeting place, professional leaders, and a centralized organization. This can change if pastors and church planters understand Jesus' expansion system and are willing to break the death grip of Constantine's structure on their conception and vision of church. It's in the two middle options of "Body Church" and "Tabernacle Church" that the church today will find expansion and life as the relational and organic form of Christ.

An Alternative Public Congregation

When beginning to develop a strategy of expansion, Jesus' simple expansion process must be separated from the traditional public cathedral model. This is true of an existing church of any size and kind, as well as of a church plant. The chart below is an adaptation of Snyder's chart and shows the large group options that are part of the church at this time. The Body Church and Tabernacle large groups must be introduced into the church in the 21st century and the existing Cathedral Church must be adjusted and given its proper place. Expansion takes place through the Body Church and Tabernacle Church.

THREE LARGE GROUP OPTIONS

1	2	3
BODY CHURCH ⟶	TABERNACLE CHURCH ⟶	CATHEDRAL CHURCH
3/12/70	50-150	-120+
Supervising	Streamlined	Traditional
Cluster	Congregation	Church
Expansion	*Support*	*Public*

CHAPTER 19: A CONVERSATION ABOUT THE LARGE GROUP

We don't need more cathedral churches but must consider the model because it dominates the church scene. We must somehow involve the cathedral church in the expansion of the kingdom or at the least neutralize its negative influence. The challenge is to produce as many "body churches" as possible that can be supported by "tabernacle churches" in expansion. The force of Jesus' relationship structure is outward as it follows His command to "go".

Jesus' expansion large group of seventy (3/12/70) can operate independently as the body church without walls. As it grows it can develop a streamlined congregation that supports the clusters of seventy. A cluster may also be part of a larger public church that is made up of several clusters of seventy. However, the larger and more public a congregation becomes, the more isolated and detached it is to the expansion mission of the seventy.

Drive through almost any section of the United States and you will see cathedral churches. The traditional cathedral church (public large group number 3 in the above chart) creates a powerful force like a black hole that sucks everything into a central point of an edifice structure, services, sermons, and programs. The question is can these cathedral churches reverse the direction of their flow, sending their people out to participate in expansion? I believe they can be part of God's expansion and that God wants to use these cathedral churches as instruments of expansion. However, Jesus' natural process is to go from the left to the right in the chart: From the Body Church to the Tabernacle Church and then to the Cathedral Church, if it is necessary. The fact is that today we have many cathedral churches and must choose to return to the Body Church. That is difficult, but possible.

For those who are ready to develop an alternative large group support congregation, I want to speak a word of caution. Until a new start or existing church successfully multiplies several seventy supervising clusters, the leaders should not start a support congregation. Once the concept of the seventy has been experienced in a new start or existing church, then leaders can think about providing a streamlined support congregation and eventually a public congregation if necessary. If started too soon, the danger is that even a support congregation (Tabernacle Church) will revert back to the old cathedral public paradigm of preaching, teaching, programs, a building, and a professional pastor.

A streamlined support congregation should operate as a mobile Tabernacle Church. Therefore, in the beginning leaders should resist the temptation to spend money for a place. It may eventually have a facility but must not depend on a building. The purpose of a streamlined congregation is to support the expansion mission of the clusters. Therefore, where it places its time, energy, and money will be different from a public Cathedral Church that is dedicated to preaching, teaching, and providing programs.

Since a streamlined support congregation is a "go" structure rather than a "come" structure, the activities in the congregation are focused outward into harvest. Because of the prominence of its friendship triads and community cells, a streamlined support congregation is about relationships rather than programs. A streamlined support congregation is organic in nature while providing enough organization to have a public witness and to support its clusters in expansion. In a streamlined congregation, the producers are mobilized as agents of expansion rather than providers of programs.

COLOR JESUS' PICTURE OF THE CHURCH

In nature there are seven colors in the color spectrum: red, orange, yellow, green, blue, indigo, and violet. The primary colors are: red, yellow and blue. From these seven basic colors, an infinite number of color combinations and shades can be made. In creation, God has colored different objects with an infinite array of colors and we do the same when we paint or color pictures. We color different pictures but use the same basic colors. Think about it: If I give you an uncolored picture of a ship and your friend an uncolored picture of a tiger, you can use the same colors for the ship and for the tiger. However, you still know which is the ship and which is the tiger no matter what colors you use. Color the picture of a ship pink and green and it is still the picture of a ship. It is the shape and form of the object that gives identity, not the color.

I recently illustrated this truth about shapes and colors with three pastors during breakfast at IHOP. I asked the receptionist for a child's activity kit that many restaurants provide. The kit was a piece of paper with some black and white pictures and a red, green, and blue crayon. The black and white pictures provided in restaurants usually follow a theme such as animals, boats, or cars. IHOP's coloring sheet that day was pictures of a space station and a space rocket. I colored the space station one color and then colored it another color. The pastors agreed that no matter what color I colored the picture, it was still a space station. Color does not change form. Horses come in many different colors but we still call them "horses."

The ministry elements of the church are the colors that are applied to every picture of the church (form). The fact is that all church strategies consist of the same basic ministry "colors" of discipleship, Bible study, prayer, worship, evangelism, leadership training, equipping, gifts, and groups. It is the picture of the church that is different. Your strategy will be colored within the lines of the church picture in your mind. If my outline of the church is Christ's relationship model then, using the same elements/colors (discipleship, Bible Study, prayer, worship, evangelism, leadership, training, equipping, gifts, and groups) my picture will resemble the Early Church.

I am not talking about nuances and shades of the ministries that we all use for the church. I am talking about the outline and shape of the church. We must recognize the difference in how Jesus forms the Church and how Constantine forms it. The spiritual elements of the church take the shape of the design of the church. If your picture of the church is Constantine's organizational model then no matter what combination or shade of ministry colors you use, the picture will be Constantine's model.

We can color the traditional Constantine picture with a new program of discipleship and it is still a picture of Constantine's church. We can paint a new coat of prayer or worship and it is still a picture of Constantine's church. This is what we have been doing for decades. Denominational offices and special ministries provide another shade of ministry and we apply it to our church. However, nothing substantially changes because the new program is applied to the same old system picture.

Our problem is not with the colors we are using but with the Constantine cathedral picture we are painting! Every year pastors are offered new programs that promise to increase the growth of the church or to make it work better. Providing these programs has become an industry supported by denominations and independent religious organizations. The idea is to paint the church with a new program shade of prayer, worship, discipleship, worship, or outreach. Seminaries train pastors how to paint a different style of sermon that is more interesting, entertaining, and generationally friendly. All these programs are good but will not substantially change the organizational picture of the church no matter how appealing and colorful they may be. The centralized church will continue to function as a maintenance system because that is what it is no matter what colors you use.

Jesus' system is a different picture. The same colors are applied but the system is different. It is absolutely essential to have the end picture in mind before developing a strategy for coloring in between the lines with the wonderful spiritual elements we see in the New Testament. We can't change the picture of the church by using different shades of ministry colors. Constantine's picture of the church will not look like Jesus' New Testament picture, no matter how much you color it with the same beautiful ministry colors of preaching, worship, teaching, ministries, bible study, social programs, and evangelism projects. The picture is still of Constantine's consumer church, not Jesus' expansion system.

We must change the picture itself! We must stop painting Constantine's picture of the church and expecting it to look substantially different. We must paint Jesus' picture of the church. The colors we use will be the same ministry colors we see in the New Testament, and the ones we have used for years.

The Choice

Pastors and members are not greatly alarmed when new or repackaged ministry programs are introduced because these programs do not substantially change the structure of the church. They just put a different color and layer on the church form. However, pastors and members will not easily give up their consumer system for the opportunity to participate in a producer system because that requires a change in the form of the church.

The familiar large group with its public worship, preaching, teaching, program ministries, and event centered service is too convenient for members and too familiar to pastors. In addition, pastors have too much invested in the traditional public model to change without a working model to replace it. People change for practical, not theoretical reasons. No one wants to change something for nothing, no matter how good the new idea sounds in theory. That means we must have a prototype of an alternative large group that will expand beyond the walls of the traditional church building.

Contrary to what many believe, the church can change and has changed. For example, the music style of worship has dramatically changed over the past several decades. In the past, church worship meant choirs, robes, hymns, organs, congregational singing, and pianos. Today churches have worship bands, contemporary songs, guitars, drums, keyboards, and spectators in blue jeans and caps watch. This is evidence that the church can change over a period of time.

The church also changed in its attitude toward and use of small groups. Over a period of fifty years small groups have become an accepted ministry method. In time, God can add an expansion large group to the church as well. It may require some time but the church can incorporate an expansion system of seventy as described in this book.

In terms of expansion the church has no choice. Either the church will find some kind of producer system that will mobilize a greater number of its members in expansion harvest or it will continue to retreat into its consumer enclaves of preaching, programs, professional leaders, and buildings. However, a producer expansion system and consumer traditional system are not necessarily mutually exclusive. A church with a public worship center can support the kind of expansion I am talking about in units of seventy ... if its leaders have the will to do it and can prototype a working model! A strategy based on Jesus' principles will have (1) a small group unit through which the lost can be contacted in friendship relationships, (2) a community group in which people can live out the basic life of Christ, and (3) a group that can supervise and organize the triads and cells for expansion.

If your church is going to expand, you must use Jesus' expansion system of 3/12/70. It is this expansion system I want to talk about in the remaining chapters of this book. Jesus' simple system will increase capacity, maximize growth, manage quality, produce leaders, support vision, reinforce values, focus on productivity, simplify strategy, and streamline organization.

Chapter 20

A CONVERSATION ABOUT TWO STRATEGIC POINTS

"In absence of clearly defined goals, we become strangely loyal to performing daily acts of trivia."
• Unknown

In order to develop a successful strategy, we must first nail down two points: Where we are and where we want to be.

```
WHERE                                    WHERE WE
WE ARE                                   WANT TO BE
X ───────────────────────────────────── X
```

The first point for developing strategy is to determine where you are. I have talked about this beginning point over and over in this book in order to give you time to internalize what I am talking about.

So, let me sum it up: You are in the middle of an elaborate and powerful organizational system that was conceived by Constantine in the fourth century and refined by brilliant and sincere Christian leaders throughout seventeen hundred years. To this day the traditional cathedral church continues to morph into new forms, but always with the same core organizational nature; it requires a building, a public meeting, a professional leader, and a product that will attract consumers. If you are a cell church you live out this kind of church in your large group public expression. If you are a house church you use the same worship, teaching, and preaching model but scale it down to fit into a house setting.

The second point in developing strategy is to have some kind of idea of where you are going. I have sought to describe that end destination in previous chapters. Let me sum it up: Jesus' church is an organic body that is unhindered by walls, funding, programs, and professional leaders. It expands through relationships that are nurtured and supervised in an integrated group system of 3/12/70.

However, let me be honest about Jesus' church: Each of us faces an Abraham moment about the Church. The place to which Christ is calling us requires an act of faith. God pointed Abraham and his descendants in a direction and gave a general vision of a land "flowing with milk and honey" (Ex. 3:8; 33:3). However, it was not the vision that got them to the land but their faith in the One Who gave the vision promise. In Hebrews chapter 11, the writer describes the journey of Israel as a walk of faith with God. Yet "none of them received what had been promised. God had planned something better so that only together with us would they be made perfect" (Heb. 11:39-40).

As they traveled toward the place God promised, they became their destination. That is why their journey was so long and painful: God had to shape them into the form of the vision. Best-selling author and motivational speaker Zig Ziglar personalized the process of implementing goals: "What you get by achieving your goals is not as important as what you become by achieving your goals."

ASSUMPTIONS

Without these two points, our strategy has no point of reference or set course and is pushed from side to side by historical assumptions that become our values and shape our strategy. A large portion of this book has been devoted to comparing assumptions about the traditional church that is building-centered and come-structure (where we are) with Jesus' mobile expansion model that is relationship-centered (where we want to be). I have made this comparison over and over using different images in order to clarify and sharpen the vision for me personally and for you as a reader. This redundancy is necessary because an idea must be considered from a variety of different vantage points and methods of explanation so that it may be internalized and owned.

All strategy is based upon assumptions. Therefore, how successful you and I are in developing an expansion strategy for the church will largely depend on our church assumption.

> *Lying behind all strategies are assumptions, which often remain implicit and untested. Frequently, these assumptions have internal contradictions. When they do, the strategy also has internal contradictions, which will prove to make it difficult or impossible to implement. One benefit of microworlds is bringing these assumptions into the open and discovering these inconsistencies.*[193]

In order to develop a successful prototype of the New Testament church (Senge's "microworld") it is necessary to understand the basic assumptions about where we are and where we are going. If our hope for expansion lies in making the traditional large group work better then it will be difficult to develop a successful

---
193. Senge, 316.

expansion prototype. There are two basic assumptions in this book that I've been building a case for in order to help you step forth in faith into a new dynamic of expansion: (1) The greatest strategic obstacle to expansion in the 21st century is the traditional large group and (2) Jesus designed the church to expand through His relationship and self-organizing unit of 3/12/70.

WHERE WE ARE

The chart, *Traditional Large Group Public Model*, is a snapshot of where the church is at this time in history. This chart represents the large public group of all models, including the cell church model. In the interior box at the top of the chart you see buildings, professional pastors, programs, ministries, and events that characterize the traditional church public model. All churches today use some variation of this box.

TRADITIONAL LARGE GROUP PUBLIC MODEL

LARGE GROUP		
-100 to 1000+		
BUILDINGS		PASTORS
PROGRAMS	ACTIVITIES	EVENTS
BIBLE STUDY	**SPECIALIZED SMALL GROUPS**	**COMMUNITY CELLS**
Graded	Bible Study Group	3
Buildings	Fellowship Group	12
Education	Ministry Group	70
Organization	Discipleship Group	120

At the bottom of the chart you see three types of small groups that have developed over the years to supplement and support the traditional public system. Traditional denominational churches focus on Bible study, creative contemporary churches use specialized small groups, and cell churches organize in community cells. Some churches now use a combination of the three supplement group ministries. For instance, a church may continue to have Sunday Bible classes while also using small groups or cells during the week.

The fact is, all models today (large and small churches) continue to use Constantine's large group public model: Preaching and programs in a building that will attract seekers and hold Christians. As I have stated previously, the traditional large group model is high-maintenance, expensive, low-expansion, and requires extraordinary and professional leaders. Under the proper extraordinary leader it can produce contained, controlled, and centralized growth. It will grow in place but will not expand in space. This is the reason we must find an alternative large group that is low maintenance, high growth, works with ordinary leaders, and will expand beyond a church building. Jesus' mid-sized large group of seventy can operate as an expansion extension of a traditional model or can operate as a separate independent unit.

Pastor, church leader, and church planter, we must honestly acknowledge where we are. We start with Constantine's traditional large group model that has been used for seventeen centuries. If you are familiar with my ministry you may have read my first book, *The Second Reformation*, in which I advocated the cell group as the wineskin structure that would restore us to the New Testament Church. I did not realize at the time the power of the Constantine conception of the church in its large group form. My greatest surprise in preparing to write this current book has been the realization that the Cell Church also uses the traditional large group public model.

The Cell Church replaces Sunday school or small groups with cells. (See the above chart.) However, Cell Churches continue to utilize the traditional large group preaching, teaching, and building centered model for church planting. (I must add, *unsuccessfully* utilizes the traditional model for church planting). Consequently, Cell Churches have grown internally but have not expanded externally.

Even the house church model employs the same basic preaching, teaching, and worship model, just in a smaller version in a house. In addition, traditional church planting models are also tied to this public model. This is why we don't today see exponential expansion as a people epidemic. The only exceptions are pioneer church planting and areas of persecution where the church is forced into using some form of Jesus' organic system of 3/12/70. We will consider church planting in detail in Chapter 22.

END POINT: A CHURCH NOT DEPENDENT ON WALLS

Yogi Berra, the great New York Yankee baseball player and amateur sage, stated an insightful truth in his own way. "If you don't know where you are going, you'll end up someplace else." Seneca, the Roman philosopher and statesman, put it this way: "If a man knows not to which port he sails, no wind is favorable." We must know our destination for the church. The end is important because in the "absence of clearly defined goals, we become strangely loyal to performing daily acts of trivia." Motivational speaker Zig Zigler warns business leaders "if you aim at nothing, you will hit it every time."

This end point is not our strategy but our destination. It is a picture of where we want the strategy to take us. But, as Abraham Lincoln observed: "A goal properly set is hallway reached."

Can you envision a church unit that can survive without a Sunday service in a building and without a traditional worship, preaching, and teaching program? Imagine there is a cataclysmic event

CHAPTER 20: A CONVERSATION ABOUT TWO STRATEGIC POINTS   363

and you can no longer meet in your building in public. What will you do? This actually happened in New Orleans when hurricane Katrina hit with such devastation. Churches that were organized in cells, such as Celebration Church in Metairie, Louisiana, were able to deal with the traumatic situation because they were already organized to function outside the walls of the church buildings that were flooded or destroyed. Pastor Dennis Watson mobilized Celebration Church through its cell structure to be a communication and distribution center for the storm ravaged area. Can your church survive in its current form, no matter what political, social, or natural events may occur?

In order to develop a successful expansion strategy, pastors, church leaders, and church planters must visualize the end point of the strategy. Even if we change the way we begin a strategy, we will have the same result if the end point does not change. If our end point is a version of Constantine's public worship service, that is what will develop no matter what new strategies we use in the beginning or in the process.

Clusters of seventy are freed from the traditional brick and mortar congregation and can be an expansion extension of an existing church. This allows the expansion force of the 3/12/70 to continue unimpeded by the organization or leadership required to maintain a large group. The following chart, *New Large Group Expansion Model*, shows the end point of a church that is expanding as a people movement. An expansion strategy will develop supervising clusters of seventy. Each cluster will form from the smallest expansion unit (3) to the largest expansion unit (70). A cluster doesn't need a congregation to exist and expand but can continue to multiply clusters by multiplying friendship triads and community cells. If necessary for logistical support, two or three clusters can eventually form a streamlined support congregation.

However, a streamlined support congregation is different from the traditional public large group. A streamlined support congregation of 120 does not require an extraordinary or professional leader. In fact, a leader of a support congregation should rise up out of the ranks of the cluster leaders who are forming the congregation. It is not dependent on a building and therefore is able to support the cluster expansion mission. It is a "go" rather than a "come" structure. A support congregation functions as a "private" support unit to train followers rather than a public unit to attract seekers. It is a body church or tabernacle church that can exist outside of the walls of a building. (See Snyder's four approaches of the church in the previous chapter.)

NEW LARGE GROUP EXPANSION MODEL

3-12-**70**	Church Without Walls		Church With A Public Face
A cluster **3-12-70** may operate without a congregation.		**1**	STREAMLINED
	3-12-70	**2**	SUPPORT
		0	CONGREGATION

A streamlined support congregation of 120:
Works with ordinary leaders.
Is not dependent on a building.
Operates as a Tabernacle Church.
Supports the cluster expansion mission.
Is a "go" rather than a "come" structure.
When needed, forms out of clusters of 70.
Is about relationships rather than programs.
Is balanced between organic & organization.

Strategy Continuum: Stuff in between

Once leaders establish where the church is and where it is going, they can develop what goes between: a strategy continuum. The continuum must have both the dynamics (presence, prayer, and edification) and mechanics (friendship triad, community cell, and supervising cluster) necessary to produce expansion. (The different parts of the continuum are covered in Section II about prototypes.)

The arrow in the chart below represents the process of the strategy: What is between the starting and end points. The dif-ferent elements overlap and flow along together. The continuum isn't a rigid step-by-step sequence but a dynamic process that allows flexibility.

STRATEGY CONTINUUM

While developing an expansion prototype, the pastor or catalytic leader will do the following.

TWO OR THREE TRIAD .... COMMUNITY CELL .... SUPERVISING CLUSTER

Personally experience the mechanics and dynamics of life in a triad and cell
Provide a Bible reading plan for triads and discussion questions for cells
Develop a personal discipleship study for new believers
Form two prototype Friendship Triads: men and women
Multiply the friendship triads into full triads of 3 and then 4 persons
Grow the triads into a pastor-led prototype cell of eight to ten persons
Prototype the mechanics & dynamics (Body Life/edification) of a cell meeting
Develop cell leaders & assistants in on-the-job training and mentoring
Multiply the initial prototype community cell into two cells
Mentor two cell leaders to be cluster leaders In a mentoring triad.
Form the three prototype cells into an initial supervising cluster
Meet as a cluster to cast vision, train, deploy, debrief, and encourage
Grow to six cells (a mature cluster) and multiply into two smaller clusters
Evangelize through friendships, *oikos*, person of peace, and net fishing events
Develop courses for Evangelism (3), Body Life (12), and Supervision (70)

In the remaining chapters I want to have a conversation with you about this continuum and the surprisingly simple strategy for implementing Jesus' New Testament model.

Chapter 21

A CONVERSATION ABOUT STRATEGY BUILDING BLOCKS

"Without strategy, execution is aimless. Without execution, strategy is useless."
   • Morris Chang CEO of TSMC[194]

Previously I promised to show you a surprisingly simple strategy for implementing Jesus' New Testament expansion model. However, even though Jesus' strategy is simple, the current traditional model complicates the implementation of His strategy. We must have a paradigm shift in vision, values, and concepts before Jesus' simple strategy can cut through the complexity of the current traditional model. Revelation is necessary to make this paradigm shift!

Versions of Jesus' strategy have worked throughout history wherever the church has used it. Some leaders return to Jesus' expansion strategy because of theological and practical conviction. John Wesley in the 18th century used a system of groups that gave him and his associates "the ability to give minute supervision to a vast army of growing Christians. As the architect of a well-disciplined movement, he was able to assimilate large population blocs into his organization in a

---

194. Morris Chang is Chairman of Taiwan Semiconductor Manufacturing Company Ltd. that he founded in 1987. TSMC pioneered the "dedicated silicon foundry" industry and is the largest silicon foundry in the world.

short time, train them effectively in the rudiments of Christian discipleship, and mobilize them into an ardent corps of social change agents." [195]

Sometimes circumstances such as persecution have forced the church to return to Jesus' strategy. This happened in the first century and in China in the last century. Where political and religious persecution and pressure is strongest today we see the expansion of the Gospel. Persecution is not the cause of expansion per se but persecution forces the church to return to Jesus' original expansion design of 3/12/70. The successful church planting movements we hear about today are examples of the church returning to Jesus' basic expansion building blocks.

This raises a question for the church in the West. Is persecution the only thing that will force the church in the West to implement Jesus' design of the church? Or, will we follow Wesley's example and implement Jesus' design because we are true to His theology of the organic church and His simple group strategy of 3/12/70?

Details have a way of making our eyes glaze over and our minds go into neutral. So, please bear with me because the details in this chapter are essential for implementing Jesus' simple strategy.

Interchangeable Building Blocks

Jesus' simple strategy is built upon the three interrelated groups that He modeled in the first century and that the church has used (wholly or partially) every time it has produced an expansion movement in history. This three-stage model works in

---

[195]. D. Michael Henderson, *John Wesley's Class Meetings* (Napanee, IN: Evangel Publishing House, 1997), 15.

every situation in which I have applied it as a pastor, a church planter, missionary, and as I now mentor pastors. These three units can be used to grow internally and expand externally as well. This is possible because of the integrated nature of Jesus' system.

The same type of building materials and architectural principles are used whether constructing a small house, a larger building, or a huge skyscraper. The application differs only in scale and architectural design. This analogy from architecture can be applied to Jesus' design of the Church.

EXPANSION BUILDING BLOCKS

Jesus said He would build His church. As the divine architect, He designed the church to operate with the same basic building blocks in every situation. Jesus' expansion strategy is interchangeable, no matter the size, age, place, or type of church. Also, every expansion church uses the same building blocks to develop strategy no matter the surrounding environment, educational level, cultural situation, demographic makeup (urban or rural), social class and condition, economic circumstances (rich or poor), or political context (restricted or free).

Jesus' interrelated group system operates as a whole unit but with each part able to stand-alone. Therefore, in this book I have written the expansion unit as "3/12/70" in order to show it has separate parts that are connected. Jesus designed these three groups to operate as an integrated and interchangeable body system, not as independent parts. From what I have seen and experienced, the Cell Church has come closest to integrating Jesus' group system so that all the tasks of the church function as a whole. However, the Cell Church has also been held hostage by the large group public paradigm that adversely affects church planting and the transition of the brick and mortar church into a more New Testament expansion model.

Jesus' building blocks require no other special ministries or programs to expand. When you use Jesus' expansion building blocks of 3/12/70 you will be able to reproduce Jesus' system and His fruit: You will form Jesus' groups, produce Jesus' leaders, implement Jesus' strategy, internalize Jesus' values, provide Jesus' supervision, and participate in Jesus' expansion results. The building blocks interelate and complement each other beginning from the smallest to the largest: The triad to the cell and to the cluster.

Each group contributes a special aspect of Christ's expansion strategy to the church. The triad is the contagious unit: The place where believers are infected with a strong dose of the Gospel. It is the basic unit that God uses to spread the gospel as an infectious epidemic. The cell is the family unit. God's fathers, young men, and children are nurtured, protected, and prepared in the community cell. The cluster is the mission/task unit where the Holy Spirit organizes, supervises, and mobilizes the triads and cells for expansion harvest. God needs each aspect of His three units to fullfill His plan to penetrate Jerusalem, Judea, Samaria, and the ends of the earth.

These three building blocks produce sufficient leaders from within the system to operate the system. The moving parts operate through relationships without walls. Jesus' three expansion building blocks are an extremely simple but extraordinary and powerful system that operates with ordinary leaders and people.

STRATEGY OVERVIEW

The startup plan I am proposing is a way for a pastor or church planter to prototype the mechanics and dynamics of Jesus' organic strategy. The chart below, *Triad, Cell & Cluster Prototype*, is a strategy picture that shows the five steps necessary to develop an expansion prototype:

1. Begin friendship triads
2. Form a prototype community cell
3. Multiply into two cells
4. Form the first cluster team,
5. Multiply the cluster.

Now, lets break down the five steps in an implementation strategy. The prototype will include a disciple triad of two or three, a prototype of a community cell of twelve, and a prototype of a supervising cluster of seventy. Each prototype is necessary to complete the next prototype. Without hindering factors from the existing model, the units will naturally self-organize: The triad prototype forms the community cell prototype and the community cell prototype organizes into the cluster prototype. Each of these prototypes was discussed separately in earlier chapters in this book.

While developing these three prototypes, leaders must experience the dynamic disciplines in Jesus' organic system: Abide in the presence of Christ, acknowledge the Lordship of Christ, learn to listen to God in prayer, apply scripture to life, follow and obey the Holy Spirit, follow and obey the Spirit, spur one another on toward love and good deeds, participate in edification through practical prophecy, live together in body life, multiply through natural friendship evangelism (the person of peace, the *oikos* sphere of influence, and those "caught" in net fishing events). In addition, leaders will model the roles of cell nurture and cluster supervision.

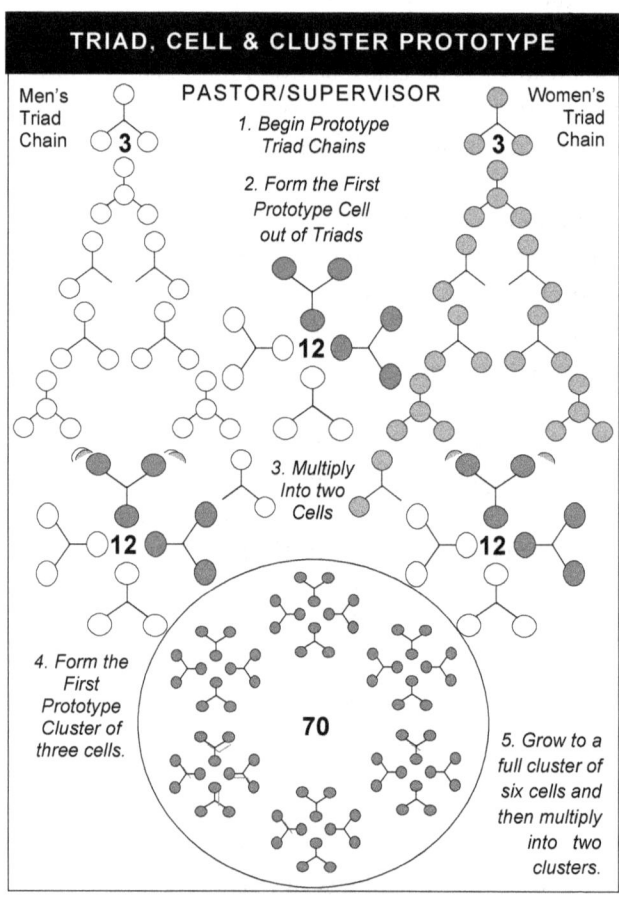

The next chart, *Friendship Triad Process*, shows the stages in the development of a friendship triad. (It was introduced in chapter 11.) A pastor or church planter must begin at this point and experience (prototype) the life and multiplication of a friendship triad with a group of followers. This process is repeated in the life cycle of each triad and is the multiplication and expansion catalyst in Jesus' strategy for today. These four stages explain the practical application of the two or three core unit.

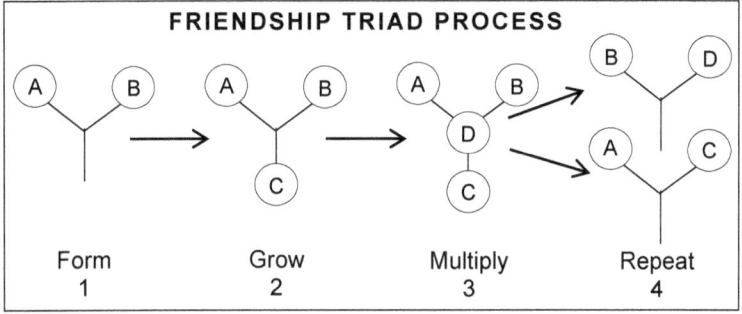

STRATEGY STEP ONE: BEGIN PROTOTYPE TRIADS

Form a triad with one other person. In the case of a new church plant or a church that is beginning cells, the pastor/leader chooses another leader to help prototype a friendship triad. Begin prototype triads by forming a men's triad and a women's triad. (See Chapter 9 for a background study of the Friendship Triad.) As the initial triads grow, they will form two triad chains that contain the DNA material for the community cells, and clusters. It is imperative that the pastor or church planter forms the first triad in order to personally experience the dynamic of a friendship triad.

The triad experience includes the personal and community disciplines listed above: Abiding in the presence of Christ, applying scripture to life, listening to God in prayer, confessing the Lordship of Christ and personal sin, spurring each other on toward love and good deeds, following the Spirit, edifying one another, being accountable to and for each other, activating friendship evangelism, reproducing by adding one more friend and then another, and then multiplying into two triads.

The objective is to form a men's chain and a women's chain as pictured in the Triad Chains chart. The spouse of the pastor or church planter can lead one of the initial triads.

The two persons in the first prototype triad connect in relationships, meet regularly, talk to each other on the phone, use Skype, text, and send emails. In other words, they use all the normal means 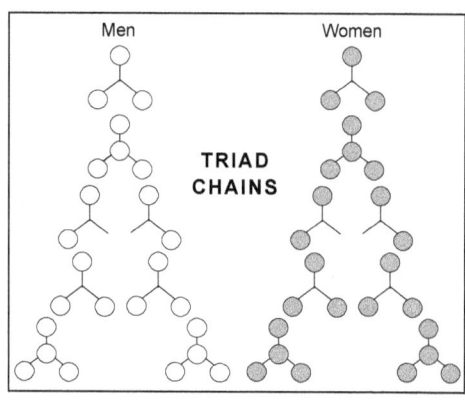 of relationship, written and verbal correspondence, social media, and face-to-face activities that family and friends use. They bond in a relationship of friendship around the written Word (the Bible) and living Word (the Holy Spirit). In churches that already have community cells or small groups, it is better to allow them to continue while developing a separate triad prototype and starting the initial triad chains. Once the friendship triad chain is prototyped (men's chain and women's chain), a strategy can be devised for forming community cells or incorporating triads into the existing cells or small groups. In a church that already has cells or groups, the pastor may, after the initial triad is completed, form a seed prototype triad in each existing cell or group.

Grow by adding a friend. The objective is to bring another person (C) into the friendship triad so that the original two become three. The new person can be a relative, friend, or acquaintance. The friend may be a Christian, a new follower of Christ, a prodigal believer, or a person of peace seeker. The triad continues to do the same thing: Apply scripture to life, pray for one another, confess Jesus Christ is Lord, confess sins, spur each other on to love and practice, and edify and encourage each other. In other words, be a Christian friend. The triad experience is a great atmosphere for friendship evangelism. Continue growth by adding a fourth person into the triad. The second friend can come into the triad in the same way as the first friend: from friendship evangelism, *oikos* sphere of influence relationships, person of peace seekers, and cell net-fishing events.

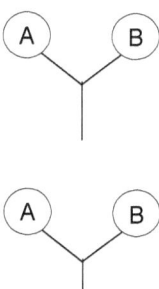

Multiply when the fourth person (D) is added. The triad remains together for four to six weeks as a group of four and then multiplies into two basic friendship triads of two. Form the new triads along natural relationships. Look at the process chart again. I am assuming that "A" invited "C" into the triad and that "B" invited "D". Therefore, one new friendship triad is formed out of "A" and "C" and the other triad is formed out of "B" and "D". Relationship is the central principle in friendship. Therefore, the simple rule of a triad is to grow along relationship lines.

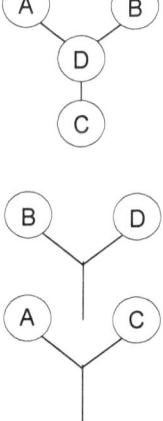

Repeat the process. The two new triads of two persons go back to the second step and repeat the process: grow to four, multiply into two, and repeat the process. The goal is to keep multiplying the two or three unit. Triads are always connected to community cells and the initial prototype triads lead to step two in the process: the prototype community cell. Triads will not multiply at the same pace.

The pastor or church planter must develop the initial triad prototype. This does several things: (1) involves the pastor and spouse in developing a triad prototype, (2) maintains the integrity of the mechanics and dynamics of the triad, (3) raises the commitment level of the pastor to friendship triads, (4) internalizes the values of Jesus' expansion system in the leaders, and (5) gives the personal experience and necessary time for the pastor to develop a triad Bible reading plan and to provide a basic study for new believers.

I agree with Neil Cole's appraisal of evangelism in triads. "These groups spread like wild fire because the breath of God blows on obedient disciples who find fuel in dry lives longing to burn for the Lord. Because the system is simple enough to pass on with one easy description the flame spreads unhindered. Ordinary Christians are empowered to do the most important work any of us can do."[196]

Strategy Step Two: Form the First Community Cell

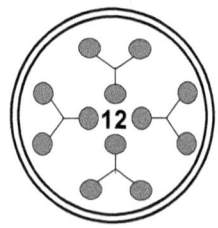

Form the first prototype cell out of the triads. The first cell should be made up of around nine persons: three or four triads. Some triads will be just beginning with two persons, some may have three persons, and some may be ready to multiply with four persons. Any combination that adds up to eight or nine persons will work. This will give the first cell a strong core but also give space for it to grow through its triads that will continue to function. A full cell will have four triads of three or four persons

---

196. Cole, *Cultivating a Life for God*, 94.

in each triad, depending on the pace of growth of each triad. The cell meeting is a place where relationships come together in community. A triad is a relationship of friends who communicate and meet as friends.

Unlike the gender specific triads, most cells will be mixed with men and women. However, cells are flexible and gender, age, and life needs can be factored into how they are formed. When prototyping the community cell, the nature of the triad must be protected because triads provide the first experience of the dynamic life that will be fully experienced in a community cell. During the cell prototype, the pastor and leaders will experience the mechanics (nuts and bolts) and the dynamics of cell community life that was experienced in embryo in the triads: Christ in the midst (2 Cor. 14:24), using the application questions, being accountable to each other, experiencing edification through practical prophecy, and following up on the friends, oikos, and persons of peace that became part of the triads. In addition, during the community cell process, leaders will be reproduced and the community cell will multiply into two cells through the growth of the triads. Cell leaders will emerge out of the friendship triads.

This is not a formula but a community experience with Christ and each other. Chapter 10 gives the theological and practical foundations necessary to understand the mechanics and dynamics of a community cell. The pastor or church planter must do the following things while leading the first prototype cell:

1. Model a cell agenda. Many use a version of the 4 W's: Welcome, Worship, Word, and Works. The cell agenda should facilitate three experiences: (1) experiencing the presence of Christ in prayer and worship; (2) experiencing the power of Christ in New Testament edification through practical prophecy; and (3) experiencing the purpose of Christ of fulfilling the

Great Commission through friendship evangelism, cultivating the *oikos* sphere of influence of cell members, contacting and following up on persons of peace, and reaching the lost in net fishing activities of the cell.

2. Lead the cell into the presence of Christ. "Where two or three gather in my name, there I am in the midst." Begin each meeting by acknowledging the presence of Christ.

3. Provide application questions about a passage from the Bible that will be used in a discussion time during the cell meeting. These should be why (root) questions and not what questions about the details of a personal story line. In a triad, Scripture is personally applied. In a cell, Scripture is also applied within the community through New Testament edification.

4. Help cell members experience New Testament edification. Edification is the central experience of the cell because God, through the work of Christ and the administration of the Holy Spirit, builds up individuals, the cell, and the church. Edification is God's wellness program for the church.

5. Identify two or three potential cell leaders as they function in the triads and cell and mentor them in a leader triad.

6. The cell leader and assistants nurture the triads in order for a cell to grow and multiply.

7. The cell leader makes sure every person in a triad completes a new believer study for Christian living.

Let me include a word of caution for a church that already has groups or cells. The temptation is to immediately organize the existing groups or cells into triads. This is the fast way but not the best way. It is preferable for the pastor and spouse to prototype a men's triad and a women's triad so that they multiply through two or three cycles and form into a cell. Then, using the prototype triads as a model, the pastor can seed a prototype triad in each existing group or cell. In this way, each community cell will observe up close and in real time the benefit of a friendship triad.

STRATEGY STEP THREE: MULTIPLY INTO TWO CELLS

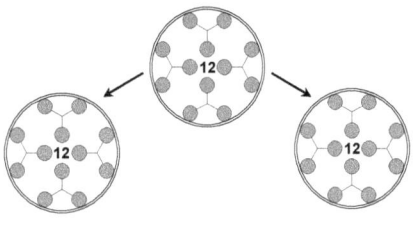

Expansion in the New Testament began when the first church became smaller. The 3,000 and 5,000 new believers were assimilated into community groups that met in the homes of Jerusalem Christians and seekers. There they experienced the life of Christ and learned what was necessary to return home and repeat the process they experienced in Jerusalem.

Jesus built the DNA of multiplication into His community group system. Therefore, multiplication is the natural inclination of a cell. If a cell is not growing it is dying. In the case of a Cell Church, a cell multiplies into newer and more manageable smaller groups that have the potential, vigor, and space to grow. "If we were to identify any one principle as the 'most important,' then without a doubt it would be the multiplication of small groups."[197]

---

197. Schwarz, 32.

A cell can multiply through biological multiplication or through generation multiplication. Biological multiplication follows the growth principle of cell division/multiplication that is the natural growth process of a biological cell. The original cell splits and becomes two new cells made up of half of the members of the original cell. Generation multiplication grows as a family. Each member in the cell is prepared to go out and begin a new cell. Children from the parent cell begin a new "family." The "father" of the new family continues to be part of and receive support from the parent cell. A combination of biological and generation multiplication may also be used. Two or three mature Christians in the original cell form a triad and begin a new "family." Both methods depend upon the triad to generate multiplication because the triad is the contagious factor in Jesus' strategy.

Andrew is the model of friendship multiplication. (See chapter 9.) "The first thing Andrew did was to find his brother Simon" (John 1:41). "Go home and tell how much God has done for you" (Luke 8:29). "Some Greeks came to Philip. He went to tell Andrew; Andrew and Philip in turn told Jesus" (John 12:20-22). "So the churches were strengthened in the faith and grew daily in numbers" (Acts 16:5).

Multiplication in a community cell naturally flows out of a friendship triad. The objective is to bring another person into the triad so the original two become three. The friendship triad is the place of basic evangelism: The first contact with friends who are "person of peace," the penetration of an individual Christian's *oikos* (sphere of influence), and the cultivation of those "caught" in the net fishing activities of the cell. The new person invited to be part of a triad can be an unbelieving seeker, a hurting Christian, or a person finding their way back to God. The triad is the natural place to assimilate new believers and to provide extra grace for hurting people who are not ready to function in a community cell. Cells cultivate, assimilate, and follow up on the persons of peace that are uncovered in friendship triads.

STRATEGY STEP FOUR: FORM THE FIRST CLUSTER TEAM

The primary factor in developing a prototype that will expand and multiply is leaders, not numbers. You can have thirty to forty people in a beginning prototype of three or four cells but still be unable to form a cluster team because you do not have the proper leaders. The cluster of seventy is the functional leadership group for expansion through 3 to 6 cell leaders and a supervising leader.

Once leadership is defined and modeled and leaders are prepared, the multiplication process can be set into motion through a supervising cluster. The initial cell should by this time have twelve to fifteen persons (4 to 6 triads) and will multiply into two cells along natural relationship lines. The pastor or church planter of the prototype may continue to be one of the cell leaders but as quickly as possible after this point should step into the role of supervisor of the emerging cluster. That is the next step.

The key to forming your first supervising cluster is to model the different leadership roles that are already operating in the prototype in the life of the pastor or church planter. Think of these roles as different hats. Hats have a functional role for the person who wear them. We

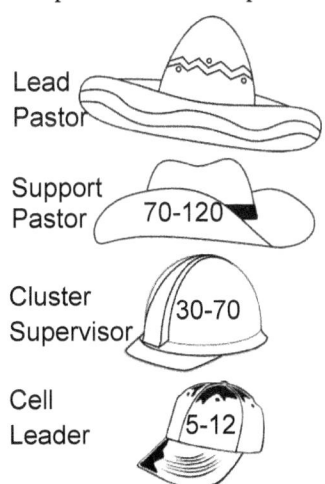

identify certain tasks or roles with certain types of hats. Baseball players wear caps, cowboys wear wide brimmed hats first made by J. B. Stetson or in Mexico the sombrero, construction workers wear hard hats, and women wear fashion hats.

A fully developed expansion system will have four leaders with four distinct hats (roles): Nurturing (cell leader), supervising (cluster team leader of seventy), supporting (streamlined congregation), and coordinating (lead pastor). Note: Persons in a triad do not operate in a leadership system but in a friendship relationship. In the beginning of a prototype all of the leadership roles are present in the person of the pastor or church planter. The coordinating role of senior pastor, the supporting role of congregation pastor, the supervising role of cluster team leader, and the nurturing role of cell leader can all be seen in the pastor. At step four of a prototype the pastor or church planter must help followers properly visualize the different leadership roles. If this is not done, the impression will be given that it takes a professional pastor to lead and supervise a community cell. This reinforces our current problem of needing an extraordinary leader in order to expand.

In teaching this important leadership concept I have used four different hats to demonstrate the different roles: A baseball cap, a regular hat, a cowboy hat, and a sombrero. In this demonstration I ask the senior pastor to come to the front of a group and one-by-one stack all the hats on his head. Remember: even in a small church the pastor fulfills the role of coordination. This is true also of a church plant. Coordinating a church, supporting a congregation, supervising a cluster, and nurturing a cell are all taking place in the life of the church planter during the initial stage.

After I put all of the hats on the pastor, I demonstrate how the pastor puts the cell leader hat on some one else, then the supervising hat on someone else, and the same with the congregation hat when it is necessary.

A cluster of seventy begins with three cells that are identified as the darker circles in the picture. The light circles represent the cells that will be added by multiplying the first triads and cells. A full cluster team has six cells. The pastor or church planter will begin to supervise the process from step one when the first triads are formed and therefore must have

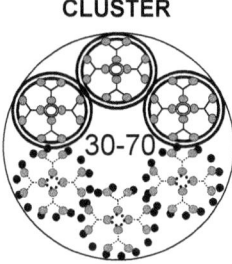

the end picture clearly in mind before beginning. The pastor or church planter will model the cluster supervisor role from the very beginning, not the role of pastor or church planter.

As I explained above, the supervising leader of the cluster team is the key to Jesus' simple strategy. If the cluster of seventy is properly prototyped in the natural sequence of the triad, the community cell, and then the cluster, everything else will work properly. When three cells are functioning, the leader (pastor or church planter) will model the role of supervisor as he/she coaches the cell leaders and cell members. The role of supervisor must be separated from the role of pastor or church planter so cell leaders will understand it doesn't take a pastor gifting to be a supervisor. Therefore, at this point in the process, the pastor or church planter must make the followers understand that he/she is operating as a cluster supervisor, not as a pastor or special church planter. This is a critical point because expansion only happens if supervisors can be naturally produced from the ranks of cell leaders.

The cluster supervisor (pastor or church planter in the beginning) will mentor the community cell leaders and assistants and will test out all necessary materials and protocols during the development of the first cluster. When the cluster is working properly, cluster supervisors will have access to and know how to use the following simple materials:

1. A Bible reading guide for applying Scripture in the triads.
2. Application questions for the cell meeting.
3. Simple materials and methods for guiding new believers into discipleship and initial Bible understanding.
4. A Friendship Evangelism Retreat (course) for teaching the members of triads how to apply Scripture to life, how to witness and explain salvation, how to walk in sanctification in basic Christian living, and how to use the discipleship materials for new believers.
5. A Community Body Life Retreat (course) for teaching cell members how to live together in Christ's presence, how to edify the Body, and how to interpret and apply Scripture.
6. A Supervising Retreat (course) for training cluster leaders how to identify, nurture, and supervise cell leaders and potential cluster leaders to expand through triads and cells.
7. Model the leadership hats of cell leader, supervisor, congregation pastor, and church pastor.

STRATEGY STEP FIVE: MULTIPLY THE CLUSTER

The final strategy step is to multiply into two cluster teams when the prototype cluster reaches six cells. Large churches using Jesus' 3/12/70 relationship model will continue to grow internally and expand externally because they organize growth around these units. Personnel must be dedicated to these units rather than to the brick and mortar model with its centralized preaching, teaching, and program system.

The following profile of a functioning supervising cluster of seventy helps us understand what is happening when a healthy cluster prototype is completed.

1. *The pastor or church planter is supervising five to seven healthy community cells (thirty to seventy) that are functioning as a cluster.*
2. *The cluster meets periodically in a retreat type setting for training, deploying, debriefing, prayer, and worship.*
3. *A leadership team, consisting of cell leaders, supports the catalytic/cluster leader.*
4. *Interns are functioning in every cell.*
5. *There is a supervisor for each cluster of three to six cells.*
6. *The pastor provides a daily scripture application plan for the friendship triads and prepares application questions to be used in the community cells.*
7. *Cell leaders oversee a discipleship study for new believers.*
8. *The pastor has developed three courses that can be taught in retreat settings by cluster supervisors:*
   a   *Friendship evangelism: Discipleship Course, personal study of the Bible, abiding in Christ and experiencing Christ in the midst, listening to God in prayer, preparing and giving a three minute testimony (my life before becoming a Christian, how I first became aware of God, how I made my decision to be a Christian, and my life now as a Christian), using friendship as natural evangelism, touching those in oikos sphere of influence relationships, and contacting and cultivating the person of peace seeker.*

  b *Community Body Life: edification, exercising spiritual gifts, fruit of the Spirit, how to lead an unbeliever to make a decision, evangelizing through community net fishing events.*

  c *Leadership supervision: leadership gifts, principles of supervision, mentoring cell leaders to be cluster leaders.*

9. Every friendship triad is growing by adding friends, relatives, and persons of peace. Cells are growing through "persons of peace" (seekers) contacted in triads, through the oikos relationships of the members in cells, and through periodic net fishing contact events and ministries.

INSTRUMENTS OF EXPANSION

When broken down into its individual steps as I have done above, the process may appear to be complex. However, the natural flow of the process once it begins is simple: triads become cells and cells become clusters. When confused about what to do, go back to the three working parts of Jesus' expansion strategy: 3/12/70. Leaders emerge out of the process: cell leaders come out of triads and cluster leaders emerge from cell leaders. This is true for an existing church and of a church plant. These three groups will integrate and simplify the ministries and programs that are part of the traditional church and that complicate the working of the church. Return to Jesus' three working parts that integrate everything else.

Pastor or church planter you must have a touch from God, a revelation word, a simple vision, and a sense that God is directing the church, or a portion of it, to become the organic body of Christ that can operate without buildings, professional leaders, programs, and a public service. This is the faith step I want to encourage you towards in the prototyping. You may have questions and reservations, however, if you feel that this is the direction God is taking you, and your church, trust God to inform every decision and answer every doubt along the way. If you will learn to live in the three groups of Jesus' strategy (3/12/70), you will be His church when you arrive at the end of your ministry journey of faith.

Listen until you get revelation! Too often we have followed the newest programs and methods in the hopes that the church will produce New Testament growth and expansion. A new approach tacked on to the existing traditional model will not change the result. The church must return to the New Testament conception of the church as a relationship expansion paradigm in order for the results to change. Only through revelation will you believe that God's simple groups of 3/12/70 will result in expansion.

I believe if you use the five simple strategy steps introduced in this chapter, God can use you and your church as His instruments of expansion in the 21st century. Every expansion strategy will have some version of the five steps that take place within the three building blocks of 3/12/70.

The prototype is completed when these five simple steps are completed and have resulted in a supervising cluster. Just keep growing through friendship triads, nurturing in cells, and supervising in clusters of seventy. The church can now survive political persecution or privilege, economic prosperity or poverty, and social peace or turmoil.

Chapter 22

A CONVERSATION WITH CHURCH PLANTERS

"Every form of organic growth sooner or later reaches its natural limits. A tree does not keep getting bigger; it brings forth new trees, which in turn produce more trees. This is the biotic principle of 'multiplication,' which characterizes all of God's creation."
• Christian Schwarz

Ross and Shirley Mackin were new church planters in Thailand just before Mary and I returned to the United States in 1989. After their required language study in Bangkok, they moved to the area in Northeast Thailand where we served during our last term. The Mackins have enjoyed a fruitful ministry for almost three decades. Along with a recent newsletter, Shirley shared the following story about her experience growing papaya trees.

> *Apparently everyone else around us knows papayas have female and male seeds and only female seeds produce fruit. So we have been nurturing up to twenty papaya plants at a time for months, not realizing some of them are male. In fact, the biggest tree with beautiful leaves is a male and continues to flower, but will never produce fruit. There must be a lesson in here from all of this. My lesson is to pick the darker female seeds to plant in the future.*

Experts say the only sure way to identify a papaya tree that will produce fruit is its flowers, not its seed. A male tree produces impressive flowers and pollen but never fruit. A female tree reproduces fruit if it cross-pollinates with a male tree. Some papaya trees have both male and female flowers and will self-pollinate. Shirley's papaya tree experience taught her the importance of having a tree that will cross-pollinate or self-pollinate. Obviously, a self-pollinating plant is preferred.

A deeper lesson from Shirley's papaya story is found in the agriculture analogies in the New Testament. Christian Schwarz believes these analogies confirm that multiplication is a "biotic principle" that God has built into all of creation ... including the church.

> *Every form of organic growth sooner or later reaches its natural limits. A tree does not keep getting bigger; it brings forth new trees, which in turn produce more trees. This is the biotic principle of 'multiplication,' which characterizes all of God's creation.*[198] *Just as the true fruit of an apple tree is not an apple, but another tree; the true fruit of a small group is not a new Christian, but another group. The true fruit of a church is not a new group, but a new church.*[199]

Pastors and church starters plant seeds that will grow into some kind of church tree. It is imperative to plant the proper seed if we want to produce a church tree with expansion fruit. Church starters can plant three kinds of church trees:

1. A church tree that will not produce fruit on its own. This is the male papaya tree. The tree has beautiful leaves and flowers and can pollinate another tree but will never produce papaya fruit itself. This is the traditional cathedral tree that grows large and beautiful but will not reproduce expansion fruit.

---
198. Schwarz, 68.
199. Ibid.

2. A church tree that will cross-pollinate. This is the female papaya tree that has only female flowers and therefore must rely upon an outside male tree with flowers to produce fruit. This is a church that must have outside leadership and/or financial help from a church planter or mother church in order to produce fruit.

3. A church tree that will self-pollinate. This is a special papaya tree that has both male and female flowers and therefore produces papaya fruit (and trees) from within itself. This is Jesus' church expansion tree of 3/12/70 that self-pollinates and naturally reproduces. This is the church tree I am talking about in this chapter.

CHURCH PLANTING CONTRAST

New churches have historically started as small groups. However, that does not mean church plants are using a different model from the traditional church. The cathedral picture is in the mind of the typical leader of a church plant. Look at the chart, *Cathedral Church Plant*.

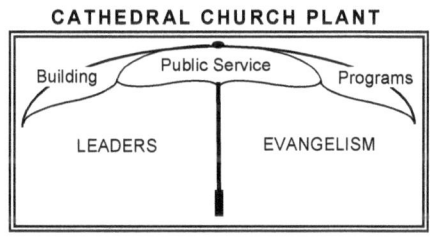

Even in the initial meetings in houses, schools, or commercial buildings, Sunday looks like a traditional public service with worship, preaching, and programs. The only difference from a traditional church is the new start has not yet developed special ministries underneath the large group because its leaders are busy attracting an initial core group through evangelism. Most house churches also use a scaled down version of the cathedral church plant model, just in a house.

Once a church planting team steps outside the large group support system of a cathedral mother church, it must provide its own large group system. Unfortunately, the only large group that most church planters know is Constantine's centralized model that is high-maintenance, building-centered, expensive, and requires an extraordinary leader to work. These new church plants begin a consumer system of programs and ministries designed to attract and hold consumers in a public worship service. They are baby cathedral churches.

This fixation on a traditional Sunday worship service has caused Pastor Bob Roberts to ask leaders who talk with him about starting a new church, "Do you want to begin a church or a worship service?"[200] If we are honest, most leaders have a worship service in mind when they talk about starting a church.

The cathedral preaching and teaching paradigm restricts church growth and eliminates the possibility of expansion. So much time, energy, and effort is directed to producing the traditional preaching and teaching programs that little is left for relationships that will produce expansion. It is not in the nature of a cathedral church plant to cross-pollinate or self-pollinate.

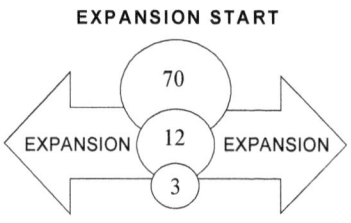

Contrast the *Cathedral Church Plant* chart above with the *Expansion Start* chart that has no public large group umbrella. An expansion church start operates without

---

200. Dr. Bob Roberts is pastor of church in Keller, Texas. His church has helped start 40 churches in the area. God is also using him in a powerful ministry of building bridges into the Muslim world. He shared this statement with me while we were together in a recent conference in Brazil.

a preaching, teaching, and program large group and is mobile, relational, self-organizing, and self-pollinating.

This expansion paradigm of church planting releases a church start from the maintenance of a public system. Therefore, the church planting team can focus on relationships instead of programs. It organizes around several manageable small groups rather than one large group. It does not require a building, is led by ordinary leaders, and produces leaders out of its system. In addition, Jesus' expansion seventy is the method for external expansion.

CHURCH PLANTING MOVEMENTS

Praise God for the church planting movements that have broken out in different parts of the world in the 21st century. The success of these movements is often attributed to special methods such as telling the stories of the Bible, one-on-one discipleship, using a certain kind of witness, or the innovative technology of the Internet.

The perception is that a successful movement grows because of a special method. Then those committed to the movement teach that "successful" method to desperate church planters who are looking for anything that works. It is important to understand the real root cause of these movements. Let me explain in more detail what I have suggested earlier in this book about the factors that cause church planting movements.

In the movie, *The Jerk*, Steve Martin plays Navin R. Johnson, an extremely naïve person who was adopted into a black family. He leaves home when he turns eighteen, gets a job and a place to sleep at a gas station, and has his name "in print" in the phone book. A lunatic randomly flips through the phone book and chooses his name as his next victim. The man scopes in on Navin with his rifle from across the freeway and starts shooting. He hits several cans of oil on display between the gas pumps. Navin's first reaction is: "These oil cans are exploding!" After more shooting, he concludes: "Someone is shooting at these oil cans!" He warns: "He hates these cans. Stay away from the cans!" Finally Navin realizes someone is shooting *at him*. His initial perceptions did not fit the reality of the situation.

It is easy to misunderstand why church planting movements are successful. We think these movements grow because of a particular ministry method. In reality, the success of these church-planting movements is due to New Testament factors rather than to modern methodology. These movements are successful because persecution or circumstances force them to return to the New Testament form of the church. Leaders do not easily or voluntarily give up the organizational form of the Church; the government or circumstances take away the organizational form.

One common factor is part of almost all church-planting movements today: They are found in areas of persecution. Persecution drives the church underground so it must gather in small groups and operate with ordinary leaders. Public meetings are restricted or impossible and this forces Christians to pour their time, energy, and resources into community life and relationship witness. They are compelled to operate in some form of Jesus' expansion system of 3/12/70. It is persecution that forces them to be the organic church of relationships rather than a new or rediscovered method.

The only exception to persecution as the primary factor in modern movements may be in a few pioneer rural areas. However, the same underlying cause is at work: In sparsely populated rural areas, Christians are not close enough together to build buildings and organize into consumer churches. Consequently they spread through the New Testament form of the church of small groups and relationships.

Because of political freedom in the West, pastors must choose to return to the organic form of the Church. That is not easy because the impressive and powerful organizational form of the Church overwhelms Jesus' simple and organic form of the Church.

This New Testament form of the church is the form of Christ. Paul wrote to the Galatians that he was in "the pains of childbirth until Christ is formed in you" (Gal. 4:19). The "you" is plural and means "you all" and is made plain in Texas English as "y'all". Christ is not just formed in me as an individual. Christ is formed in community, in us all.

> *To be conformed to the image of Christ is not an ideal to be striven after. It is not as though we had to imitate him as well as we could. We cannot transform ourselves into his image: it is rather the form of Christ which seeks to be formed in us, (Gal. 4:19) and to be manifested in us. Christ's work in us is not finished until he has perfected his own form in us. We must be assimilated to the form of Christ in its entirety, the form of Christ incarnate, crucified and glorified.*[201]

Jesus' church is a form through which God conforms us through community into the form of Christ. This is the great mystery and hope of Christ in us (Col. 1:27). The triad is the friendship form of Christ. The community cell is the family form of Christ. The supervising seventy is the expansion supervision form of

---

201. Dietrich Bonhoeffer, *The Cost of Discipleship*, (New York: Collier Books, Macmillan Publishing, 1963), 341.

Christ. The congregation is the public form of Christ. Current church planting movements that expand have been forced to take the form of Christ and therefore:

- Escape expensive and stationary buildings
- Use ordinary people and leaders
- Move along relationships as a people movement
- Live in the presence, power, and purpose of Christ in small reproducible groups
- Apply Scripture to life instead of just studying it
- Take the main message and activities into homes of persons of peace
- Mobilize all believers for evangelism
- Go and make disciples.

THE CELL CHURCH'S FLAWED CHURCH PLANTING SYSTEM

Several years ago, I detected a weakness in cell churches in the area of church planting. Churches with cells were no more successful in starting new churches than traditional or seeker churches. This realization came to me as I watched dynamic and growing cell churches send their first missionaries to begin new churches beyond the large group ministry arm of the mother church.

These cell church planters had already successfully reproduced the small group pattern of 3/12/70 internally within the structure of the mother church. However, they struggled to develop expansion momentum or even to duplicate the growth of the mother church in a new start. They failed because they tried to reproduce the large group model that was embedded in their mind and experience.

Consequently, these church planters too quickly looked for a building in order to have a Sunday worship service (musical band and worship team) with stimulating and motivating messages, teaching programs, and traditional paid leadership positions for pastor/preacher. A significant amount of their time, energy, and resources were invested in a public worship, preaching, and teaching large group. (The cluster of seventy I am suggesting is a large group. However, it is not public and does not require a special building or professional preachers and musicians. Its focus is outward in supervising and organizing expansion. So even while these cell churches had experienced supervising clusters internally as part of the organization of the church, they had not conceptualized the church in a large group of seventy outside of the existing structure.)

Why can a mother cell church grow internally while using the cathedral large group system and it's church plants cannot expand externally beyond the umbrella of the mother church?

In a large mother church, a relatively small percentage of the leaders and productive members (in relation to the total number of members) are required to put on the Sunday program. This releases a large percentage of members to give their time, energy, and resources to expanding the church internally through community cells. However, in a new external start, a large percentage (often 100%) of the team and early converts is required to put on the public Sunday program or to sit in the pews and be the audience for the programs.

This significantly reduces the time, energy, and resources available for expansion activities. The new starts spend so much time trying to duplicate the large group activities of the mother church that the power of expansion is dissipated in the large group activities.

This is also a danger for a community cell that does not use friendship triads. The cell meeting becomes so time consuming and emotionally intensive that natural witness is hindered. The cell meeting becomes a small come structure and a therapy office for listening to problems rather than listening to God. This sucks the time, focus, and energy away from natural friendship witness.

Even the best leaders of growing cell churches cannot produce external expansion through cells that are tied to Constantine's public large group worship, preaching, and teaching model.

I am convinced God is preparing cell church leaders to expand the church through Jesus' expansion strategy of 3/12/70. Cell churches already use these supervising seventies internally within the worship, preaching, and teaching model of Constantine. Now, cell churches need to expand externally through groups of seventy that are not trying to produce Constantine's fruit and model, but rather the fruit and model of Jesus' organic groups.

Germination

Jesus often explained the spread of the Gospel with the agricultural picture of seed sowing. Viewing the triad of two or three as the seed of the Gospel gives a simple basis for understanding the natural growth process of the Church.

> *This is what the kingdom of God is like. A man scatters seed on the ground. Night and day, whether he sleeps or gets up, the seed sprouts and grows, though he does not know how. All by itself the soil produces grain---first the stalk, then the head, then the full kernel in the head. As soon as th grain is ripe, he puts the sickle to it, because the harvest has come. (Mark 4:26-29).*

Germination is the process by which a plant grows from a seed to a plant. It is the growth of the potential plant contained within a seed that results in the formation of the seedling. Germination can be thought of in a general sense as anything expanding into greater being from a small existence or germ.

Seed germination depends on both internal and external conditions. Water and temperature activate germination in a seed and the enzymes within the seed are activated. This sets into motion the energy necessary for the growth process.

The Triad is a spiritual seed and the disciplines or experiences contained within the seed are the catalytic hydrated enzymes that cause the seed to grow. The chemical process begins to germinate in the disciplines within the triad and then the seed becomes a small plant in the form of a community cell and a full mature plant producing fruit in the cluster.

THE TRIAD SEEDING PRINCIPLE

The seeding principle is to plant a triad seed of a two or three unit that Jesus specifically promised to indwell: "Where two or three gather in my name, there am I with them." (Matthew 18:20.) This means that the seed of two or three is the most basic unit of the Body of Christ where the life and power of Christ is first activated.

The triad seed grows into a cell, a cluster, and a church. The seeding principle can be used in three church situations:

1. *In an existing church the pastor can prototype a triad seed and then seed triads into groups that already exist in the church.*
2. *An existing church can plant a seed of (1) two or three*

> Christians, (2) a cell seed of three or four triads, or (3) a cluster seed of several cells into a geographic or demographic setting outside of the mother church.
> 3. A church planter can be the seed for a new church by starting a triad that grows into a cell and then grows into a cluster.

The same mentoring stages and process are used with an existing church or in a church plant. However, the beginning point is different: A church plant is beginning a church in a new area and an existing church is developing a prototype for internal growth and external expansion within an existing church.

The roles of the persons involved in a church plant and those mentoring a movement of churches are also different. Mentoring a church movement focuses on pastors of existing churches. Mentoring a church plant focuses on a church planter and its core leadership team. A church plant becomes a mentoring model for a movement when it multiplies its first cluster of seventy.

A Church or a Worship Service?

Using Jesus' simple strategy, churches of all sizes and models can begin new churches and support worldwide expansion. In order to do this, pastors and church planters must uncoupled from the public large group worship system of the mother church. This is necessary because a new start will not expand if it remains tied to the public large group expression while trying to implement the cell system. Even a growing cell church cannot make a new start grow when it is tied to the traditional large group system.

Remember Bob Robert's question to potential church planters: "Do you want to begin a worship service or to begin a church?" This is why I believe the major obstacle to expansion church planting is the traditional large group public model. This model turns the focus, time, energy, and resources of a church plant inward toward growing the large group instead of outward toward expansion. A daughter church plant copies the mother church and mobilizes its members to provide programs and ministries for consumers.

The traditional public large group preaching and teaching, building and brick, consumer and come structure model dooms church starts, even those of cell churches, to ordinary growth or stagnation. This is the reason most churches never grow beyond the 100-member barrier. (In truth the majority of churches are much smaller.)

The large group system is too expensive, immobile, high-maintenance, ingrown, and dependent on an extraordinary leader. It reverses the Strachan principle of mobilizing its total membership for witness and instead mobilizes all of its producers to provide a public large group service for the remaining consumers. The organization large group system of the church competes with the organic church body for the time, energy, and focus that are essential for expansion.

THE LIFE-FLOW OF A CHURCH PLANT

Several years ago I suffered a walking heart attack. That means I was still walking around for several days while some serious stuff was happening to my heart. I was teaching conferences in London and in Frankfort, Germany. In London, my friend Laurence Singlehurst treated me to a wonderful meal at a great Chinese restaurant. Then he dropped me off at my room at the Highfield Oval that is the YWAM base at Harpenden.

As I climbed the stairs to my room at one of the guest houses, a pain hit me that took me to my knees. That night the pain did not subside until early morning. This repeated itself several times during the week, usually at night after eating the evening meal. Later after I returned to Houston and had surgery, my cardiologist explained the connection between my eating and my pain.

I had several blocked arteries and my blood was not getting to my heart. At night after I ate, the blood was flowing to my stomach to digest food and my clogged arteries could not deliver enough oxygen-rich blood to my heart. The result was a dangerous and painful condition.

When a church or church planter tries to plant a church with the traditional large group, there is a problem with the life flow. The life that should be flowing into organic relationships goes to large group activities. The spiritual life-blood of the church goes to the organization rather than to the organism. Consequently, there is not enough life flow for both the organizational activities and the cells. The large group sucks all of the life out of expansion. This is a dangerous and painful condition for the church and the church planter.

Church planter: if you want to be part of an expansion movement, minimize the activities used for the large group and maximize the focus and activities of relationships and cells. Forget about planting a traditional large group with a building, pulpit, and pews, instead, prototype Jesus' three relationship groups of 3/12/70. Never get larger than seventy until you have multiplied into three or four clusters and absolutely need a streamlined forward operating base to support continuing expansion. At that point, use the body church or tabernacle concept of your large group instead of the popular cathedral model.

Pastor of an existing church: Plant Jesus' expansion model

inside your church as a prototype and then transplant it into Jerusalem, Judea, Samaria, and the ends of the world. Make sure the transplant uses the body church or tabernacle concept of large group and not the mother church cathedral model.

This brings us to our next conversation with pastors of existing churches.

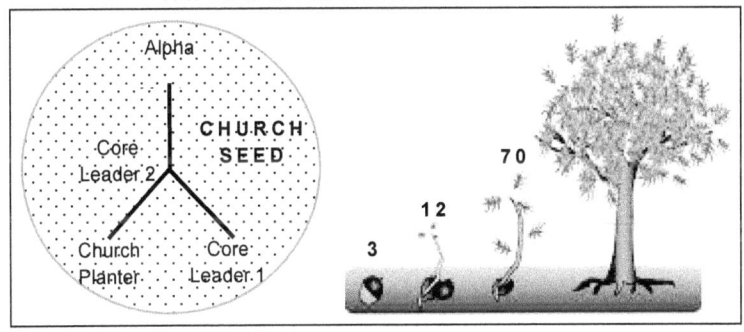

THE TRIAD IS THE CHURCH PLANTING SEED

Chapter 23

A CONVERSATION WITH PASTORS

"Strategy without tactics is the slowest route to victory. Tactic without Strategy is the noise before defeat."

• Sun Tzu

When I was a young boy, I saw Eric Brenn perform his classic spinning plate routine on the Ed Sullivan Show. The central feature of his act was spinning five glass bowls on top of five flexible sticks that were four feet long and attached to a table. Between the spinning bowls on the same table he had eight spinning plates.

While keeping the bowls on the long sticks moving and the eight spinning plates rotating, he would do other amazing balancing features with eggs, drinking glasses, and spoons. All of this, of course, was done while keeping the glass bowls spinning atop their sticks and the plates spinning on the table.

As a glass bowl or plate began to slow down, it would wobble uncontrollably. The audience would become alarmed, thinking the bowl or plate would fall and smash to a million pieces. Just in the nick of time, Brenn would run in and give the glass bowl or plate a new spin. Back and forth he would go trying to keep up with the demands of the spinning bowls and plates. I was exhausted by the time he finished the act, always with no broken bowls or plates.

Pastors identify with the spinning plate illustration in my conferences. It seems to express the desperate multi tasking required in the ministry. The ministry feels like a mad dash of running back and forth in order to keep the plates of ministry spinning. Pastors know the panic of keeping the activities spinning or everything comes crashing down. Good news: Jesus' expansion system of 3/12/70 is your way out of the spinning plate circus act.

The Umbrella Large Group

Instead of the spinning plate routine, let's see if we can at least get the church's large group system into a neutral position. Look at the large group of today's church as an umbrella. Umbrellas protect from the elements and give a place of shelter. The psalmist uses this picture of God's protective covering. "He who dwells in the shelter of the Most High will rest in the shadow of the Almighty" (Psalm 91:1).

The large group umbrella represents all of the ministries and services provided by a church for its members. This includes worship services, music programs, counseling, youth activities, children's ministries, Bible study, administrative support, and a public identity. The large group umbrella is used in all of the primary models of the church: Cathedral (traditional) Church, Creative (contemporary) Church with Small Groups, Cell Church, and even some versions of the House Church. The umbrella analogy gives a practical way to understand the Church today.

When used properly the large group can be a protective support for the expansion of the church. However, the church umbrella also has the inherent danger of sucking everything into its orbit of activities and influence and hindering expansion. It becomes a spinning plate circus and the pastor is the main attraction running back and forth trying to keep the plates spinning.

The large group of the church today is the greatest obstacle to expansion because so much of the life of the church is invested in it. Therefore, it is imperative that we understand how to use the large group in a positive way for expansion, or at least to neutralize it so it does not hinder what God wants to do in the 21st century.

OBSERVATIONS

Let me make some important observations about the church umbrellas pictured in the accompanying charts. Observation one: The umbrellas in the pictures are essentially the same in all three models: A public service, ministries, programs, and a building. This conclusion may be a surprise for some cell church pastors who assume the cell church operates with a different large group model because it uses cells. The

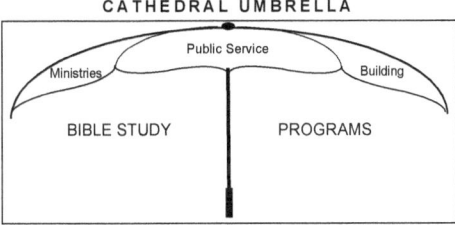

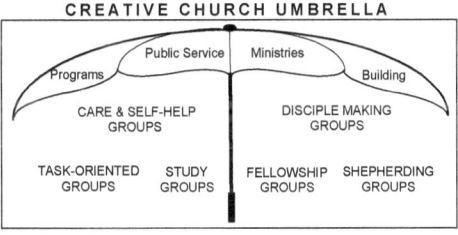

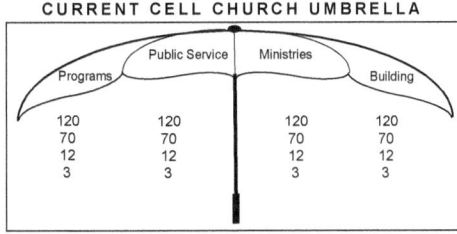

truth is the majority of churches over the world operate with this large group model, including the cell church.

Observation two: Underneath the large group umbrella of each model are different groups, ministries, and activities. These ministry activities change periodically as they are packaged in new terminology and given new bells, whistles, and shiny objects. The newly packaged ministry programs may focus on prayer, worship, discipleship, leadership, Bible study, or evangelism. (Small groups may be one of these packaged ministry programs). Mainline Protestants, Baptists, Pentecostals, Catholics, and Independents selectively apply the ministries that support their particular theological and denominational prism. However, all use the same large group umbrella, regardless of the size of the church or the flavor of its worship service. The introduction and excitement of a ministry package in a fresh and creative way may temporarily help the church. However, the umbrella system itself remains the same. A ministry fad has a short shelf life and eventually loses its appeal and effectiveness and is replaced by another ministry fad. These ministries only slightly and temporarily increase the growth of the church and since they are designed for the large group come-structures they are incapable of contributing to expansion.

Observation three: The large group umbrella model will grow internally but it is not designed to expand externally. The umbrella model is too rigid, high maintenance, expensive, and dependent on a building and professional leaders for effective church planting. We should not be surprised that leaders protect the familiar ministries and programs under the large group umbrella and neglect ministries such as church planting that are outside of the large group cover. This does not mean the large group has no place in the church today. Jesus used the large group in His ministry as the public place where He was lifted up before the crowds and multitudes, even those at the temple. The large group today is the public expression of Christ where He is lifted up in the world.

Observation four: The large group umbrella is the picture imprinted in the mind of most pastors and church planters who are starting a new church, no matter the situation: urban or rural, free or persecution, dense or sparse population. The cathedral large group umbrella is the paradigm that is so dominating today that most pastors and church leaders cannot visualize the church in any other way.

Observation five: The house church uses a version of the large group umbrella. The only difference is the place: A special leader preaches and teaches in a house. In my opinion this is why house churches in the West have not produced a movement like in other places and periods of history. They operate as one group rather than with Jesus' exponential expansion units of 3/12/70. They are hidden away in a house in a small version of the traditional large church with which they are so disappointed and angry. Consequently, without Jesus' expansion group system of 3/12/70, house churches in the West have no way to organize, supervise, and expand as a movement.

OPTIONS

Pastor, I am convinced your church, no matter the size or type (traditional church, creative church with small groups, cell church, and house church), can participate in expansion. Let's look at five strategy options or courses of action that you can use in order to participate in expansion: Plant, transition, stretch, share, and transplant. Now, let me speak to each option in a little more detail. A pastor can choose the best option for his/her situation.

**FIVE OPTIONS FOR THE CHURCH
TO PARTICIPATE IN EXPANSION**

1. PLANT an internal expansion unit in your church.
2. TRANSITION current small groups into expansion units.
3. STRETCH your umbrella to the edge of the large group.
4. SHARE your umbrella with area church planting teams.
5. TRANSPLANT an expansion unit of 3/12/70.

Option One: *Plant an expansion prototype inside your church.* The best way for some churches to participate in Jesus' expansion system is to first develop an internal expansion cluster under its large group umbrella. Use the church planting steps in the previous chapter.

1. Begin a men's and women's triad.
2. Form the first prototype cell out of triads.
3. Multiple the prototype cell into two cells.
4. Form the first prototype cluster of seventy with three cells.
5. Grow to a full cluster of six cells and multiply to two clusters.

Using a parallel strategy, a pastor can prototype Jesus' expansion system of 3/12/70, while continuing Sunday public worship and even existing small groups. That is the beauty of developing a prototype: You do not disrupt everything else that is going on. Prototype triads first and the triads will allow you to prototype a healthy community cell and a small cluster of thirty or forty persons (three or four cells).

Option Two: *Transition your small groups within your church into cells.* This is necessary because groups may grow but will not expand. Pastor, begin by prototyping a friendship triad of a men's triad and a women's triad. That is the first step in the simple strategy and is explained in detail in chapter 21. These are friendship triads that I have described in this book that operate outside of the cell meeting. They are different from the triads that are used during the cell meeting for discussion, prayer, or ministry. Triads are the contagious unit of the church that spreads the Gospel through friendships. They help change the values of selected members from groups to cells and prepare the way for developing a community cell prototype. This is a first step that can lay the foundation for external planting. Then,

CHAPTER 23: A CONVERSATION WITH PASTORS 411

plant a triad as a seed in selected groups or bring members out of their groups and form them into triads.

Option Three: *If you already have cells, stretch your umbrella.* Move expansion units as far as possible to the geographical edge of your large group. Focus on introducing the new concept of Jesus' expansion unit of 3/12/70 into your church mission vision. God has placed within every church some producer members with the gifts of evangelism and ministry. You have a choice to use these members to provide programs, ministries, and events for a Sunday consumer system, or you can thrust them into the harvest in Jesus' expansion groups of 3/12/70. These are special-forces commando Christians. They are going to do something on the cutting edge, like enter a parachurch ministry. You will either use them or lose them. Give them a way to do Jesus' expansion strategy. Turn the producers loose! Provide necessary large group support ministries so your producers can expand in triads, community cells, and supervising clusters. A creative small group church might have the goal of tithing 10% of its small groups to become expansion cells in the harvest beyond the large group umbrella. This is a way a traditional or creative church can organize and supervise expansion at the edge of their large group umbrella.

Option Four: *Share existing large group facilities and ministries with church planting teams* that are not part of your church and that do not yet have a large group public service. These church-planting teams can share in the overflow of your large group umbrella. With your large group help, these church-planting teams can focus on relationship expansion instead of on duplicating a time consuming and expensive large group that you already have in place. We have enough cathedral churches for many church planting teams to share in their support large group while expanding the church with Jesus' 3/12/70.

Option Five: *Transplant an expansion unit of 3/12/70.* Once a church has planted an expansion unit of 3/12/70 within the church, it can begin to transplant that model in total or in part. A church that is already organized internally around Jesus' 3/12/70 system or a church that has just planted an internal 3/12/70 unit can transplant an expansion unit of 3/12/70 as a mission, satellite, or hive into a geographical area beyond the large group umbrella. Transplanting strong churches instead of planting seeds is a strategic paradigm for worldwide revival in the twenty-first century.[202] I learned firsthand about transplanting when my father retired and planted a peach orchard with 1000 trees. Orchards are not planted from seeds but from transplanted trees that are at least two years old. These trees have been carefully selected and cared for in a nursery. A transplanted tree is larger, stronger and reproduces more quickly than a planted seed. Transplanted fruit trees are also healthier because they are grafted into a special stock that is resistant to root disease.

A church can transplant a friendship triad, transplant a community cell, or even transplant a functioning small cluster of thirty persons or a full cluster of seventy persons. This substantially changes the exponential equation of expansion. In this way, a church can use Jesus' expansion units to plant a church that will expand beyond the large group umbrella of the central church.

CATHEDRAL AND CREATIVE CHURCHES

Cathedral (traditional) churches and creative (small group) churches make up the majority of churches in the world. They are the same basic model, heavily invested in a public worship, preaching, and teaching structure. The only difference between the two is that creative churches may also include small groups in addition

---

202. William A. Beckham, "Transplanting Strategy" in *Redefining Revival* (Houston, TX: TOUCH Publications, 2000), Chapter 17.

to an organized program of studying the Bible. Compare the two pictures: *Cathedral Church* and *Creative Church with Small Groups*.

As you can see in the pictures, the same options are open to both models: Plant a 3/12/70 unit under your umbrella, transition your existing groups into cells, stretch your umbrella farther into harvest so your cells don't have to replicate

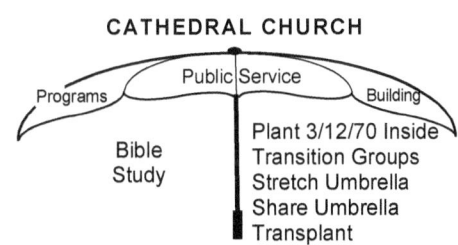

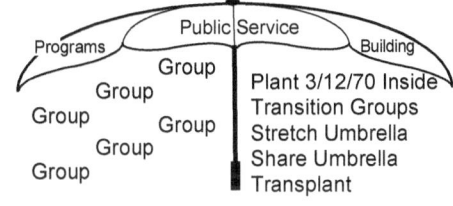

large group activities, share your umbrella with church planting teams, and transplant an expansion unit outside your umbrella.

Pastors of large churches today usually treat small groups as a program and have special pastors on staff assigned to oversee them. These churches explain the importance of small groups in their vision and mission statements. From the pulpit, the pastors of these churches extol the benefits of small groups. Pastors of these impressive churches are visionary leaders who have found a way to grow the church. However, creative churches use small groups as a ministry and holding container, not as a vehicle of expansion. Many of these creative churches with small groups are growing and are able to hive off into missions or satellite daughter congregations.

If you are a growing mega church in this category of creative churches, you have several things in common with pastors of other large churches. (1) You are a gifted communicator and extraordinary leader. (2) You have a favorable demographic location. You must have a certain density of population to grow. (3) Your church appeals to the needs or wants of a niche market. You scratch an itch and provide a spiritual service. (4) You are TV and media savvy. (5) You operate a well-oiled organizational machine. (6) You use some kind of groups to hold members, to give members a sense of belonging, and to provide spiritual ministry. (7) You are a good CEO and everything is done with "excellence." (8) You are a general and have an impressive headquarters. You have hundreds of officers and enlisted people in your army and are recruiting many more every year.

Nevertheless, you are not taking new territory. You are waging a war from your headquarters with stirring parades, impressive marching bands, spit and polished activities of excellence, and a show of strength. No matter how large you grow you are not expanding as a people movement like Jesus' relationship strategy in the first century. Implementing Jesus' expansion unit of 3/12/70 will maximize your ministry and move you from a good growth model to Jesus' great expansion system. You will move from your headquarters parade ground to God's frontlines where the battle for the souls of men rages.

If you are the pastor of a creative church with small groups, you are positioned to participate in expansion. You have a large group umbrella through which you can support internal growth and external expansion by using Jesus' simple building blocks of 3/12/70. You can break out of your come structure organization and become part of the organic expansion we see in the New Testament. Then, you will be an expansion mission church, not just a supplier of money and members to organizations, agencies, and boards that send missionaries. You can expand into Jerusalem, Judea, Samaria, and the world through Jesus' expansion unit of 3/12/70.

CELL CHURCH

Cell churches are some of the largest churches in the world. An operating cell church is the best working model of internal growth and has the potential for external expansion. Cell churches grow large by organizing in cells and clusters of seventy under the large group umbrella. Some cell churches also have a broader organizational unit of a congregation that consists of several clusters of seventy. These "congregations" provide another layer of leadership under the umbrella of the church. In the chart below I show the basic expansion unit of 3/12/70 without the "congregational" level because the congregational concept tends to overshadow the more important and smaller unit of seventy.

A cell church has unlimited potential of producing both internal growth and external expansion. A cell church should look like the chart below. It is stretching its umbrella with seventies just as far as it can go. It is sharing its umbrella with independent church planting groups that need large group ministry support. It is transplanting seventies beyond the umbrella of the mother church. And, after several seventy clusters have multiplied, they form a separate body or tabernacle congregation that is streamlined, mobile, and designed to support expansion. These support congregations are lean, mean, and expanding machines.

CELL CHURCH INTERNAL GROWTH & EXTERNAL EXPANSION

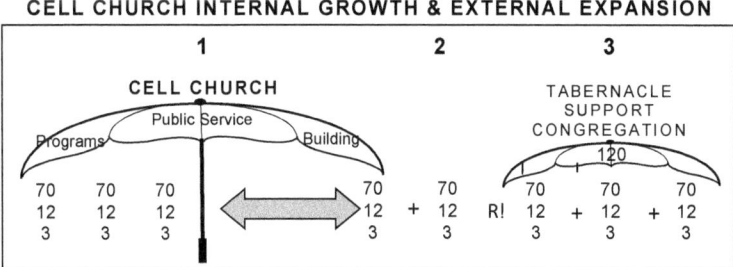

There are two reasons the cell church model has not reached its potential as the expansion church that I describe above: Church planting and cells. (1) It uses the traditional cathedral large group to plant churches and starts worship services instead of a church.[203] (2) It puts undue pressure on its community cells because it does not support them with the basic unit of friendship triads. The cell (small group) must do everything.

CELL CHURCH WEAKNESS ONE: CHURCH PLANTING

I became aware of the church planting weakness of cell churches several decades ago when I recognized a disturbing contradiction among cell churches. (I introduced this concept in the previous chapter on church planting. However this weakness is so important that I am including it again in this conversation with cell church pastors.) Dynamic and growing cell churches have had problems reproducing outside of the campus umbrella of the central church.

These cell churches grew faster and larger through triads, community cells, and supervising clusters of seventy under the umbrella of the central church. However, once a cell or several cells were planted outside the umbrella with the intention of becoming a separate church plant, they lost the growth vigor that was evident in the 3/12/70 structure within the umbrella of the central church. This is still the case. Cell churches that have impressive internal growth produce ordinary growth when they began new units outside of their large group umbrella.

What causes the difference between internal and external growth in cell churches? Clusters and congregations under the umbrella of a central cell church are not required to develop a separate large group with expensive buildings, high maintenance programs, and

---

203. I introduce the church planting weakness of the Cell Church in Chapter 22, "A Conversation with Church Planters," pages 390-392.

extraordinary leaders. The central cell church provides all necessary large group support: worship, Bible study, events, ministries, and programs. Therefore, the internal clusters of seventy are released to grow under the protection and provisions of the large group umbrella of the central church. This accounts for the internal growth and large size of some cell churches. Internal growth continues as long as the small group units of 3/12/70 enjoy the large group benefits of the central umbrella organization.

Cell churches organize internally in several large group forms: As a body church of 70, as a mobile and organic tabernacle church of 120, and as a cathedral with a large group public face. Unfortunately, cell churches use the more expensive, immobile, and complex cathedral large group as its model to plant churches. Cell churches plant Constantine's large group model along with the small group system of Jesus. Consequently their church plants are crushed by the weight of the large group and are only able to survive at the growth rate of traditional churches. The cell church must use Jesus' mid-level group of seventy in order to organize and supervise external expansion. This will remove the weight of the traditional large group preaching and teaching model.

CELL CHURCH WEAKNESS TWO: PRESSURE ON THE CELL

Let me address the second weakness of the cell church: Pressure on the community cell because of the lack of triads of two or three. The cell church must increase natural growth by supporting cells with friendship triads. This will take pressure off of the cells and introduce a relationship expansion force within the movement. Cell Churches must install friendship triads of two or three into the existing cell system. The triad is the contagious unit of Jesus' expansion strategy for both Christians and those who are not Christians. Two or three Christians continue to infect each other with the good news of Christ's friendship and they infect their friends who are immature Christians or unbelievers who do not yet realize that they are the friends of God. I believe the contagious friendship triad is the most important factor in the expansion of the church.

Cell church pastor: Stretch the umbrella. Begin expansion units of 3/12/70 outside your umbrella, and retrofit triads into your internal cells. Extend your large group umbrella as far as possible and begin new mid-level expansion units of seventy. Share your large group umbrella with independent church planting teams. Transplant Jesus' 3/12/70 expansion unit.[204]

God's Preparation for the Church Today

God has invested 60 years in preparing the church for this time in history. Through these decades He has gradually turned the church back toward His small group expansion system. If God has patiently worked with the Church for 60 years to restore groups, I believe He will take whatever time and steps are necessary to complete this change in the design of the church by adding the contagious two or three unit and the church planting unit of seventy.

Jesus' 3/12/70 unit gives concrete and straightforward steps for moving the church into expansion. The expansion seventy contains the contagious element of the triads, the nurturing family element of the community cells, and the mission element of the supervising seventy. Within a prototype 3/12/70 are the elements of Christ necessary to produce epidemic expansion. It is a contagious unit that maintains the infectious nature of the Gospel in the triad of three. It is a family unit that nurtures and maintains the wellness of those infected with the Gospel in a community cell of twelve. It is a mission task force that

---

204. William A. Beckham, "Expansion Analysis" in *The Second Reformation: Stage 2* (Moreno Valley, CA: CCS Publishing, 2014), Chapter 10.

organizes, supervises, and mobilizes those who are infected with the Gospel in the mission of expansion in a cluster of seventy.

God has given a way that every church and every church leader can be part of expansion in the 21st century. This is not possible as a method or as a program. It is not even possible as a ministry of prayer, worship, evangelism, or even a ministry of small groups. It is possible because it is the form of Christ.

UN-STICKING MINISTRY

God has placed me in a mentoring ministry with a group of Spanish-speaking churches in Houston. I regularly meet with a group of pastors, attend the worship service of one of the churches, and debrief every Tuesday with the pastor of the church I am attending. In addition, after worship on Sunday during the first two or three months I attend a church, I eat lunch with two or three different men chosen by the pastor so I can get to know them and share basic concepts about ministry through relationships. It is a challenge because we usually need a translator. This mentoring ministry has been a great blessing and a practical confirmation of the truths I have shared in this book.

At a recent Sunday lunch in a Mexican restaurant with two church leaders and the pastor, I asked the leaders to tell about their experience with God and the church. After sharing about his conversion and early experience in the church, one leader explained that in his early experience with God he wanted to become more involved in "ministry." However, ten years later, sitting across the table from him, he said, "I feel like I am stuck!" He is a faithful member of his church, attends worship service every Sunday, takes up the offering, tithes, and is recognized as one of the leaders of the church. However, he feels stuck. With the translator's help we formed the following sentence about

Christians and their experience with the church: "Many people in the Church know God but don't know how to ministry for Him."

I have found this to be a common feeling among faithful leaders in our churches. They feel stuck in a church building, in programs, in Bible study, and in the latest good program. They are stuck in the audience as other people minister to them through music and the Word. They are stuck in our pews; stuck listening to sermons; stuck taking up the offering; stuck as a spectator watching a performance. This is the nature of the organizational church: Ordinary Christians get stuck doing the jobs that keep the organizational system working. If the problem of pastors is keeping the plates of ministry spinning, the problem for laypersons is watching the spinning plate performance and/or working behind the scenes so the performance can take place. In any case, they are stuck, either behind the scenes supporting the performance or in the audience watching the performance.

One part of Jesus' ministry mission is to "set the captives free" (Luke 4:18-19).

> *The Spirit of the Lord is on me,*
> *because he has anointed me*
> *to proclaim good news to the poor.*
> *He has sent me to proclaim freedom for the prisoners*
> *and recovery of sight for the blind,*
> *to set the oppressed free,*
> *to proclaim the year of the Lord's favor.*

I am convinced Jesus wants to apply His mission statement to Christians trapped in an organizational system. We are captives of Constantine. The Roman Emperor controls our lives through the church system he developed in the fourth century. That is what this church leader was saying. He was stuck, held captive in a system that did not satisfy the promise of his salvation experience. He was oppressed in a system that did not live up to his expectation of what it meant to be a Christian and to be part of the Church.

Above everything else, Jesus' relationship system of 3/12/70 un-sticks us, both ordinary Christians and pastors. I shared with the men at that restaurant about the Christian ministry that God has given to every Christian: The ministry of reconciliation, of saying to a person "you can be the friend of God rather than His enemy." This is the ministry of friendship. Jesus' relationship system of 3/12/70 releases ordinary Christians to the primary ministry of reconciling a lost world to Christ; of saying to friends, "You are the friend of God, not His enemy" (2 Cor. 5:17-21).

> *Anyone who is joined to Christ is a new being; the old is gone, the new has come. All this is done by God, who through Christ changed us from enemies into his friends and gave us the task of making others his friends also. Our message is that God was making all human beings his friends through Christ. God did not keep an account of their sins, and he has given us the message which tells how he makes them his friends. Here we are, then, speaking for Christ, as though God himself were making his appeal through us. We plead on Christ's behalf: let God change you from enemies into his friends! Christ was without sin, but for our sake God made him share our sin in order that in union with him we might share the righteousness of God. (GNT)*

Pastor, Jesus' relationship system of 3/12/70 will set you free from the spinning plates and set your people free from the maintenance ministry in which they are stuck. That is Jesus' ministry to and through you and your people.

CONCLUSION

THE SPIRIT OF NAMAAN

*"For my thoughts are not your thoughts,
neither are your ways my ways," declares the LORD.
"As the heavens are higher than the earth, so are my ways
higher than your ways and my thoughts than your thoughts."*
• Isaiah 55: 8-9

Namaan, the victorious general of the army of the king of Aram (2 Kings 5:1-19) was infected with leprosy, one of the most feared diseases in the ancient world. (Aram was the military power in the region at the time.) A young Jewish girl in Namaan's household believed Elisha, the prophet of Israel, could heal him. The arrangement for the meeting with Elisha was handled by Naaman's king and directed to the king of Israel, head of state to head of state. It could have national repercussions if Elisha failed. The frightened King of Israel set the meeting up in Samaria and then got as far away as possible.

When Naaman arrived at Elisha's house the prophet sent a servant out to give the general his instructions. "Go and wash in the Jordan seven times, and your flesh shall be restored to you and you shall be clean." Naaman was "furious" because the prophet had sent a lowly servant to give such a ridiculous prescription for healing. The general at first refused.

Namaan's haughty reaction to Elisha doesn't make sense in light of his desperate condition. We see this same attitude in Peter on the rooftop in Joppa when in his vision he refused to eat what God sent down to him from heaven on a sheet. This was the attitude of many religious leaders toward Jesus. "Can anything good come out of Galilee" (John 1:43-46; John 7:40-53)? There is an addictive cynicism toward the small and ordinary.

For General Naaman, Elisha's prescribed treatment for his disease was too simple, ordinary, and mundane. "Bathe in the river Jordan!" It was a small, insignificant, and dirty river in his mind. Fortunately a servant talked some sense into Naaman with the argument: "It can't hurt and we have already come this far." After dipping himself seven times in the Jordan as instructed "his flesh was restored like the flesh of a little child." This story teaches us that disdain for God's simple and ordinary is a serious spiritual disease that can keep us from enjoying God's wholeness.

Namaan not only suffered from the disease of leprosy but also from the more deadly disease of pride. This was pride of position and pride of personal opinion.

The Church Analogy

The lesson in this story is: God's methods may appear to be unsophisticated, unimposing, unorthodox, and counterintuitive but they work. In Namaan's opinion, he deserved more pomp and respect than Elisha gave him, and he felt he could come up with better procedures and protocols than dipping seven times in the Jordan River.

It is easy for pastors and church leaders to get caught up in the great things of the church: Preaching sermons, teaching the Bible, publically ministering to the people, and managing the

Conclusion

wealth of the church. Large meetings, beautiful ceremonies and services, spiritual pageantry, TV exposure, and professionally trained and gifted leaders appear to be the obvious hope for the church.

The spirit of Namaan is a prideful disdain of God's ordinary and simple thoughts, ways, and solutions. It is a safe assumption that contempt and arrogance are part of the problem of the church today. The reaction of pastors to the small group expansion units (3/12/70) is an example of the Namaan spirit. Groups are small, simple, commonplace, ordinary, unimpressive, and hidden. This breeds contempt for them.

The opinion of many pastors is that simple triads of two or three, community cells of twelve, and a supervising group of seventy cannot compete with the programs and activities of the large group meetings. They are addicted to the pomp, pageantry, and visible qualities of the centralized system.

When leaders do use small groups they often subordinate them to existing structures and treat them as another program to administrate, as a way to hold members attracted in the large group, or as another group for Bible study, ministry, or fellowship. Many pastors even refuse to call small groups by their New Testament name: *ecclesia*.

Metaphorically, triads and cells are equivalent to the dirty Jordan River: ordinary and unimposing when compared to the history, complexity, visibility, great edifices, and material wealth of the organized church. God's cure for the church today is to dip seven times in the ordinary small groups used by Jesus.

I continue to be amazed at the visceral reaction against solutions that are offered that are outside the traditional paradigm.

Something is wrong deep down in the spiritual psyche of leaders that blind them to the expansion mission of the church and trap them in a growth strategy of impressive ministries, programs, and buildings. It has taken God more than half a century to get pastors to accept small groups and yet many pastors continue to use small groups as a way to build Sunday enterprises and empires, not to be an expansion people movement.

Dangerous Attitude

Leaders may not be infected with Naaman's disease of leprosy but are susceptible to his second disease of pride. The Bible warns about pride. "God is opposed to the proud, but gives grace to the humble" (James 4:6) NAS. God hates "haughty eyes, or the proud look" (Prov. 6:17). "When pride comes, then comes dishonor … " (Prov. 11:2). "Pride goes before destruction, and a haughty spirit before stumbling" (Prov. 16:18). "A man's pride will bring him low …" (Prov. 29:23).

In Namaan we observe two dangerous characteristics of pride. (1) Pride of position: Elisha offended Naaman's sense of importance and position and (2) pride of opinions: Naaman was disdainful of the prophet's procedures and protocol for healing. In his exalted opinion, dipping seven times in the dirty Jordan River wasn't necessary.

The key to experiencing God's life is accepting His thoughts and ways instead of ours. "For my thoughts are not your thoughts, neither are your ways my ways," declares the LORD. As the heavens are higher than the earth, so are my ways higher than your ways and my thoughts than your thoughts" (Isa. 55:8-9). The personal opinions of leaders are dangerous because they question and rationalize God's instructions.

Over the years I have come to understand that God is more interested in my obedience to His ways than in my opinions about them. In fact, personal opinions about the things of God are barriers to God's ways and take Christians dangerously close to declaring to God: my will, my way, my thoughts, and my opinion are more important than your will, your ways, your thoughts, and your truth.

God's expansion groups of triads (3), cells (12), and clusters (70), though ordinary and unimposing, have the power to break the Namaan spirit that infects leaders and to heal the Church. In the presence of Christ in the small groups of 3/12/70, pride, self-sufficiency, professionalism, and dependence on organization are broken. Leaders learn intimacy, confession, honesty, and transparency. Great leadership skills are not needed in a triad or community cell but humility is. The integrated small unit of 3/12/70 is Gods healing protocol for the church today.

Pastors, our pride of position and opinions must be broken so we can experience the power of God's expansion units of friendship evangelism, community cells, and supervising clusters of seventy.

THE CURE FOR THE CHURCH

For years religious leaders have been looking everywhere for a cure for what ails the Church. Expensive remedies and complex procedures have been tried and have failed. Learned men of church medicine have had their go at the illness of the church, but without success. In spite of the expenditure of great sums of money on cures as diverse as "snake oil" and high tech spiritual medicine, the church still lacks the health and vigor we see in the New Testament. We open our spiritual hospitals on Sunday. Some are like great medical complexes and some are small clinics. All are open for business and dispense information about spiritual wellness and give motivational speeches about spiritual good health. The spiritual illness inside and outside the church continues to spread unabated.

Could it be that we are ignoring the simple New Testament instructions? "Go bathe yourself in the Jordan River of small groups and your skin will be restored to you." Live in community; ask Christ to be present; listen to what He says, and see what He does.

In light of all of the great churches, magnificent buildings, elaborate services, beautiful ceremonies, great preachers, and primetime TV, how can a simple "layman" leading a small group of 5 to 12 people out in a home make a difference? How can small groups be successful when programs conceived by some of the most educated and brilliant minds of the church with unlimited resources of vast denominations regularly fail?

Small groups of 3/12/70 seem too small, disorganized, and unpredictable when compared to the familiar and formidable church organization. The traditional church, as we know it, is so powerful looking, so visible, so recognizable in its buildings, and so obviously "religious." Surely whatever cure we come up with must take place within its sanitized, sterile, and sanctified surroundings, not in small vulnerable groups out in the world.

But it is God's call, not ours. It was Elisha's call not Naaman's. God's way is not our way and His thoughts are not our thoughts. If we turn up our noses at God's simple small group structure we may be turning up our noses at God Himself. He said, "I will be in their midst" … in the midst of those small groups.

Not only did Naaman's pride get in his way but also his training. He was a soldier. Command something to be done and someone else did it immediately. Why couldn't Elisha just do it himself right there on the spot by waving a magic wand? This is typical of leaders who are looking for an immediate cure. Do it to me! Naaman's cure demanded that he be engaged in the process. This cure could not be commanded. Leaders cannot hire or command someone else to cure the church. Those in charge must be the ones to go to the river and get wet. Too often the pastor is too busy running the organization to be involved in the basic expansion units: the 3/12/70. This shows the priority of the pastor: preaching and programs in a centralized building. A church is never cured until the pastor is cured of the pride of position and personal opinions about God's spiritual instructions.

When Naaman got to the river it is to his credit that he then went all the way. Others want a half cure. Dip three or four times instead of seven. Church leaders can accept the importance of small groups to the health of the church but still be unwilling to take the whole cure. They attach small groups to all of their old church program cures. They use the cell group but refrain from the triad and the organizing cluster. Half cures and mixed cures can be worse than no cure. Dip but don't get your head wet. Dip but use a full diving suit. Going halfway with small groups will not cure the church and may be like taking a half dose of penicillin. It neutralizes the effectiveness of the medicine.

If the "skin" of the church is to be restored "like the flesh of a little child" then the church must obey the word of the Lord completely. When God says "dip seven times," six won't do.

The Small Group Cure of 3/12/70

Jesus' small group relationship cure worked in the first Century! The Early Church grew exponentially without any of the structures that are so often identified as the antidotes for a sick church. The first century church did not have any parachurch organizations, special preaching orders, denominations, seminaries, societies for missions or ministries, mass media, or what we call "programs."

Elton Trueblood described the early church.

> *It is hard for us to visualize what early Christianity was like. Certainly it was very different from the Christianity known to us today. All that they had was the fellowship; nothing else; no standing; no prestige; no honor ... but they had a secret power among them, and the secret power resulted from the way in which they were members one of another.*
>
> *There were no fine buildings. There was no hierarchy; there were no theological seminaries; there were no Christian colleges; there were no Sunday Schools; there were no choirs. Only small groups of believers...small fellowships.*
>
> *In the beginning there wasn't even a New Testament. The New Testament itself was not so much a cause of these fellowships as a result of them. Thus the first books of the New Testament were the letters written to the little fellowships partly because of their difficulties, dangers, and temptations. All that they had was the fellowship; nothing else; no standing; no prestige; no honor. The early Christians were not people of standing, but they had a secret power among them, and the*

secret power resulted from the way in which they were members one of another.[205]

The items in Trueblood's list are not necessarily wrong and may have some benefit in some way. However, they were not part of God's church architecture in the first century and are not God's cure for the Church today.

SMALL GROUPS OF 3/12/70 ARE GOD'S "MIRACLE DRUG"

Several years ago I read a magazine article with the title, *The Miracle Drug!* I was surprised to learn that some consider the "miracle drug" to be the ordinary aspirin. It is effective in treating so many different ailments. The first thing recommended in the case of a heart attack is to chew up an aspirin. Sometimes the familiar things are the most effective. I take several high-priced and high-powered pills each day for a heart condition. If I were given the choice of taking only one of these pills a day, I would choose, I think with the doctor's recommendation, to take my baby aspirin.

The small group cluster of 3/12/70 is God's miracle drug for the church because it can heal so many of the church's ailments. What is the pathology (the essential nature) of the disease of the church today?

Vertigo. The church is unbalanced between the large and the small, between worship and evangelism, between Sunday and the other six days of the week, between gathering and scattering, between growth and expansion, and between "clergy" and "laity." The small group cluster corrects the imbalance of the church and sets it on a even path.

---

205. Trueblood, *The Yoke of Christ*, 25.

Infertility. The church has a problem reproducing itself. The small group cluster approach of 3/12/70 will cure the church's problem of multiplying itself because small groups provide a delivery system for engagement with the world. Organizations are not fertile or infertile. Fertility is associated with living things. The fertility of the church depends on its relationships, not its organization. Organization, no matter how many activities are taking place within it, cannot be the Body of Christ. The living Body of Christ requires some kind of organic DNA. God provides the spiritual stuff of His Body in relationship groups of 3/12/70.

Immobility. The church is hooked up to a building life support system with all kinds of gadgets, tubes, and machines necessary for its survival. Confined to its building and unable to move out into the world (except through TV or Internet), it must be maintained and cared for by others. Small groups will pull the plug on the building life support system of the traditional church and restore it to health so that it can be active and mobile out in the world.

Anemia. The church is weak and rundown. Small groups will restore the church's strength and power by providing a place where Christ builds up His church through the working of His gifts. "The whole body, being fitted and held together by that which each joint supplies, according to the proper working of each individual part, causes the growth of the body for the building up of itself in love." (Eph. 4:16.) The wellness of the church takes place through edification in small groups.

Obesity: Doctors warn continually that obesity is one of the most prevalent and dangerous health conditions of humans today. This also happens with organizations. We are in the bloated Tower of Babel phase of the church: centralization and consolidation of the church as one giant organization that grows larger and larger. Churches that survive with the current church organization within the current cultural environment of the 21st century must get bigger and bigger. This results in what I have described as the vacuum cleaner church. Members from smaller churches are sucked into the vortex of churches that are building larger and larger buildings and organizations. These are giant religious malls with one stop shopping: they are centralizing and consolidating the church as a modern day tower of Babel in one place and led by one leader. Jesus' system of 3/12/70 gets the church into fighting shape for the spiritual battle.

Do you want your church to be truly healed so that its "skin" is like that of a baby's? Are you desperate enough yet to follow the simple instructions? Are you ready to jump into the dirty old river of groups? Then jump! The water is fine and the cure is amazing.

God can heal the church with his prescription formula: 3/12/70. Contagious friendship evangelism in triads of three + community edification in family cells of twelve + supervising leadership in clusters of seventy = expansion.

Can it be this simple? Ask Namaan and look at Jesus' model!

INDEX

A

Accountability, 184, 189, 192, 196, 198, 222
Allen, Roland, 61, 62, 63
Anatomy of innovation, 117
Assumptions, 359, 360

B

Bangkok urban strategy, 70-73
Barna, George, 86, 160
Bonhoeffer, Dietrich 45, 46, 101, 144, 151, 395
Brazil model, 76-79, 283-286
Browning, Elizabeth Barrett, 127
Building, 48
Building blocks, 367-388

C

Cell, 133, 138-141, 202-203, 205, 222, 304, 316, 318, 376, 380, 417, 418
    Discussion questions of a cell meeting, 233
    Holistic cell, 163, 208, 211, 220, 303
Centralizing, 25-26, 432
Chambers, Oswald, 91, 92
Change, 93, 94, 97 97-100, 335-336, 354, 368, 418
Church, 223-224, 267-268, 274-275, 346-349, 351
    Body church, 346-348
    Cathedral church , 348-349
    Cell church, 12, 34, 64, 73-74, 77, 282, 314, 316, 358, 361, 370,
        395-398, 407, 415, 418
    Creative church, 327, 411, 413, 414
    House church, 34, 61, 347, 362, 409

Large church, 30, 31, 33, 36, 330, 409
Mega church, 17, 29, 31, 43, 325, 333, 413
Phantom church, 346-347
Tabernacle church, 346-350, 364, 417
Vacuum cleaner church, 32, 36, 432
Church building, 34, 347-348
Church planters, 70-71, 389-391, 396, 400, 402
Church planting, 64, 315, 317, 324, 328, 362, 368, 391-403, 415, 418
Churchill, Winston, 124, 255, 269, 323, 324
Cluster, 35, 37, 46, 65-68, 72, 74-75, 78, 80, 223-233, 314, 317, 318-319, 335, 347, 349, 363, 370, 381-386, 412, 418
Cole, Neil, 23, 25, 47, 48, 185, 193, 233, 376
Coleman, Robert, 41, 50, 227, 228
Collins, Jim, 59, 83, 86, 111, 114, 299
Color, 351, 352, 353
Community, 133, 199-200, 201, 203, 205-207, 216, 244, 377
Confess sins, 191, 195, 375
Congregation, 74, 108, 224, 304, 347, 350, 364, 415
Constantine, 27-28, 42-43, 64, 100, 245-248, 261, 265, 335, 352, 361, 398
Contagious, 37, 46, 73, 315-316, 370
Conversational prayer, 145

D

Dark night of the soul, 111-124
Death, 57-59, 163, 217-219
Decentralizing, 23-26, 34, 35
Decision instrument, 94-95
Decision process, 93, 99
Discipleship, 250-252, 277- 278

E

Edification, 159-181, 192, 378
Epidemic, 35, 162, 227, 316, 370
Equipping, 107, 203, 208-209, 222
Evangelism, 184, 189, 193, 194, 213-215, 222, 305, 309
Expansion, 15, 17, 26, 27-29, 48, 61, 63, 227, 231, 286, 314, 325, 326, 330, 349, 379, 382, 386, 387, 392, 398, 412, 415

F

Flawed, 100, 396
Flywheel, 114, 115
Friendship triad, 73, 183-203, 314, 316, 320, 321, 334, 374, 375

G

Gerber, Michael, 18, 85, 292, 328, 330, 332
Gladwell, Malcolm, 34
Governing principle, 283, 284, 286
Graham, Billy, 290
Great commission, 29, 243, 253, 269, 280, 336
Group, 27, 35, 46, 74, 85, 165, 231, 233, 292, 359, 360, 361, 364, 425, 428, 429, 431
    Large group, 346, 348, 354
    Mid-level group, 35, 36, 53, 75, 79, 223, 324
Growth, 17, 27, 28, 29, 56, 57, 64, 108, 315, 325, 326, 328, 380, 390, 398, 414, 431, 432
    External expansion, 57, 63, 64, 108, 227, 246, 326, 393, 398, 400, 414, 415, 417
    Internal growth, 64, 108, 227, 245, 317, 326, 328, 400, 414, 417

H

Harvest, 67, 305-307
Holy Spirit, 42, 46, 52, 57, 104, 127, 128, 155, 162, 167, 168, 172, 176, 193, 207, 210, 257, 259, 287, 288

I

In between history, 266

J

J-curve, 113
Johari window, 174

K

Kierkegaard, Soren, 150, 306

L

Laubach, Frank, 140, 143, 150
Lay, Robert, 76, 281, 282, 292, 293
Leaders, 15, 18-20, 36, 50-52, 107, 108, 109, 116, 117, 123, 124, 141, 203,
   211, 212, 213, 222, 227, 238, 331, 334, 381, 382, 426
   Noun leaders, 51, 245
   Ordinary leaders, 36, 37, 51, 78, 317, 331-333, 361, 393
   Verb leaders, 51, 245
Leadership, 30, 32, 50, 51, 54, 75, 81, 86, 96, 106, 117, 118, 120, 188, 193,
   197, 198, 203, 206, 207, 210, 211, 219, 221, 222, 225, 227, 228,
   235, 236, 252, 276, 285, 292, 301, 302, 304, 307, 308, 309, 310,
   313, 314, 318, 319, 333, 351, 352, 363, 381, 382, 384, 385, 386,
   391, 397, 400, 408, 415, 419, 427, 433
Lewis, C.S., 61, 62, 146, 154

M

Mainframe, 188
Mallicoat, Helen, 130
Materials, 59, 72, 212, 233, 234, 235, 239, 291, 384
McGavran, Donald, 27
Ministries, 127, 187, 230, 272, 282, 411
Mission, 48, 49, 159, 223, 224, 227, 230, 232, 248, 263, 271, 273, 276,
   280, 283, 291, 319, 327, 342, 420
Mobilize, 49, 108, 226 .285, 331, 334, 354, 368, 396
Momentum, 111, 113, 114, 115, 120, 124, 304, 396
Movement, 15, 27, 36, 37, 45, 49, 63, 184, 230, 271, 281, 283, 286-292,
   315, 325, 326, 330, 393, 400, 402
Mullins, E.Y., 55
Multiplication, 184, 194, 306, 372, 379, 380
Murray, Andrew, 143

N

Naaman, 423, 424, 426, 428, 429
Neighbour, Ralph, 15, 62, 69, 79, 151, 206, 212, 215, 221, 292, 300, 335
Noonan, Peggy, 255, 256
Nurturing , 382

O

INDEX 439

Ogden, Greg, 50, 194, 202
Organic, 15, 27, 31, 41, 45-48, 50, 52, 85, 92, 109, 244, 245, 246, 247, 253, 331, 347, 348, 389, 390
Organization, 52, 66, 85, 243, 245, 246, 247, 252, 275, 347, 348, 350, 297, 417

P

Paradigm, 18, 19, 20, 26, 79, 100, 224, 245, 246, 247, 248, 249, 250, 255, 261, 265, 266, 325, 367, 393, 425
　Paradigm paralysis,,241, 255, 264
　Paradigm shift, 261, 367
Partridge, Howard, 95, 96
Pastor, 19, 36, 69, 76, 78, 106, 116, 183, 189, 194, 229, 233, 236, 238, 250, 265, 300, 301, 302, 323, 324, 325, 326, 327, 328, 337, 339, 346, 361, 372, 376, 382, 385, 387, 409, 414, 418, 421, 429
Persecution, 245, 253, 325, 362, 368, 388, 394, 409
Practical prophecy, 163, 164, 165, 170, 171, 172, 173, 175, 176, 180, 203, 220, 235, 371
Prayer, 21, 50, 54, 85, 93, 140-143, 157, 167, 174, 191, 203, 248, 258, 272
　Prayer list, 148
　Prayer listening, 152, 184, 337
Preparation, 80, 97, 124, 297, 298, 299, 301, 302, 303, 307, 418
Presence, 55, 104, 127, 141, 163, 184, 189, 215, 217, 247, 262, 319-321, 337
Programs, 27, 28, 31, 34, 35, 43, 44, 52, 73, 127, 159, 224, 232, 245, 248, 280, 323, 324, 350, 352, 353, 355, 360, 392
Prototype, 15, 16, 57, 59, 60, 85, 87,155, 157, 183, 223, 224, 233, 236, 303, 305, 336, 339, 371, 376, 377, 381, 384, 387
Prototype fatigue, 112-124
Putman, Jim, 19, 250, 252, 274

R

Ramm, Bernard, 45, 173, 259
Relationship, 17, 34, 44, 57, 105, 135, 136, 137, 165, 169, 194, 196-198 203, 210, 244, 318, 319, 320, 325, 327, 331, 336, 359, 374, 411, 421
Revelation, 19, 21, 104, 128, 146, 163, 172, 173, 256-267, 387
Richardson, Alan, 259
Rinker, Rosalind, 145

Roberts, Bob, 392
Rogers, Everett, 98

S

Schaeffer, Francis, 128
Schwarz, Christian, 29, 389, 390
Scripture Application, 219
Self-pollinate, 390, 391, 392
Senge, Peter, 283, 329
Seventy, 35, 37, 44, 46, 53, 63- 81, 210, 223, 239, 244, 314, 317, 322, 328, 335, 338, 339, 349, 355, 363, 371, 381, 398, 410, 418,
Snyder, Howard, 48, 345, 346
Spinning plates, 405, 421
Startup circle, 300, 301, 302, 303, 308
Stedman, Ray, 200, 243
Strategy, 15, 16, 17, 20, 21, 29, 34, 41, 42, 60, 66, 67, 68, 100, 225, 227, 236, 263, 269-280, 298-310, 313- 322, 323-344, 345, 346, 357, 358, 359, 363, 367, 368, 371, 373, 379, 380, 381, 383, 384, 410
Strategy continuum, 7, 364
Streamlined congregation, 68, 347, 349, 350, 382
Strobel, Lee, 131, 134
Supervision, 35, 44, 61, 63, 65, 66, 74, 88, 92, 223, 227, 232, 304, 314, 323, 370
System, 29, 30, 31, 32, 35, 36, 47, 50, 51, 52, 61, 81, 85, 100, 159, 188, 208, 227, 228, 229, 238, 253, 268, 279, 283, 317, 318, 326, 328, 329, 330, 331, 332, 333, 334, 335, 336, 337, 342, 343, 344, 345, 353, 354, 355, 369, 370, 376, 392, 401, 408, 410, 420, 421
    Consumer system, 354, 392, 411
    Producer system, 354

T

Thompson, Marjorie, 141, 147, 153
Those days, 263, 264
Time, 16, 18, 23, 37, 49, 50, 65, 83, 87, 88, 93, 99, 120, 124, 138, 196, 226, 232, 245, 250, 264, 265, 266, 288, 289, 290, 291, 292, 321, 325, 329, 360, 361, 362, 368, 392, 397, 398, 401, 418
Time, Chronos, 264
Time, Kairos, 264, 265

INDEX

Traditional, 17-20, 27-32, 34, 42, 43, 47, 50, 51, 52, 64, 69, 70, 73, 74, 75, 79, 100, 106, 109, 132, 148, 159, 200, 224, 229, 238, 244, 245, 246, 248, 249, 252, 253, 255, 256, 264, 266, 272, 278, 280, 286, 324, 326, 327, 330, 338, 345, 347, 352360, 361, 362, 363, 367, 386, 391, 392, 396, 397, 400, 401, 416, 425, 428
Transplant, 327, 403, 409, 412, 413, 418
Trinity, 44, 45, 130, 135, 275
Twelve, 44, 46, 52, 65, 66, 67, 68, 76, 188, 205, 206, 216, 224, 225, 232, 276, 303, 316, 319, 371, 381, 418, 433
Two or three, 46, 65, 133, 184, 185, 186, 192, 197, 286, 308, 313, 314, 316, 378, 417, 425

U

Umbrella, 314, 317, 392, 397, 406-418

V

Values,20, 76, 93, 100- 109, 123, 231, 234, 283, 284, 285, 294, 335, 336, 337, 338, 339, 355, 359, 370, 376
Vision, 16, 17, 19, 42, 63, 64, 77, 83-97, 113, 117, 119, 123, 124, 223, 229, 231, 234, 238, 265, 271, 274, 282, 283, 284, 285, 292, 304, 314, 346, 355, 358, 359, 387, 411, 413
Vision bus, 86, 90

W

Wellness, 150, 159, 161, 162, 163, 165, 167, 168, 172, 184, 217, 227, 378, 418, 428, 432
Willard, Dallas, 144
Wineskins, 13, 48, 346
Wuest, Kenneth, 156

www.ingramcontent.com/pod-product-compliance
Lightning Source LLC
Chambersburg PA
CBHW050059170426
43198CB00014B/2395